Fundamentals
of
Educational
Assessment

Cregg F. Ingram
Brigham Young University

D. Van Nostrand Company

New York   Cincinnati   Toronto   London   Melbourne

'd Van Nostrand Company Regional Offices:
New York   Cincinnati
D. Van Nostrand and Company International Offices:
London   Toronto   Melbourne
Copyright © 1980 by Litton Educational Publishing, Inc.
Library of Congress Catalog Card Number: 79-66016
ISBN: 0-442-25211-0

Published by D. Van Nostrand Company
135 West 50th Street, New York, N.Y.   10020

10   9   8   7   6   5   4   3   2   1

Preface

With the advent of the Education of All Handicapped Children Act (Public Law 94-142), teachers in the public school at all levels of instructional responsibility, from primary to secondary, and regular to special education, are confronted with the task of providing the most appropriate educational program for each child. An appropriate educational program requires the teacher to process information about the child more accurately in order to determine those instructional strategies that will best meet the child's educational needs. At the heart of these skills is a basic understanding of diagnostic or assessment techniques.

Fundamentals of Educational Assessment has been designed to provide teachers, primary or secondary, regular or special, with the fundamentals of educational assessment to aid them in collecting, utilizing, and synthesizing diagnostic information for program planning. Examples throughout the book have been selected from the educational world of the public school teacher. These examples illustrate real-world problems in educational assessment encountered by teachers.

The contents of the book are based upon the results of an extensive study conducted by the author among teachers, administrators, and parents of exceptional children. The results of the study are equally applicable to all teachers who have the responsibility of developing instructional programs.

The study that prompted this book had as its objective the determination of skills, competencies, or behaviors that were perceived as being most needed in successfully teaching exceptional children. The study itself was designed around the critical incident technique developed by John Flannagan (University of Pittsburgh, 1963). Following his procedures, over 1,000 persons were asked to provide critical incidents related to teaching exceptional children. More than 3,000 critical incidents were collected from teachers, administrators, and parents in the western states of Arizona, Idaho, Nevada, Utah, and the mid-eastern states of Kentucky, Indiana, and Tennessee.

These incidents were then synthesized into categories of specified teaching competencies. Educational assessment was one of those categories. Educational assessment behaviors were identified frequently as critical to teaching exceptional children. These behaviors guided the author and became the focal point in the development of this book.

Several major concerns evolved from the study relating to educational assessment. One was the skill and ability level of the teacher to educationally diagnose and remediate the child who is not performing in the classroom. Most teachers expressed a lack of training in assessment and in exposure to the role educational assessment plays in program planning. Both regular- and special-education teachers reported concern about their ability to prepare an educational program.

Another frequently reported incident involved assessment information obtained from professional staff members in the school. The school counselor, psychologists, and social workers were often reported as being unable to provide interpretive information from diagnostic measures that could be easily translated into practical and manageable classroom strategies.

Teachers reported referring a child to a psychologist or psychometrist for assessing the extent of a reading or math problem. The results confirmed the teacher's initial diagnosis; that is, the psychologist's report indicated that the child did have a reading problem. The report, however, usually contained little if any information that directed the teacher to the proper remediation strategies, instructional materials, and techniques that could be used in helping the child overcome the reading problem.

Another area of concern was based on the following frequently reported incident. Psychologists often suggested a behavior modification approach for correcting misbehavior in the classroom. This usually included placing the child on some type of reinforcement schedule. Teachers felt that this approach was an inadequate remediation strategy, since many reported having over 25 students and believed that the time involved in observing and reinforcing one child could be better spent in remediating the academic problems of several children.

These comments are not meant to imply that the psychologist, school counselor, and other professionals do not provide worthwhile services to the classroom teacher. These professionals and their services were frequently identified in this study as valuable assets for helping the classroom teacher. The incidents are presented as illustrations of: (1) The problems faced by teachers as the only diagnostician in the classroom; (2) the critical importance of teachers possessing at least a minimal level of diagnostic-prescriptive skills; and (3) the need for supporting staff (school psychologists, counselors, and others) to develop an increased understanding of the teaching techniques, methodologies, and materials needed to remediate the learning problems of children in the classroom.

The book is organized into three major parts: Part 1 provides an introduction to the fundamentals of educational assessment. The concepts of test reliability and validity are discussed. The reasons why, how, and by whom educational assessments should be conducted are given, along with discussions about standardized and nonstandardized testing methodologies.

Part 2 has as its primary purpose the development of educational assessment skills by the teacher. The student or reader completing this part of the book will be exposed to the different formal and informal methods, procedures, and instruments that are used in conducting educational assessments. Examples are provided to illustrate how the assessment information can be interpreted for later program planning. The student is given several opportunities to apply the information from each of the chapters found in Part 2 to practical, realistic problems in educational assessment.

Part 3 consists of an explanation of Public Law 94-142 and its potential impact on the teacher as an educational program planner. In light of this law, as well as of the requirements of producing an appropriate educational program, the reader is provided with samples and activities directed toward the interpretation and application of diagnostic data in the development of these educational programs.

The author would like to express thanks and appreciation to

many who have helped in the preparation of this text. The author notes with a great deal of satisfaction that those who have made primary contributions to the development of this text have been teachers and practitioners in the day-to-day world of teaching children. The author would especially like to thank Randy Lloyd and Joyce Baca for their efforts in developing the first draft of a book that became the nucleus of the present text. Special thanks are also due Nicole Mongiello and Nancy Sams Hoke for their editing and assistance in indexing and to JoAnne Ingram, Barbara Fischer, Shirley Johnson, and the secretaries from the Department of Educational Psychology at Brigham Young University for typing the original manuscript.

The author extends special thanks to Professor Edward Clark, St. John's University; Professor Daniel J. Reschly, Iowa State University; Professor Sally Antes, Western Illinois University; and Professor Maryann Bilello Schaefer, St. John's University for their helpful suggestions and criticisms of the manuscript. Appreciation is extended to all publishers and authors who granted permission to reproduce their materials in making this a more meaningful work. To Dr. Don Logan, Dr. Edward Blackhurst, and Dr. Melton C. Martinson, thanks for the intrinsic motivation to complete this text.

THIS BOOK IS DEDICATED TO
GEORGE AND LUCILLE INGRAM

Contents

Part Three   Developing an Educational Program

An Overview of Assessment

chapter

1

Introduction to Assessment

Objectives

At the conclusion of this chapter the reader should be able to:

1. define educational assessment;
2. discuss the purposes inherent in conducting an educational assessment;
3. define formal and informal assessment procedures;
4. specify who should be involved in the assessment process;
5. discuss the assessment skills needed by classroom teachers;
6. outline procedures for preparing to conduct an educational assessment.

Preparing to Conduct an Educational Assessment

"He's all yours. He can't read or write, and he's a behavior problem. The principal told me to bring him down to your classroom, and so here he is. Good luck."

This is an often-experienced example of how many classroom teachers get both special and regular children with whom they will be working. Now that "he's all yours," what are you going to do? How are you going to go about preparing an appropriate educational program?

In order to establish what you are going to do, you must first obtain certain information about the child. What is the child capable and not capable of doing? Your program for this child will most certainly have to be based on this information. How can it be obtained? Educational assessment is a method by which information can be generated to answer these questions. Learning how to conduct an educational assessment should be an integral part of any training a teacher receives. The remainder of this chapter will explore some introductory concepts involved in the assessment process.

Definition of Assessment

Educational assessment is the application of a systematic process of diagnosis that results in identification of a child's school-related problems. It also uncovers the type of remediation processes that can be used to correct the problems.

Since assessment is a complete process, all the factors that can affect performance must be taken into consideration. These factors range from the child's capacity for learning to the environmental or physical conditions that surround the learning situation (Cross, 1972). Also included is the social-emotional level of the child. How does the child feel while the task is being learned? Another factor is the child's understanding of the mechanical process of the task to be performed. How much of the task does the child understand? For example, if the task is reading based on a phonic approach, does the child have an understanding of word-attack skills, sound-letter associations, and rules governing vowel and consonant usage?

Once armed with the above assessment information the teacher is in a much better position to develop, plan, and select effective and efficient educational strategies to correct the child's problem.

Purposes of Assessment

In the literature many purposes of assessment are reported to include placement, classification, and research. When the teacher's role is considered, the primary reason for making an assessment is to plan the most appropriate education program for the child. To do this an inherent purpose of the assessment must be to determine the specific skill level of the child relative to the task to be performed, be it an academic, physical, or social task. Assessment information allows the teacher to specify more exactly the skill level of the child as well as educational strategies to be used within the program. These purposes are greatly magnified by the Education for All Handicapped Children Act of 1975 (PL 9-142) where assessment becomes more than an end in itself. Under this law the primary purposes of assessment are identified as (1) developing the most appropriate educational program for a handicapped child, (2) making decisions relative to placement of the child in the least restrictive environment, and (3) outlining the evaluation procedures that are to be used in determining the effectiveness of the child's individual educational program in meeting identified goals and objectives. (A more thorough discussion of PL 94-142 will be found in Chapter 14.) These purposes may be helpful in ensuring that the child will not suffer from the detrimental effects of placement in an improper educational setting (Dunn, 1968). Further, they provide the basis from which to determine or to account for the effects a particular program will have on the child's performance.

Who Should Assess?

Several authorities (Burnett, 1970; Meyers and Hammill, 1976; and Wallace and Larsen, 1978) have implied that the classroom teacher should play an important role in the assessment process. Utilizing the teacher in this manner is not a new concept (Smith and Neisworth, 1969) and supports the research completed by the author (see Preface) related to the skills teachers felt they needed to plan more effective educational programs. The involvement of teachers in assessment is even more critical when consideration is made of the responsibility for developing, implementing, and evaluating a child's entire educational program. In studies conducted by Chow (1978) and Buchanan (1975) teachers consistently identified diagnostic skills as one set of behaviors requisite to the development of a child's educational program. Within the regulations for PL 94-142 it is recommended that a team of professionals be responsible for conducting the child's educational assessment. The classroom teacher is identified as a member of that team, and it is suggested that the teacher be involved in the diagnosis. This involvement increases the teacher's reponsibility for knowing how to conduct an educational assessment.

For legalistic and legislative reasons, the classroom teacher should not perform the assessment alone. Higgins (1977) points out that sound educational practice calls for assessment to be conducted by a team of professionals. This concept parallels the evaluation procedures specified in PL 94-142. It appears that no one person can adequately determine and identify all the multiplicity of information concerning a child's learning performance. In Higgins' discussion of the assessment team he outlines seven points that should be considered in organizing the team for evaluation. These guidelines are based on meeting the provisions recommended in PL 94-142 and include:

1. the public agency responsible for determining that the child has a specific handicap will use a team to evaluate that child;
2. the official from the education agency responsible for the administration of special education programs will be responsible for appointing team members;
3. the composition of the team must include the child's regular teacher or a teacher licensed or certified by the state agency and appointed by the official representing the educational agency completing the assessment;
4. one additional individual certified or licensed by the state education agency to conduct individual diagnostic examinations (school psychologist, speech clinician, or resource teacher) must be included on the assessment team;
5. members constituting the team shall be chosen on the basis of their knowledge of procedures used in the evaluation of children;

6. each individual team member must be qualified to perform the specific assessment tasks they have been assigned; and

7. after the evaluation, the team should meet at least once to discuss the evaluation and to reach a decision as to the child's performance.

Even if a team evaluation effort is used, the individual classrooom teacher must possess some minimum level of assessment skills just to participate with the team or to act as an individual teacher in the preparation of a child's individual program. These skills include: (1) being able to develop or utilize assessment procedures, formal or informal, that will generate information about the child's specific skill level of performance on any school-related task and (2) to be able to interpret diagnostic data from standardized or criterion-referenced measures; or, more directly, to synthesize from a previously completed assessment information that becomes useful for program planning and development. It appears obvious that the teacher's primary role is to teach. However, to teach effectively, one must have the necessary information from which to develop an effective educational program. This information is usually identified from some kind of assessment made of the child's abilities, disabilities, learning style, and the environment from which the teaching and learning is to take place. To make the educational program appropriate, the teacher must be involved in the evaluation and, therefore, must possess the skills mentioned above.

The Instruments and Procedures To Be Considered

Assessment must be planned individually if it is to be used for the purpose of assisting the individual child to perform more efficiently and effectively in the classroom. Assessment techniques and instruments, be they formal or informal, standardized or criterion-referenced, must then be selected and used to meet that end. Reports of inappropriate use of assessment instruments and the resulting data seem to be appearing in literature on an ever-continuing basis. It appears that once a test or procedure has become institutionalized, we come to accept it without asking any further questions as to its appropriateness or asking how it can be used more productively. Deno (1972) nicely summarizes the underlying reasons for assessment when she states that:

> It seems obvious that educators cannot give up testing in all of its forms. To teach is to be judging every moment of every interaction with the child. How we can respond most productively, how we can best manipulate the factors influencing his learning so as to increase the probability of its occurring. Judging requires measuring in one form or another against criteria which are relevant to the decision that must be made. Assessment must and will occur subjectively or objectively. Our commitment should be to make the assessment as worthwhile as we can in terms of its contribution to improve learning on the part of the child (p. 362).

Given Deno's statement, two types of assessment, formal and informal, will be discussed. In a *formal assessment*, the teacher relies primarily on the administration of standardized tests. A standardized test is one that has been constructed for a specific purpose and has been "standardized" to reflect the performance of a child taking the test in relation to the performance of others who have taken it.

A standardized test is usually characterized by the following:

1. specific administration procedures;
2. definite scoring criteria;
3. distinct methods for interpreting scores outlined in detail.

The results are reported in terms of quotients, scale scores, grade equivalents, or percentiles that compare a given child's performance to a national or regional group of children who have completed the test (Hammill, 1971). Standardized tests have been designed to assess the individual, the group, the individual's achievement, the group's achievement, the individual's capacity, aptitude, and interests, or the group's capacity, aptitude, and interests.

For making *inter-individual* comparisons—that is, comparing an individual with the members of his or her peer group—a standardized test is usually the instrument selected and used. Standardized tests can also reveal information for use in making *intra-individual* comparisons—or comparing the individual perfor-mance in one area with performance in other areas. In making an intra-individual comparison, the standarized test must be thoroughly understood in terms of the tasks or behaviors to be measured by the test. A good source for determining the types of formal standardized tests available is Buros's (1972) *Mental Measurements Yearbook*. This reference provides a comprehen-sive listing of most standardized tests.

Informal assessment is usually developed and administered by the teacher. It is used when specific information is needed but no standardized test is available to provide the information. For ex-ample, a child may not understand the concept of prefixes and suffixes as it applies to spelling. A teacher will design a test to measure the child's relative ability to utilize those concepts.

The advantage in using informal devices is that there are no limits to what can be measured. When consideration is given to the tasks to be learned, informal assessment becomes a valuable technique. A child's ability to perform social, emotional, physical, and academic tasks can be assessed using these procedures. Infor-mal assessment can also provide a very distinct advantage in that the program to be developed and the student's performance to be assessed in most cases can be one and the same.

Two methods of informal assessment provide the teacher with some good general information from which to plan additional as-sessment procedures and to select remedial strategies. These methods are known as the *Case Study Method* and the *Criterion Task-Based Method.*

In the *Case Study Method,* the teacher reconstructs the child's history to determine some of the underlying causes for the child's current problem. There may be factors that exist in the home that are directly affecting the child's inability to perform at school. On the other hand, the home environment may be quite conducive to correcting learning problems. Or, there may be things outside the class that will assist the child in overcoming his learning prob-lems in the class.

There are a number of different ways for collecting case study information. However, case studies are usually constructed through an interview with the child's parent, guardian, or someone who knows the child intimately. The usual information collected includes the child's *developmental history; medical background;* the child's *physiological makeup* in terms of normal growth and development patterns; *psychological history;* and some indication of how well the child learns educationally related material.

Another informal method that is generally used in working with children having learning problems is the *Criterion Task-Based Method.* This method is much like criterion-referenced testing in that the child's ability to complete a task is measured against the requirements of the task. Consider the example of a child asked to perform a reading task successfully at a fourth-grade level. The steps of a criterion-based approach would include finding answers to the following questions. Figure 1-1 provides an example of the answers that might be found.

1. What is the task to be learned?
2. What is the criterion level to be met by the learner?
3. How will the child's performance be measured?

The child's ability to perform or not perform then becomes a diagnostic guide relative to the task. If the child can't perform the task, the task may be too difficult, the criterion level too high, or additional instruction related to the task may be needed. In other words, the teacher using a Criterion Task-Based Method has three options of assessment:

1. Examine the child's ability or inability to complete the task at the criterion level. Is the selected task too easy or too difficult?
2. Examine the selected criterion level. Is it too high or too low?
3. Examine the level of task difficulty. Should the level of difficulty be reduced (in this case, from a fourth-grade level to a third-grade level) or should the method of instruction be altered?

Such an analysis gives some insight into the remediation work that must be accomplished in order to assist the child in performing the task to the criterion level. This information gives the teacher very specific direction for program planning.

Figure 1-1 Criterion Task-Based Method

Question	Answer
1. What is the task?	1. The child will complete the following fourth-grade reading tasks: a. *Structural Analysis* (1) Know the rules for syllables to include suffixes and prefixes; each syllable must contain a vowel and a single vowel can be a syllable. (2) Know suffixes and prefixes. b. *Phonic Analysis* (1) Know rules for using vowels. (2) Match phonemes with appropriate graphemes.
2. What is the criterion level?	2. The child must complete all structural and phonic analysis tasks presented with 90% accuracy.
3. How to measure the child's performance?	3. Each of the structural and phonic analysis skills for use in this program will be measured at the end of the instructional period in which they were taught. For example, the child will be required to demonstrate rules for syllables, to identify syllables in words, and suffixes and prefixes; each syllable

Guidelines for Conducting an Assessment

The assessment to be effective at all should follow some systematic procedure. This procedure can be broken into two parts: (1) planning the assessment and (2) actually conducting the assessment. In developing a plan for the assessment, several items should be kept in mind. Perhaps at the heart of the plan for assessment is the *referral question*. The referral question is usually provided through the teacher's own concern, or, if the person is acting as a member of a diagnostic team, the question can come from a parent, a teacher, or from observing the child in the classroom. The referral question specifies or gives direction to the overall assessment procedure to include the identification and selection of tests.

In developing a plan, reasons for the assessment must be decided. This may be part of the referral question or may go beyond the referral question in that a decision must be made as to how the assessment information will be used. Will it be used for academic program planning, for altering the child's environment in the school, or for providing the child with some type of prosthetic device to assist him/her in learning? Reasons for the assessment are not based only on the referral question but on the information collected about the child's previous performance as well as observation of the child's current behavior. Instruments and assessment procedures can then be decided upon once the referral question and reasons for referral have been carefully reviewed. The determination as to the use of standardized or criterion-referenced measures can be more cogently determined.

The plan also includes the determination of the battery of tests or diagnostic procedures to be used. In a number of articles concerning assessment (Wallace and Larsen, 1978; Higgins, 1977; Meyers and Hammill, 1976; and others), the child is given a battery of standardized tests. That is, the school district or other agency selects a number of procedures or tests to be used with all children. This seems to be a common practice within public education. A practice of running a standard battery of tests on every child referred for help with their educational program may be more detrimental than helpful. Detrimentally, it seems obvious that not all the tests from the battery will be needed or will generate needed information about the child and therefore time is wasted that could be spent more productively in some other area. Further, the results from a standardized test may not always be used appropriately, and it appears that teachers, as professionals, are not always able to go beyond the test score to the area of what is really needed by the child. Therefore, it is best, when given the referral question, to use that question as a guide in selecting the tests or procedures to be used in the assessment.

Instruments and procedures will provide direction as to who should or will conduct the assessment. For example, if the identification of standardized tests has been made, this may require the services of a professional trained in the use of a specific diagnostic tool (i.e., a psychologist to administer the Wechsler In-

telligence Scale for Children, or audiogram completed by an audiologist).

In conducting the assessment several items must be considered. First, *permission*, either from the parent or guardian, must
be obtained. Second, the *conditions* under which the assessment
is to be conducted must be approved or must meet the regulations outlined within the local education agency. An *assessment
site* should be selected on the basis that it provides for the optimum conditions conducive to collecting the most valid information about the child. If a standardized test is to be used, then an
appropriate room and setting must be found. If an observation is
to be made of the child's social interaction with peers, then a
number of different environmental settings must be identified
that will allow for that type of observation. A third consideration
is *rapport*. If the assessment is to be conducted on a one-to-one
basis with the child, it becomes important that the child and the
person conducting the assessment have a good rapport and that
the child feels comfortable in that setting. Another important factor in conducting an assessment, to include the preparation
period and reporting of results, is *confidentiality* of the information collected or generated through the assessment.

Summary

The purpose of assessment should be always to improve the
child's performance. This may involve assessing the child's academic performance, the performance of the child in social situations, as well as the environment in which the child is attempting
to learn. It appears also that the teacher is at the heart of the assessment process since the teacher is most directly involved with
the child. Considering assessment from a legalistic or legislative
standpoint, in conjunction with the responsibilities for program
planning for each child, the teacher has a need for possessing a
minimum level of assessment skills. When planning an assessment, the referral question and reasons for the assessment must
be carefully reviewed. In conducting the assessment parental permission, developing rapport with the child and confidentiality of

the assessment information must be in the forefront of the teacher's mind.

Can You Answer These Questions?

1. What are the purposes of educational assessment?
2. What is an assessment?
3. How would you differentiate between inter- and intra-individual comparison?
4. What are the seven points to be considered in organizing an assessment team?
5. What are the characteristics of a standardized test?
6. What reference document is appropriate for finding information about standardized tests?
7. What would you consider in planning an assessment?
8. What are some considerations to be made by the teacher in conducting an assessment?
9. What are the disadvantages of a preselected battery of tests?
10. Who should be involved in the assessment process?

References

Buchanan, M. *Identification and Validation of Special Education Competency for Noncategorical Teacher Preparation Programs.* Unpublished doctoral dissertation, University of Utah, Salt Lake City, Utah, 1975.

Burnett, R. W. "The Classroom Teacher as a Diagnostician." In D. L. DeBoer (ed.), *Reading Diagnosis and Evaluation.* Newark, Delaware: International Reading Association, 1970.

Buros, O. K. (ed.). *The Seventh Mental Measurements Yearbook.* Highland Park, New Jersey: Gryphon Press, 1972.

Chow, N. Y. H. *Special Education Teaching Competencies: An Investigation of the Difference of Perceived Importance of Teaching Competencies between Teachers and Categorist Areas of Special Education.* Unpublished doctoral dissertation, Brigham Young University, Provo, Utah, 1978.

Cross, D. *Manual for the Educational Assessment Clinic.* Lexington, Kentucky: Department of Special Education, University of Kentucky, 1972.

Deno, E. "Reflections on the Use and Interpretation of Tests for Teachers." In E. Meyers, G. Uergason, and B. Whelan (eds.), *Strategies for Teaching Exceptional Children: Essays from Folks of Exceptional Children.* Denver, Colorado: Love Publishing, 1972.

Dunn, L. M. "Special Education for the Mildly Retarded: Is Much of it Justifiable?" *Exceptional Children,* September 1978, 35, 5–22.

Hammill, D. D. "Evaluating Children for Instructional Purposes." *Academic Therapy,* 1971, 6, 341–353.

Higgins, J. P. "Present Levels of Performance and Assessment: Some Basic Considerations." In S. Torres (ed.), *A Primer on Education Programs for Handicapped Children.* Reston, Viriginia: The Foundation for Exceptional Children, 1977.

Meyers, P. I., and D. D. Hammill. *Methods for Learning Disorders* (2nd ed.). New York: John Wiley, 1976.

Smith, R. M., and J. T. Neisworth. "Fundamentals of Informal Educational Assessment." In R. M. Smith (ed.), *Teacher Diagnosis of Educational Difficulties.* Columbus, Ohio: Charles E. Merrill, 1969.

Wallace, G., and S. C. Larsen. *Educational Assessment of Learning Problems: Testing for Teaching.* Boston: Allyn and Bacon, 1978.

chapter

Fundamentals of Assessment

Objectives

At the conclusion of this chapter the reader should be able to:

1. differentiate between Norm- and Criterion-referenced testing procedures;
2. define and discuss reliability and validity as it applies to the use of tests in planning educational programs for children;
3. define split-half, test-retest, and equivalent forms methods of reliability;
4. define content, concurrent, and predictive validity procedures;
5. define and give examples of mean, mode, and median;
6. discuss the importance of a standard deviation, percentile, standard scores, age and grade norms, and the standard error of measurement.

Introduction

Assessment requires the application and use of systematic procedures or instruments to generate information about a child's ability to perform prescribed tasks. The assessment techniques and instruments are constructed following specified fundamentals used in measuring human capacity, ability, behavior, or performance. Several of these fundamentals of assessment will be discussed in this chapter to include norm- and criterion-referenced tests, reliability and validity, measures of central tendency, and other normative measurement concepts.

Norm- and Criterion-Referenced Testing

Norm-Referenced Testing. In norm-referenced testing, an individual's performance is measured against that of his or her peers. That is, the individual's score on a norm-referenced test is compared to a score that reflects how the individual's peer group would have answered that question. Salvia and Ysseldyke (1978) point out that in norm-referenced assessment acquisition or learning of content is important only to the extent that differential learning allows the tester to rank-order individuals from those who have acquired many skills to those who have acquired few. In other words, the emphasis in norm-referenced testing is on the relative standing of individuals representing different chronological ages, usually from different parts of the country, and representing a variety of cultural and demographic backgrounds. The items are then normed following either an age or point-scale procedure. The items from the test are scaled in terms of the percentages of individuals who represent a particular age group that has responded correctly to the items presented. Test items in an *age scale* would differentiate between younger and older children. That is, a test item that had been normed on eight year olds should not be correctly answered by a five year old; only a small percentage of six- and seven-year-old children should be able to answer the item correctly, while a very high percentage of eight-year-old children should be able to correctly answer the item, and that all older children (older than eight) should be able to correctly respond to the item.

Point scales are constructed by ordering the test items into different levels of difficulty. Theoretically the levels of difficulty are not age associated and should reflect the person's performance in terms of a grade equivalent (Salvia and Ysseldyke, 1978). The grade equivalent represents the average performance expected at a particular grade level. For a more detailed discussion of the concept of age and point scales, refer to Salvia and Ysseldyke (1978), Anastasi (1976), Thorndike and Hagen (1977), and Gronlund (1972).

Criterion-Referenced Testing. The criterion-referenced test has as its purpose the measurement of an individual's mastery of a specific skill. The criterion test measures how well a person has mastered the necessary skills needed to complete a specified task successfully. The test is usually composed of items that reflect the individual skill or tasks that comprise the overall task to be learned. Wallace and Larsen (1978) characterize criterion-referenced testing as that test which measures the individual's performance or evaluates the individual's performance in terms of an absolute or specific criterion that has been selected for that individual. For example, the criterion set for one individual may be 80 percent correct spelling of a list of words selected from a fourth-grade reader. An advantage of criterion testing is that it allows the teacher to identify not only the task to be performed but the skills and the acquisition of those skills by the individual relative to successful mastery of that task. As Salvia and Ysseldyke (1978) point out, the items on criterion-referenced tests are usually directly associated to, or with, specific instructional objectives for the teacher to identify the beginning point of instruction as well as the direction or sequence the instruction will take.

When To Use Norm or Criterion Tests. The most functional use of either a norm- or criterion-referenced test lies in the expected or intended use of the test information. If the intent of the teacher is to evaluate the effects of an instructional program in reading and the teacher wants to compare students' performance against a regional or national norm, then a norm-referenced device should be used. It is not uncharacteristic to find a majority of special education placement decisions made on the basis of norm-referenced test results. A number of states require the utilization of norm-referenced measures as a part of the evaluation of a student before placement in a special education program can be made. Norm-referenced tests are also valuable tools in the screening of students, particularly in the academic areas where a child's score can be readily compared to those of other children within the class, giving direction to the teacher for further assessment or program planning. The author feels that the use of the norm-referenced tests in screening may be the most valuable reason for using a test of this nature. For example, in the development of a comprehensive math program for a large group of children with varying degrees of ability, a standardized or norm-referenced math test to identify the performance levels of all the students could be administered. Grouping of students could then be made on the basis of performance and noted deficiencies could then be further analyzed for use in programming more specifically to individual or small group needs. As Salvia and Ysseldyke (1978) illustrate, norm-referenced tests are designed primarily for one purpose: to separate the performances of individuals in order to allow the teacher (in this case) to discriminate among those performances. From this information the teacher can make more appropriate program development decisions.

If the intent of the classroom teacher is to plan an individual program for the child, then the use of criterion-referenced devices should be considered as the vehicle in reaching this end. As mentioned earlier, the criterion-referenced test reflects information relative to the skills or criterion needed to complete a specific task. Both the criteria and the task can be tailor-made to meet the individual child's needs. Using a criterion-referenced measure, the teacher is able to more readily identify the specific skills that the student possesses or does not possess relative to completing that task. Once this information is identified, the teacher has a distinct criterion for selecting and developing instructional strategies. Since most criterion-referenced tests are composed of skills that are sequenced in level of difficulty from simple to complex, the teacher can also identify where the instruction should begin and what direction that instruction should take. Further, with the use of a criterion-referenced measure the evaluation of effect of the instructional strategy is obvious in that the child either can now master the task or cannot master the task. If the instructional strategy is adequate the child can be seen moving along the curricular sequence toward mastery of the entire task. If the instructional strategy is not appropriate, the child is still at or close to the entry level of that instructional sequence, thus necessitating a change in strategy which may involve changing the entry level to one more easily accomplished by the child or changing the method of instruction.

Reliability and Validity

Reliability. Reliability is synonymous with dependability or stability (Kerlinger, 1973). If a test is reliable, it continues to test and give the same scores over and over again. In most standardized testing a statistical procedure has been applied to determine the reliability of the test. This is accomplished by correlating different test scores from the same instrument to determine if the tests are stable—that is, to determine the degree of fluctuation from one set of test scores and another. The greater the fluctuation, the greater the instability of the test. If the correlation is high, the relative stability of the test can be said to be good. A perfect correlation would be considered $+1.00$; an exact opposite correlation between two sets of data would be -1.00. A relationship reflecting no correlation at all between two sets of data would be 0.0. In a manual for a standardized test in which the reliability data were reported to be .95, it could be concluded that the test was very dependable since the closer the correlation reaches 1.00, the more reliable the test is said to be.

The reliability is an important component of a standardized test. It has been found in looking through many administration manuals for a number of different "standardized tests" that the reliability and validity information has been omitted. Without this information, the test's reliability has to be considered suspect at best. When the reliability data are included, the higher the correlation coefficients are and the closer they approximate 1.00, the more reliable or stable the test should be.

A number of methods are used for determining reliability. Those methods most commonly found in the author's review of standardized tests and test manuals were the *split-half, test-retest,* and the *equivalent form methods.* In the *split-half* procedure, the test items are divided into two parts. A method for doing this is to simply number all the test items sequentially and then to select out the odd numbered items and compare them to the even numbered items. For example, a test is administered to a group of children; upon completion of the test, the scores obtained on the odd items are correlated with the scores of the even numbered items to determine their stability in measuring the performance of the children on that particular test.

In a *test-retest* method the test is administered to a group of children and then, after a specified period of time, the test is readministered to the same group or a like group. The results are then correlated between the first and second groups to determine how stable or how consistent the results were in measuring the performance of those taking the test. A critical factor in the *test-retest* methodology is the interval of time used between the two administrations of the test. Generally, the time interval should be as short as possible, thus increasing the reliability of the data obtained from the two administrations.

The *equivalent forms* method of reliability is accomplished by administering alternate forms of the same test to the same population. That is, two equivalent tests reflecting equal levels of difficulty but composed of different items that measure the same skill is administered to a population, half of the population receives one form and the other half of the population receives the other form of the test. Scores are then correlated and the reliability of the equivalent forms determined.

In selecting any standardized test, the teacher should review the test manual and locate that section that provides the reliability and validity data. Those data should then be reviewed thoroughly to determine the reliability of any particular test. As stated earlier, a test manual that does not provide these types of data should be considered suspect as to what the test is actually measuring.

Validity. Validity can be simply defined as the ability of a test to measure what it purports to measure. For example, if a test was designed to assess mathematical skills, then the results of the person taking the test should provide an indication of that person's mathematical ability if the test is to be considered valid.

Some tests lend themselves to validations better than others. For example, to validate a math test one need only look at the test to determine if it is composed of math computation items. From that, at least a surface face validity can be ascertained. Other tests, such as those that are designed to measure aptitude or intelligence, do not lend themselves to this surface validation. Therefore, it is important for a teacher using any test to consult the administration manual for the validity data for that particular test.

There are several methods for determining the validity of a test. Those to be reviewed here will include content, concurrent, and predictive methods of validation. *Content validity* is an indication of the adequacy of the test in covering sufficiently a sample of the behaviors under consideration. A beginning step in content validity is a clear and distinct understanding of what the content should be. Salvia and Ysseldyke (1978) outline three factors used to establish content validity. Within the first factor the questions "Are the test questions appropriate?" and "Are the test questions really measuring the behavior under consideration?" must be answered. The appropriateness is based upon a number of possible variables: (1) the age level the item is to measure; (2) the developmental level of the item must be considered; and (3) the actual content of each item understood. One would expect that the content of a math achievement test would be composed of math achievement test items. Further, if the math test is to measure fourth-grade performance levels, then test items should be composed of information appropriate to that age and developmental level. Salvia and Ysseldyke's (1978) second factor in determining content validity is the completeness of the item sample. The test items should sample a broad range of tasks. In the example of the fourth-grade achievement math test, the expectation would be to find more than a test of basic addition facts but would include a broader range of computational skills to include multiplication and division items appropriate to the fourth grade. The third factor in establishing content validity is how the test items assess the level of mastery of the content. Assessing the level of mastery can be completed in a number of different ways, to include having the person being tested recognize the correct answer in multiple choice array, to compute a correct answer, or to apply a procedure in generating the correct answer.

Concurrent validity involves comparing the test under investigation to a test of the same type which is already accepted as an accurate measurement device. If, for example, we were to develop a test of intelligence, the scores for that intelligence test can then be compared with those scores obtained from an already accepted measure of intelligence. To do this, a sample group of persons is selected to which the new test is administered as well as the accepted intelligence test. Both scores obtained from this one group are then correlated as a means of determining concurrent validity. The first step in obtaining concurrent validity is to find an existing valid measure with which to compare the new test.

Predictive validity allows for making accurate estimations about a person's performance in the future based upon that person's score from a predictive test. To determine predictive validity, the test score is measured against future performance (Kerlinger, 1973). For example, the predictive validity of an aptitude test is validated by checking the future performance of individuals who reportedly scored high or low on that aptitude test. If the aptitude test score was high and a high score was used to predict relative success in a particular area, then checking the performance of individuals who scored high to ascertain if they were in fact successful in that predicted area would be a means of determining predictive validity.

Another method of determining predictive validity would be to compare the results from a test against those of an already-existing test or against the judgments of experts representing that particular area under question. For example, if a test is developed to determine if a child is learning disabled and the test is used to predict or identify who is learning disabled, the validation of that test can then be made against the opinions of noted authorities in the area of learning disabilities. That is, given those children who were identified as learning disabled by that test and then it is found that "experts" also identify them as learning disabled, it can be concluded that our test has some predictive value for identifying learning disabled children.

Test validity information is important in determining the accuracy of the test to be used. Evidence of validity should be presented in the test manual or report (Salvia and Ysseldyke, 1978). Without evidence of test validity, the test should be considered suspect. Another consideration that should be made in determining the validity of the test is that the reported information dealing with the limits of generalized ability of the data presented. In other words, a test designed to measure intelligence should have reported somewhere in the administration manual or description of the test construction any information relative to how the test results should be interpreted and used to appropriately reflect the population that was used to construct and validate the test. Without this information, the teacher is at a loss as to how the test data or results can be interpreted, and inappropriate decisions about developing instructional programs or placing children in appropriate educational settings may be made.

Measures of Central Tendency

Measures of central tendency can be most useful when a teacher is attempting to sort test data into meaningful descriptions of the performance variability of students. Measures of central tendency allow for the systematic organization of scores or performances beginning with the *mean*, which is simply the arithmetic average of all the performance scores. The mean allows for comparison against that average, and a student's score can then have more meaning in terms of instructional program direction for the teacher. The mean is computed by simply adding all the scores available and then dividing the total by the number of scores obtained. If fifteen scores have been collected and the fifteen scores total 45, the mean or average would be computed as 3.

$$\text{Number of scores} = 15$$
$$\text{Total of scores} \quad = 45$$
$$\text{Mean} = \frac{45}{15} = 3$$

The next measure of central tendency is the *median*. The median is merely the point at which half of the scores are above and half the scores are below. The median can be a point of reference and does not necessarily have to be an actual score; it merely reflects the mid-point of all the scores in the distribution. For example, a series of scores could be 21, 22, 23, 25, 26, 27. The median for this distribution would be 24. In a distribution of scores of 87, 84, 81, 80, 78, 78, 75, the median would be 80. That is, half of the scores are above and half of the scores are below 80. The median is used to determine relative position of a person's performance.

Another measure of central tendency is the *mode*, which is simply the score that occurs the most often. It may be of value if a group of scores occurs frequently enough to indicate central tendency. In the distribution of scores of 24, 20, 15, 9, 9, 9, 5, 3, the mode would be 9. It is an indication of the frequency of the occurrence of that particular test score on the test administered. The mode could be useful to the classroom teacher in interpreting the test scores and making decisions about the performance expectancy of the individuals taking the test. However, the mode is a very poor indicator for use in interpreting test scores. The median or mean is recommended to represent typical or average performance (Thorndike and Hagen, 1977).

Normative Data

Within formal testing there are a number of different procedures that can be used to identify where a child's performance fits in relationship to those of other children taking the same test. These include the use of percentiles, standard deviations, standard scores, grade and age norms, and standard error of measure. For the sake of classification, these procedures are being identified as *normative data*.

Standard Deviation. As Thorndike and Hagen (1977) point out, it is almost impossible to say what a standard deviation is. Simply stated, it is an indication of how scores can be distributed and interpreted. Salvia and Ysseldyke (1978) illustrate the deviation as a unit of measurement used in statistics similar to other units of measurement, such as an inch or ton. In other words, scores from a normal distribution can be measured in terms of standard deviation units from the mean. In the interpretation of test scores it is most important to know about the means and standard deviations computed for each individual test. Figure 2-1 illustrates the standard deviation in relationship to a normally distributed curve. In

Figure 2-1 Normal distribution and the Stanford–Binet and Slosson Intelligence Test Standard Deviation Distribution

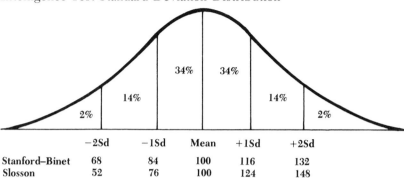

	−2Sd	−1Sd	Mean	+1Sd	+2Sd
Stanford–Binet	68	84	100	116	132
Slosson	52	76	100	124	148

the figure, it can be seen that between +1 and −1 standard deviation (Sd) can be found 68% of the total population. At +1 Sd from the mean can be found 34% of the population and at +2 Sds can be found 48% of the population. From +2 to −2 standard deviations from the mean would contain 96% of the total population.

Different tests have different standard deviations and therefore require making different interpretations of the test results. The significance of a score in a distribution is dependent upon the mean and standard deviation. That is, a score from one test may not necessarily have the same value as a score from a like test if the standard deviations and means are different. An example of this is provided in Salvia and Ysseldyke (1978) where a Stanford-Binet IQ score is compared to a similar IQ score from the Slosson Intelligence Test. The Stanford-Binet score of 80 is 1.25 standard deviations below the mean of 100 while the IQ score of 80 from the Slosson Intelligence Test is .83 standard deviation below the mean. Even though the two tests provide a similar IQ score, when consideration is made of the standard deviations, the two scores cannot be equally valued (see Figure 2-1). The standard deviation for the Stanford-Binet is 16 with a mean of 100. The Slosson Intelligence Test while having the same mean has a standard deviation of approximately 24, thereby creating a difference in the value of each IQ score when standard deviation is considered. Referring to Figure 2-1 placement of the individual score from each of the tests on the normal distribution indicates that the scores are not equally distributed. This comparison is provided to illustrate that the teacher who is going to be making decisions based upon normative test data should take time to consult the administrative manuals of the test to determine the means and standard deviations that should be found within.

A *percentile* merely delineates where a child performs within a group in terms of the percentage of those who perform either above or below. For example, with a student scoring in the 45th percentile, it can be said that 55% of the population had a higher score and 44% of the population had lower scores. The percentile acts as a ranking of the child in relationship to all other children that have taken the same test.

Age and Grade Norms. These norms refer to the child's position relative to either age or grade placement. Thus, a score of 21 on a particular test could be interpreted in two ways. One, it could be translated into an *age norm*. For example, the score 21 is a score obtained more frequently by persons who are in the same age range. A *grade norm* reflects the score most frequently obtained by a particular grade level. In other words, a grade score of 21 could be obtained most frequently by, say, ninth-grade students. Many tests provide age and grade norm data. The teacher should be aware of those data, especially if program decisions are being made. In using achievement test data, the results of which are usually presented in either age or grade norms, the teacher's awareness of what a child's score reflects in terms of age or grade norms will provide better direction for making program decisions.

Standard Scores. Standard scores are much like age, grade, and percentile norms in that they allow the teacher to determine the student's relative position in the distribution of all scores. However, unlike age and grade norms, the standard score allows for better control of predicting where a student's position is. Standard scores translate seemingly diverse raw scores into comparable entities. The standard deviation is used in the computation of standard scores. Standard scores in the form of either *z scores* or *T scores* are usually found in the administration manuals of standardized tests. A *z* score is a standard score that has a mean of zero and a standard deviation of 1. The individual's raw score from the test is converted to a *z* score to illustrate relative position. For example, given two raw scores, 50 and 45, it appears that these scores are in close proximity of each other. However, in computation of the z score it is found that the raw score of 50 has a deviation of $+1.5$ from the mean while 45 is found to be a $-.5$. Using this illustration, it can be seen that the relative position of the two scores is perhaps greatly different than on the initial scrutinization of those scores. A z score is computed with the following formula.

$$z = \frac{\text{Raw Score} - \text{Mean of All Scores}}{\text{Sd}}$$

A T *score* is a standard score having the mean of 50 and the standard deviation of 10. Like the z score, a T score can be computed on raw data to provide a more meaningful picture of what the raw data mean. A raw score can be computed to show relative position. Using the z scores in the example above, T scores can be computed using the formula

$$T \text{ score} = 50 + 10z \text{ score}$$

Let it be pointed out that raw scores do not always reflect relative position and that in comparing raw score data, caution should be given to making comparisons between two scores as in the example above. If the teacher wishes to find the relative position of any child's particular score then the standard deviation, the z or T score can be computed to illustrate that position more dramatically.

Figure 2-2 illustrates the T and z scores relative to a normal distribution while Figure 2-3 illustrates the computation of z scores into T scores.

Figure 2-2 z and T Scores Relative to a Normal Distribution

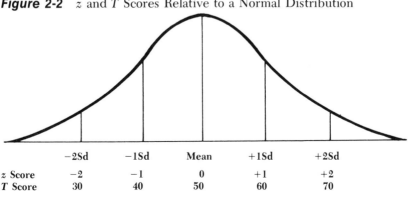

	−2Sd	−1Sd	Mean	+1Sd	+2Sd
z Score	−2	−1	0	+1	+2
T Score	30	40	50	60	70

Figure 2-3 T Scores Computed from z Scores

Raw Score	z Score	T Score (T Score $= 50 + 10(z)$)
50	$+1.5$	$65 = 50 + 10(+1.5)$
45	$-.5$	$45 = 50 + 10(-.5)$

Standard Error of Measurement. The standard error of measurement is an attempt to account for the possible variability or error involved in the test. In other words, an individual's score may not be that individual's true score due to the presence of error within the test and/or test results. To help account for this error, the Standard Error of Measurement (SEM) is determined for each test. The SEM then is used to provide a range within which the individual's true score can be said to exist with greater confidence. A good example of the application and use of SEM is found in the Keymath Diagnostic Arithmetic Test (Connolly, Nachtman, and Pritchett, 1971). In this test the SEM for the total test raw score is 3.3 points. An individual's true score on this test should exist somewhere between plus 3.3 points and minus 3.3 points from the individual's raw score. For instance, a raw score of 175 would provide a range of scores from 171.7 to 178.3 in which the individual's true score should exist. The SEM is a necessary tool for helping the teacher decide on the relative reliability of a particular test.

The fundamentals of assessment discussed above are essential in the understanding and interpretation of standardized test scores or in the selection and utilization of norm-referenced standardized measures. As mentioned earlier, in reviewing tests for inclusion in this text, the author identified a number of standardized tests that lacked the normative data discussed above. Many tests do not have validity and reliability data available. In utilizing standardized tests for the purpose of program planning or for any reason other than the development of appropriate educational programs for the child, it seems ludicrous to administer and rely on any test that has not been properly normed or does not provide information relative to its reliability and validity. The importance of having reliability and validity data is greatly enhanced when a standardized test is being considered for use as a placement criterion for determining the type of educational setting, special class, resource room, or other, in which to place the child.

Figure 2-4 is a reflection of those standardized tests which were identified by the author as not having enough adequate normative data contained with their test manuals from which sound decisions concerning either the reliability, validity, or both could be determined. The tests reported in Figure 2-4 are those discussed in this text and are not an inclusive list of all tests that may have questionable data. The reader is referred to Salvia and Ysseldyke (1978), Thorndike and Hagen (1977), Anastasi (1976), Gronlund (1976), and Buros (1972) for further information as to the normative data available for specific tests as well as to the individual test manuals that report reliability and validity information. Further, it is not to be implied that the tests appearing in Figure 2-4 should not be used in the instructional process or that they won't reveal some important information about a child's performance. The information obtained from them or any other test result should be used cautiously in planning instructional pro-

Figure 2-4 Standardized Test with Limited Normative Data

Arthur Adaptation of the Leiter International Performance Scale
California Achievement Test
Developmental Test of Visual-Motor Integration
Developmental Test of Visual Perception
Diagnostic Reading Scales
Gates-MacGinitie Reading Tests
Gates-McKillop Reading Diagnostic Tests
Gilmore Oral Reading Test
Goodenough-Harris Drawing Test
Gray Oral Reading Test
Illinois Test of Psycholinguistic Abilities
Metropolitan Achievement Test
Peabody Picture Vocabulary Test
Primary Mental Abilities Test
Slosson Intelligence Test
Stanford-Binet Intelligence Scale
Wide Range Achievement Test

grams. However, the author believes that only those tests or devices with strong validity and reliability data should be administered for the placement of a child into a categorical special education classroom, such as for the mentally retarded or emotionally disturbed.

Can You Answer These Questions?

1. What is meant by norm-referenced testing?
2. What is meant by criterion-referenced testing?
3. When would it be appropriate to use a criterion-referenced test? Norm-referenced?
4. What is reliability?
5. What is validity?
6. Can you define split-half, test-retest, and equivalent form reliability?
7. Can you define concurrent, content, and predictive validity?
8. What are the measures of central tendency? Define them.
9. What is the value of the standard deviation and standard scores?
10. Can you illustrate the use of the standard error of measurement, percentile, and age and grade norms?

References

Anastasi, A. *Psychological Testing* (4th ed.). London: Macmillan, 1976.

Buros, O.K. *The Seventh Mental Measurements Yearbook*. Highland Park, New Jersey: Gryphon Press, 1972.

Connolly, A., Wl Nachtman, and E. Pritchett. *Keymath Diagnostic Arithmetic Test*. Circle Pines, Minnesota: American Guidance Service, 1971.

Gronlund, N. *Measurement and Evaluation in Teaching* (3rd ed.). New York: Macmillan, 1976.

Kerlinger, F. N. *Foundations of Behavioral Research*. New York: Holt, Rinehart and Winston, 1973.

Salvia, J., and J. E. Ysseldyke. *Assessment in Special and Remedial Education.* Boston: Houghton Mifflin Company, 1978.

Thorndike, R. L., and E. Hagen. *Measurement and Evaluation in Psychology and Education* (4th ed.). New York: John Wiley and Sons, 1977.

Wallace, G., and S. C. Larsen. *Educational Assessment of Learning Problems: Testing for Teaching.* Boston: Allyn and Bacon, 1978.

chapter

3

Conducting the Assessment

Objectives

At the conclusion of this chapter the reader should be able to:

1. outline a systematic procedure to be followed in conducting an educational assessment;
2. identify and discuss factors that affect a child's school performance;
3. specify procedures for conducting a task analysis.

Organizing for Assessment

To be productive, educational assessment must be conducted systematically and purposefully (Bateman, 1965; Smith, 1969; Gearheart, 1976; Wallace and Larsen, 1978; and others). It appears that the assessment process is composed of identifiable steps. These steps reflect a systematic, planned approach to the assessment of a child's abilities and disabilities and resulting information that can be used for planning an educational program. The steps include having the teacher:

1. realize and identify that a problem exists, whether academic, social, or physical;
2. analyze the problem in terms of the requirements of the task and the child's behavior in relationship to those requirements;
3. specify the problem by conducting an analysis of all elements or factors that could be affecting the problem;
4. synthesize the results of the above information into a program plan that specifies and outlines strategies for correcting the problem;
5. continually monitor and evaluate the effectiveness of the instructional program in remediating the problem.

All of the above steps appear to be critical in conducting an educational assessment. They will be further discussed in the following sections.

Locating Potential Problems

To assist the teacher in locating the potential learning problems of a child, a *discrepancy analysis* can be conducted. This type of analysis involves using information collected from both formal and informal assessment procedures. The first step in the discrepancy analysis is a determination of the child's *expected* capacity or potential for learning as well as the child's *actual* performance. For determining expected levels of performance, a teacher can refer to age and grade norms that outline or clearly depict what the cognitive, academic, social/emotional, or physical expectations should be for a child at a particular age or grade level.

References for age and grade expectations can be found in the chapters covering each of these areas. In terms of cognitive capacity, the teacher must possess a knowledge of those behaviors expected of a child at a specified age level or found within the growth and development stages that a child progresses through. Academic expectations consist of knowing the expected behaviors of a child in the areas of reading, math, spelling, oral and written expression for each age and grade level. Having this information gives the teacher a basis from which to judge a child's performance at a particular age or grade level of proficiency. Socially and emotionally, the teacher must be aware of the expected behaviors of the child at any particular stage of development. Knowing the social patterns of development is essential to assess whether the child's social behavior is appropriate or not. Emotionally it is important to understand the fears, anxieties, and periods of emotional highs and lows of the child at different stages of development. An understanding of the child's physical growth and development patterns will be valuable for determining if the child's fine and gross motor activity is appropriate or if the child's motor coordination is comparable to that expected of other children at the same age or grade level.

The use of *standardized tests* such as the WISC-R or the Stanford-Binet provides a formal way of identifying expected performance behaviors in that these devices are norm-referenced or comprised of items that reflect the behaviors characteristically found in children at a specific age or stage of development. These devices allow the teacher to analyze a child's performance in relationship to those expected or normed behaviors. These standardized tests provide the teacher with a means of identifying specific behaviors that characterize a child's cognitive abilities. Standardized tests can also be used to determine the actual achievement level of the child. However, being aware of the curricula of any particular academic scope and sequence is vital for the classroom teacher. Further, to assess a child's actual performance in the motor, social/emotional, or cognitive area, the teacher should be aware of the myriad of informal procedures and devices that could be used to assess that performance.

The selection and use of standardized tests either as a determinant of expectancy or achievement must be made in light of the recent controversy being expressed as to their utility in public education. As Moran (1976) points out, the use of some standardized achievement test results in information that is of relatively little value or assistance to teachers in instructional planning. The time involved in using such tests in essence will only delay the teacher's own assessment of the same skills in or through more informal means. Even though Moran's reference was directed primarily to general achievement tests and not to those standardized measures designed to assess achievement within a specified academic area, the statement illustrates a potential disadvantage in using a standardized measure that generates information that may have little value for program planning. Any information that is to be used from a standardized test should be selected on the basis of assisting the individual teacher in planning and implementing programs that directly result in helping the child to learn in the most efficient and effective manner possible. Several authors have identified several limitations of standardized tests (Wallace and Larsen, 1978; Salvia and Ysseldyke, 1978; Ekwal, 1976; and others). The use of these formalized measures is usually time consuming and requires the person administering the test to be specially trained. There is not always enough time for the classroom teacher to administer a standardized test individually, nor has the teacher been specifically trained to administer many of the tests.

Concern has been expressed over the use of standardized test data for making decisions about children as to the type of educational program in which they should be placed. The contention is that standardized tests were designed using only majority ethnic children in the normative process. The result has been that many standardized tests are perceived as being culturally biased and unfair to minority populations. Further, it appears that the use of the data or results from standardized tests has been misused or is used inappropriately. In other words, the test scores become a means of classifying and labeling children which have relatively little value in the development of educational programs. Further, even though some tests have been standardized, the reliability and validity information on these "standardized tests" is lacking (Salvia and Ysseldyke, 1978). Wallace and Larsen (1978) report that many standardized tests do not report adequate reliability information in their test manuals. The author has found this to be very true in the preparation for this text; as indicated in Chapter

2, several of the tests identified for reference in this document were found to be lacking adequate information as to their construction, reliability, and/or validity. However, many of these tests are acceptable standards of measure that are used continually throughout the educational community. In light of the discussion presented above, caution must be taken in the use of standardized tests.

On the other hand, Scannell (1978) indicates that standardized tests have some distinct values and uses in the educational world. He emphasizes that standardized tests are designed to reflect national views of the traits measured. They provide comparable scores across the different traits measured, and they provide comparable scores across time. The use of standardized measures allows for a continuity in measurement and that from standardized test data, local performances can be compared with that of various reference groups. In terms of Scannell's last statement and in relationship to performing a discrepancy analysis, wise use of a standardized test would be to compare the performance of a child against that of the child's immediate peer group and not a national norm.

Informal devices are usually of most assistance to the classroom teacher since they are designed to assess specific skills in specific areas. To construct or use informal devices adequately the teacher must be aware of expected levels of achievement. These are either determined through observation of children performing a particular task at a particular age or grade level, or through a thorough task analysis of the behaviors needed to complete the task.

After the teacher has used either a standardized test or an informal one to determine the child's expected as well as actual performance, these two factors are then compared to determine if a significant discrepancy exists between the expected and actual performance. A discrepancy between the expected and actual performance assists the teacher in pointing out more exactly the type of problem the child is experiencing. What constitutes a significant discrepancy? As a general rule of thumb, the following guidelines can be used to establish the seriousness of a problem for different age levels of children.

1. Primary grades: actual performance one year or more below age or grade peers.
2. Intermediate grades and junior high: performance one and a half years or greater below age or grade peers.
3. High school: performance two to three years or more below age or grade peers.

At all three levels these conditions should generate concern about the educational program in which the child is presently participating. Both the child's abilities and the program should be analyzed further.

Two types of comparisons are made in a discrepancy analysis. One is an *intra-individual* comparison where the child's performance is compared with the child's own estimated, expected level for learning. In the other, *inter-individual* comparison, the child's performance is compared to what is expected of children of the same age and ability level. Depending on the teacher's program planning intent, either of these methods of comparison will be valuable for selecting instructional strategies.

The discrepancy analysis, then, is simply a measurement of the child's expected level of performance against the child's actual level of performance. It involves having the teacher make a determination as to what the expected level should be, which can be accomplished through the use of standardized as well as informal assessment techniques. The child's actual performance or achievement level is next assessed. This assessment requires the teacher to be able to select, administer, and to interpret information from standardized instruments. Results from the child's actual achievement performance are then measured against the expected level of performance to determine whether a discrepancy exists between the two.

The following case study is an example of how a discrepancy analysis can be conducted. In this example, information from formal standardized tests has been selected for illustration. The selection and use of this type of formal test data were made on the basis of the author's study (see Preface), in which teachers identified as one of their weaknesses an inability to utilize information from standardized tests—especially IQ and mental age data provided from the WISC-R and Stanford-Binet intelligence tests. These examples are illustrative only of *one* use that the teacher may make of formal test data. The point must be stressed that in a discrepancy analysis the aim or intent is to determine what the expected behaviors are and what the child's actual behavior is in relationship to that expected level, to compare these two sets of information, and then to use the comparison as a guide in planning an appropriate educational program.

A Discrepancy Analysis Case Study

Mary has a chronological age (CA) of twelve years zero months (12.0) and the test results from a Weschler Intelligence Scale for Children, Revised (WISC-R), indicates that her IQ score is 112. What is her expected level of achievement?

By determining mental age (MA), a manageable score can be generated to answer this question. MA is defined as what would be expected of children of a specific age in performing a particular task. For example, a child six years of age has a score of 110 on the Stanford-Binet Intelligence Test. The child's mental age would be approximately seven years of age or, in other words, the child's anticipated performance level would be comparable to that expected of a child seven years of age. The formula used to compute the MA is:

$$\frac{IQ \times CA}{100} = MA$$

In Mary's case:

$$\frac{112 \times 12.0}{100} = \frac{1344}{100} = 13.4$$

From the MA, an expected level of academic achievement can be predicted. This is accomplished by simply equating the mental age with the corresponding grade level. For example, a child of six years of age usually attends the first grade, an eight-year-old attends the third grade; therefore, a child with an MA of six years would be expected to perform academic tasks at the first-grade level whereas a child with an MA of 8 should be expected to at least complete third-grade level tasks. An easy method of determining grade expectancy is to subtract 5 from the MA. In Mary's case:

$$MA - 5 = \text{Grade Expectancy}$$
$$13.4 - 5 = 8.4 \text{ Grade Expectancy}$$

Translating a relatively unmanageable IQ score into mental age enables you to predict on a cursory basis what could be expected of Mary in completing academic tasks.

After grade level expectancy has been established, the actual level of performance is compared. Mary's achievement test results indicate she is functioning in math at the fifth grade, six month level (5.6) and her reading and grade levels are 8.3 and 8.4, respectively. Use of this information will enable a more thorough analysis to be made relative to academic strengths and weaknesses. By comparing achievement test scores to her expected level, it can be determined that Mary is functioning below grade expectancy in math (expected 8.4; actual 5.6) and at expectancy in reading (expected 8.4; actual 8.3) and spelling (expected 8.4; actual 8.4). From this intra-individual analysis it appears that math may be a problem area for Mary.

How does Mary compare with her age level peers on selected academic areas? Comparisons on an inter-individual basis alter the perception of Mary's academic strengths and weaknesses. Inter-individually, the math score of 5.6 is not sufficiently below her grade level placement to indicate a problem (grade level 6.4; actual performance 5.6). Reading and spelling scores are above grade placement and indicate distinct strength. The initial intra-individual analysis of Mary's math performance becomes one of less concern when an inter-individual comparison is made. However, when planning an appropriate educational program, both sets of information are critical for stating objectives and selecting instructional materials. Figure 3-1 provides a graphic display of Mary's discrepancy analysis. This profile correlates age, grade placement, and specific test results into a more easily understood comparison of expected and actual performance behaviors.

Discrepancy analysis provides assessment information that can be used for eventual program planning and selection of media and

Figure 3-1   A Correlation of Mary's Chronological Age (CA) with Grade Placement (GP) and Academic Performance Scores

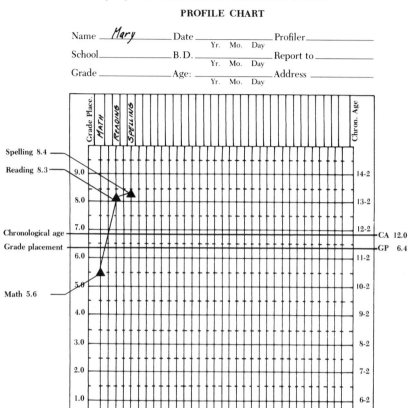

PROFILE CHART

Name __Mary__ Date _____ Profiler _____
                Yr.   Mo.   Day
School _____ B.D. _____ Report to _____
                Yr.   Mo.   Day
Grade _____ Age: _____ Address _____
                Yr.   Mo.   Day

materials. In Mary's case, the teacher has to make a decision relative to maintaining Mary in the current math program or developing a new program to stimulate Mary to perform closer to her expected level of achievement.

Task and Behavioral Analysis

The second step in assessment is to analyze the problem in terms of the requirements of the task and the child's behavior in relation to those requirements. The purpose of such an analysis is to diagnose the learning problem further. Using the preceding discussion of Mary as a continuing example, it is concluded that "she has a problem in math." Certainly a program cannot be established on the basis of that statement alone. An understanding of the math task is essential before a worthwhile program can be written. Task analysis can help teachers in better understanding the task as well as in generating information for use in program planning.

Task analysis is defined by Wallace and Kauffman (1978) as being "a sequence of evaluative activities which pinpoints the child's learning problem and guides the teacher in planning an effective remedial sequence of instructional tasks" (p. 105). Theagarajan, Semmel and Semmel (1974) indicate task analysis is an important preliminary step in the development of any instruction and outline five steps instrumental in conducting an analysis. These are:

1. *Specify the main task.* This entails a comprehensive statement of the task and the task objectives. The skill that is expected to be acquired upon completion of instruction is clearly identified.

2. *Identify sub-tasks* at the preceding level of complexity. In this stage the skills needed to perform the main task are determined. These are supporting or subordinate tasks required for successful completion of the main task.

3. *Treat each sub-task as a main task* and repeat the analytical procedure.

4. *Continue the analysis* until the sub-task reaches the entry level of the student: that is, when the behaviors have been so delineated that they reach a level that is easily completed by the student. At this point the task analysis can be concluded.

5. *Complete the task analysis.* This step is merely a listing of all the major and minor tasks that can then be used as a guide in developing the instruction and evaluating the effects of that instruction.

Moyer and Dardig (1978) provide guidelines for conducting a task analysis. They identify that the first step is to limit the scope of the main task and to be cautious of selecting a task that is too large and unmanageable. Second, the sub-tasks supporting the main tasks should be written in observable terms. This ensures agreement between observers in measuring the task. Third, the terminology descriptive of the task should be written at a level that is understood by the potential user of the task. A fourth guideline is to write the task in terms of what the learner will be doing. Finally, the task, and not the learner, should be the focus of attention. That is, focusing on the specific way in which the learner completes the task is counterproductive. The general characteristics of the population are considered when the analysis is being conducted; however, the behaviors to complete the analysis, not how the learner manifest those behaviors, are what should be observed.

In their work, Moyer and Dardig identify several methods of conducting task analysis. Selected methods from their work are found in Figure 3-2.

In the case of Mary, it would be necessary to identify the math level at which she is to function. Since she is performing at the fifth-grade level and it is anticipated that her performance should be at the eighth-grade level, the main task becomes having her perform math computations at an eighth-grade level of proficiency. Each of the supporting tasks is then identified down to a level that permits Mary to function successfully. Figure 3-3 provides an illustration of how a task analysis of one of the sub-components of math could be further delineated. Once a task analysis has been completed, the teacher then analyzes Mary's behavior in relation to those specified skills.

The teacher's task and behavior analyses progress in these four stages:

1. The student has a problem in reading. This becomes the main task.
2. The problem is analyzed and found to be specific to the area of phonics skills, specifically those skills involving consonant blends, long and short vowels, and the oi, oy, aw, and au sounds and usage.
3. The student's behavior is then analyzed in relationship to that task, and it may be found that the child does not know the consonant blends or the short vowel sounds.
4. This information leads directly to specific objectives from which the instructional program can be written.

Figure 3-2 Task Analysis Methods. [Summarized from Moyer and Dardig (1978)]

Method	Description
WATCH THE MASTER	This method is especially well suited to the analysis of psychomotor tasks. The person conducting the task analysis simply watches a person proficient in the performance of the task such as setting a table or riding a tricycle, and writes down in correct tempo order all the steps that the master performs. Every step should be recorded excluding only those judged to have no relevance to the major task. The steps should be written as accurately and concisely as possible.
PERFORM THE TASK	This is a variation of "Watch the Master" in that the person performing the analysis performs the actual task and records or monitors his/her behavior as the task is being completed. (Using a tape recorder and recording verbatim the steps that the analyst goes through in completing the task is suggested by Moyer and Dardig for this method.)
BRAINSTORMING	In this method the analyst simply writes down all the sub-tasks involved in a particular goal without regard to order. The sub-tasks are then arranged in as logical an order as can be ascertained. It is suggested that this method is useful when a number of individuals are analyzing the same task. When comparison of results is made, sub-tasks are either added or deleted as necessary.
GOAL ANALYSIS	It appears most accepted with goals from the affective domain. In goal analysis in the area of affective domain, the sequential list of sub-goals is a means of identifying behaviors that signal attainment of the goal. Frequently teachers set goals such as "Will have a good self-concept," or "work hard." Until the behavior is identified that describes this goal, it is difficult to measure the attainment of this type of goals objectively. Mager (1962) described the assessment of goal analysis into the following steps: (1) write the goal on

paper; (2) list the observable behaviors a person would exhibit to show that he or she has obtained the goal; (3) review the list, discarding behaviors that should not be included or those that need further clarification; (4) describe what is intended for each goal by determining how frequently or how well the behavior must be performed; (5) test the statements for adequacy and completeness by determining whether the behaviors in the final list represent comprehensive attainment of the goal.

Figure 3-3   An Example of Task Analysis of Fraction Skills

Task	Sub-Tasks
Developing Skills in Understanding Fractions	

1. Describe relationship of a quart to a gallon as a fractional term.
2. Describe relationship of 2 quarters to a dollar as a fractional term.
3. Describe relationship of 6 inches to a foot as a fractional term.
4. Describe relationship of 6 months to a year as a fractional term.
5. Compare simple fractions.
   Ex. $1/2 = 2/4$ $1/4 = 2/8$
       $1/2 = 4/8$ $1/4 = 4/16$
6. Identify and write mixed numbers using fractions previously taught.
7. Change improper fractions to mixed numbers.
   Ex. $3/2$ $5/4$
8. Add fractions with like denominators having sums less than denominator.
9. Add fractions with like denominators having sum larger than denominator.
10. Add fractions with unlike denominators having sum less than common denominator.

Analysis of Factors Affecting the Problem

This technique is termed *process analysis*. It establishes the *method* in which the task is to be learned. One of the most important components of this process is determining how best the child receives (input) and gives information (output). It is an analysis of how well the child uses sensory channels and attempts to answer the question: "Does the child see, hear, and understand the task well enough to complete it?" If not, several changes must be made:

1. A change in the child's ability to process sensory information. This may necessitate having the child wear eyeglasses or a hearing aid. It may also require training of some sensory channels to make them more efficient.
2. If this is not possible, a change in either the teacher's presentation of the task requirements or the requirements themselves must be made. For example, if the requirement includes learning a phonics approach to reading, a child having difficulty hearing and processing auditory stimuli may have to have this requirement changed to accommodate his or her learning style better.
3. Another important factor to consider is whether the child understands the mechanical operations of the task. In Mary's case, merely teaching her the mechanical operations of addition and subtraction may be enough to eliminate her math problem.
4. Other factors that may influence learning problems include how the child feels about him/herself or how others feel about the child. Is the child comfortable enough, both socially and emotionally, to learn? Mary's lack of success in math could have caused an uncomfortable feeling about math and prevented her from being able to complete tasks. If this information is known, the curriculum can be adjusted to provide successful math experiences.
5. The final step in the process analysis involves study of the physical environment in which the task is to be performed. The child must be physically comfortable in order to complete the task. Inappropriate lighting, temperature, and noise level can be factors which affect a child's performance. The teacher should assess these factors and make adjustments as part of the instructional program.

Synthesize Results into a Program Plan

The fourth stage in conducting an assessment is to synthesize the results of the discrepancy, task, behavioral, and process analyses into a program plan. To be effective, this plan must identify and implement strategies for correction. Evaluation must be specified for determining the effects the strategies are having on the behaviors being corrected. Information on how to synthesize these results into an educational plan is contained in each of the following content area chapters, and program planning is the topic of Chapter 13.

Monitor and Evaluate the Program

This final step measures the effectiveness of the four steps that precede it. This evaluation should be ongoing and based on the objectives of the program.

Inappropriate Assessment

It is important for the teacher to remember that assessment procedures provide a means of thoroughly analyzing a child's behavior. Without thorough analysis, teachers too often assess a child's behavior incorrectly. A child who acts out in the classroom may be perceived by the teacher as a behavior problem, but in reality the child's disruptive behavior may be related to other factors. This behavior may be stimulated by an inability to hear, to see, or to reproduce assigned tasks; or environmental factors such as lighting or noise may be interfering with the child's ability to complete the tasks. Any of these factors may be contributing to the child's acting out. By eliminating the factor(s), the problem can be eliminated. It becomes paramount that the teacher make a thorough, complete assessment. Misassessment can lead to unwarranted assumptions about the child that lead to inappropriate program planning.

Can You Answer the Following Questions?

1. What are the systematic procedures to be followed in conducting an educational assessment?
2. What are the factors that affect a child's performance?
3. What are procedures used to conduct a task analysis?
4. Can you define the following terms:
   a. intra-individual comparison;
   b. inter-individual comparison;

 c. formal assessment;
 d. task analysis;
 e. behavioral analysis.

References

Bateman, B. "An educator's view of a diagnostic approach to learning disorders." In J. Hellmuth (ed.), *Learning Disorders*, Vol. 1. Seattle, Washington: Special Child Publication, 1965.

Ekwall, E. E. *Diagnosis and Remediation of the Disabled Reader.* Boston: Allyn and Bacon, 1976.

Gearheart, B. R. *Teaching the Learning Disabled: A Combined Task-Process Approach.* St. Louis: C. B. Mosby, 1976.

Mager, R. F. *Preparing Instructional Objectives.* Palo Alto, California: Fearon Publishers, 1962.

Moran, L. *Assessment of the Exceptional Learner in the Regular Classroom.* Denver, Colorado: Love Publishing Company, 1978.

Moyer, J., and J. C. Dardig. *Practical Task Analysis for Special Educators Teaching Exceptional Children*, 1978, *11*, 16–18.

Salvia, J., and J. Ysseldyke. *Assessment in Special and Remedial Education.* Boston: Houghton Mifflin Company, 1978.

Scannell, D. P. "A positive view of standardized tests." *Focus on Exceptional Children*, 1978, 10, 5, 1–10.

Smith, R. M. (ed.). *Teacher Diagnosis of Educational Difficulties.* Columbus, Ohio: Charles E. Merrill, 1969.

Theagarajan, S., D. Semmel, and M. Semmel. *Instructional Development for Training Teachers of Exceptional Children: A Source Book.* Reston, Virginia: The Council for Exceptional Children, 1974.

Wallace, G., and J. M. Kauffman. *Teaching Children with Learning Problems* (2nd ed.). Columbus, Ohio: Charles E. Merrill, 1978.

Wallace, G., and S. C. Larsen. *Educational Assessment of Learning Problems: Testing for Teaching.* Boston: Allyn and Bacon, 1978.

Assessing Learning Problems

chapter

4

Cognitive Assessment

Objectives

At the conclusion of this chapter the reader should be able to:

1. provide a rationale for conducting a cognitive assessment;
2. identify standardized tests commonly used in the assessment of cognitive abilities;
3. specify some of the strengths and limitations of standardized tests of cognitive abilities;
4. provide examples of how to use data from a standardized cognitive measure in the planning and preparation of individual education programs.

Introduction

There exists a growing controversy over the use or misuse of devices used to assess one's cognitive or intellectual capacity. Hallahan and Kauffman (1976) have indicated that tests designed to measure intellectual capacity (IQ) are culturally biased. Deno (1972) indicates that intelligence testing, even for research purposes, constitutes an unacceptable invasion of privacy. Wallace and Larsen (1978) have concluded that IQ tests are neither accurate predictors nor sensitive guides to the development of educational programs. Moran (1978), on the other hand, suggests that the IQ score provides a limited frame of reference for revealing gross discrepancies in a child's performance. Stellern, Vasa, and Little (1977) indicate that the results of formal intelligence measures—namely, the WISC-R (Weschsler Intelligence Scale for Children—Revised)—can be interpreted for program planning in more specific ways than just the global measure of intellectual capacity. Gearheart and Willenberg (1974) have stated that intelligence tests, especially the Stanford-Binet, can be very useful instruments in measuring the potential for learning in the typical formal academic program.

As stated by Biehler (1974): ". . . the score on an intelligence test is merely a qualified guess about how successful a child is as compared to other children in handling certain kinds of problems at a particular time" (p. 581). The intent for this present chapter is not to build a case for or against the use of the IQ test as a measure of a child's or anyone else's cognitive capacity but one that provides some indices of that person's academic aptitude. More important, the discussion *will not* focus on the use of an IQ score for classification or labeling purposes as the author feels that the IQ score per se is of little value to the classroom teacher. It does appear, however, that the IQ test is widely used and will continue to be used within the educational community. This concept is supported even more in light of the research conducted by the author in preparation for this text (see Preface). It was found that teachers of both special and regular classrooms who were serving exceptional children had in many cases been given only an IQ test score as the primary reason for placement of the child in the special program. It was more a rule than an exception that the teachers had only this little bit of information from which to plan an educational program for the child. Teachers indicated that they were ill prepared to interpret IQ test data and to use the data in a functional way. Given the premise that IQ tests will continue to be used and that teachers will be given this type of test data, the purpose of this chapter will be one of assisting teachers in the examination of the role that could be played by the data in planning and developing educational programs for children.

Standardized Tests: Proponents and Opponents

Standardized tests exist, and many cases provide the clues from which more comprehensive educational programs can be developed. That is, standardized tests, IQ or achievement, are designed to measure a set of specific behaviors with these behaviors representing some functional aspect of human endeavor, such as how to make mathematical computations or reads, how well one reasons or solves problems, and many others. It seems only logical, then, to use the performance of an individual on a given test as a measure of that person's ability to perform the task being tested.

As mentioned before, an IQ score by itself means nothing, but if one is familiar with the tasks required of the person in completing the test and is familiar with the research available concerning the test scores, then a greater reservoir of information is available to analyze the individual's performance and to generate more specific information for planning an educational program. It is the author's intended purpose throughout this text to emphasize that all the data collected, either from standardized tests, teacher observation, criterion measures, or through other means, have one primary and important purpose: that that data be used in the development of an individual program that will assist the child in improving skills, performances, and attitudes and better prepare that individual for a fuller and more functional life experience. The remaining contents of this chapter are organized into two sections. In the first section, cognitive assessment is defined and discussed. In the second selected IQ tests are described, and each test is discussed in terms of the type of information that can be generated or interpreted in assisting the teacher in developing an appropriate educational experience for the child.

Definition of Cognitive Assessment

Jean Piaget (1963) indicates that cognitive development is dependent upon maturity, experience, and heredity. The stage of cognitive development that a child has attained appears to be a major contributing factor to what the child has learned and should influence the types and kinds of materials to be presented to the child in learning new information. That is, if the stage or level of development can be ascertained, this information will be of great assistance in selecting what the child can and will learn as well as the materials and strategies that will best assist that child in learning those new concepts and ideas. Cognitive assessment is more than an assessment of intellectual capacity as measured by an intelligence test. It is a composite look at the child's maturity, experiential background, and, as Piaget has indicated, the child's heredity. In planning an educational program, it is imperative on the teacher's part to take into consideration these areas of cognitive development.

Cognitive capacity has been differentially defined as the ability to deal with abstractions or the global capacity of the individual to act purposefully, think rationally, and to work effectively within the environment (Wechsler, 1944). Even a cursory analysis of the comments of Piaget, Terman, and Wechsler reveals that a person's cognitive capacity is perhaps more than can be measured with a single instrument. Even in the work of Alfred Binet (Deno, 1972), his intent initially was to develop a test not so much to measure intelligence as to develop an instrument that could predict how well a child might do within the French school system. It appears that over time his intent and purpose have been lost. The test Binet devised has become to some a viable predictor as well as an indirect measure of overall capacity to perform when in reality the test does not measure all that is involved in a person's cognitive capacity to perform.

Given Piaget's theory that cognitive development is dependent upon maturity, experience, and heredity, these elements must be considered before a statement of capacity can be made. Merely looking at the score from one standardized IQ test will yield an unjust indication of one's overall cognitive capacity. If a test score is to be used, it must be combined with observation of the individual's actual performance in a number of different areas, social/emotional, academic or physical, as well as an understanding of the person's experiential and environmental background. Combining all of this information into a composite whole will yield a better and more exact estimate of a child's cognitive capacity to perform.

In conclusion, in planning a child's educational program and in conducting an assessment of cognitive capacity, there must be information generated as to the type and kinds of experiences that the child has had relative to social/emotional, academic, and physical development as well as the environmental influences that have surrounded the child throughout his or her life. This information is a necessity for appropriate educational program planning and will require the teacher to go beyond the classroom to identify this information. It will require in-class observation of behavior, out-of-class observation of behavior, interviews with persons intimate with the child and observations of the community from which the child comes.

Planning Programs Using IQ Test Data

Teachers sometimes receive merely an IQ score from a Wechsler Intelligence Scale for Children—Revised (WISC-R), Stanford-Binet, or other intelligence test. As such, the IQ score means relatively little. For example, receiving an IQ test score from a Stanford-Binet of 75, or from a WISC-R with a verbal score of 98, a performance score of 104 and a full-scale score of 102 provides the teacher with very little information that can be used for program planning. However, if these scores can be combined with a knowledge of the child's age, present grade placement, a little about background and experiential level, decisions relative to the type and kind of program for the child can be made with greater benefit. Knowing the child's present grade placement and the expectations that surround that grade placement, in terms of social/emotional, academic, and physical performance expectancies coupled with the IQ score can assist the teacher in selecting the most appropriate educational strategies for the child. To continue the example, the child with a Stanford-Binet score of 75 who is placed in the fourth-grade classroom: in observing the child's social/emotional behavior, it is found that these expectations at the fourth-grade level seem to be met very well by the child, that he is performing close to the level he is expected to in this area. It is also observed that the child's physical and maturational abilities are at or even exceed the expectancy level of children in that grade placement. However, when the academic tasks are viewed, it is found that the child is lacking fundamental skills in academics. The teacher in this case is faced with the dilemma of selecting the most appropriate kinds of instructional materials. Utilizing the IQ score from the Stanford-Binet, Mental Age (MA) is computed. The MA is an indication or reflection of the performance level, in this case academics, that a child should be able to reach successfully. The MA is computed from an IQ score by the following formula:

$$MA = \frac{IQ \times CA}{100}$$

Once the MA is found, applying the rule of MA minus 5 is a gross indication of the expected level of academic performance from which materials should be selected and used for programming. In this case, the fourth-grade child's Chronological Age (CA) is 9.5. Applying this information to the formula, an MA of 7.1 is generated.

$$MA \quad 75 \times 9.5 = 7.1$$

Applying the expectancy rule of MA minus 5, a cursory idea of the skill level at which the child could be functioning successfully is determined, in this case 2.1. The academic teacher now has several bits and pieces of information from which to plan an educational program. In terms of social/emotional and physical/motoric areas, the child is to continue in the program that is presently being offered. In the area of academic skill development it becomes necessary to make adjustments in the existing curriculum so that it can be functionally and successfully completed by the child. The child appears unable to handle or deal with fourth-grade academic materials; therefore, the materials must be selected at a level more easily completed by the child. Utilizing the IQ score, the teacher can make an initial decision as to a beginning place from which to observe the child's performance that is more accurate than having the child perform and fail fourth-grade academic tasks.

Following this procedure more appropriate techniques, strategies, and materials can also be identified and given to the child from which further observation of performance can be made. Caution should be given to the selection of instructional materials, however, especially if the materials are perceived by the child as being below the child's social maturity level. In this case, first-grade materials may be insulting to the child; therefore, the teacher must be careful to select materials that are at the appropriate success level of completion but are not insulting to the child's maturity level. Reading materials, for instance, should probably be selected from high interest-low vocabulary materials, that is, materials that have a level of appeal equal to that of the child's maturity but are developmentally at a level that can be successfully completed by the child.

Formal Assessment Measures

In the above example the IQ score is merely one part of the information that is used or can be used in helping the teacher make decisions relative to the development and selection of instructional strategies. It appears that in the above case, as is found in all types of assessment, the purpose is to develop or generate as much information as possible concerning the child and through these increased amounts of information the chances of making incorrect instructional decisions will be reduced. Following are a number of selected intelligence tests that are commonly used throughout the educational community. These are presented as a means of assisting the teacher in better understanding what the tests measure as well as to increase a knowledge as to the tasks required to complete the test.

The Stanford-Binet (Sattler, 1965; Terman and Merrill, 1972) was the first and perhaps the prototype of all the IQ tests that followed it. This test was developed by Alfred Binet in France. His original purposes were to make an instrument to predict which of the children attending Paris schools would most likely succeed and which would not. Essentially, Binet's initial work was a sampling of achievement of critical school tasks that had been defined by teachers. Later, when comparisons of performances of children were made, it became evident that comparisons could be made between children of specific ages as to how other children of the same age had performed. And then it was hypothesized that how most children learn at a particular age might be used as an indication of what a child would be ultimately capable of learning within that age group. It was from the work of Terman in the early 1900s utilizing Binet's information that the Stanford-Binet Intelligence Test was devised (Deno, 1972). From this test two new elements in the measurement of cognitive capacity came into vogue: (1) the intelligence quotient (IQ) was coined and (2) the concept of mental age (MA) was introduced. The Stanford-Binet is considered a developmental age scale and is used primarily with younger children because it is a more sensitive measure for children prior to age six. The test is also considered a measure of global or general intelligence even though it is primarily a verbal test, or a test of understanding verbal constructs and concepts. Gearheart and Willenberg (1974) indicate that some authorities have established a framework for the subtests of the Stanford-Binet by grouping them into memory, discrimination, and other categories. They conclude, however, that the Stanford-Binet is a most useful instrument for measuring learning potential in a formal academic program (p. 27).

The Wechsler Scales. Wechsler (1955, 1967, 1974) devised three tests to assess intelligence at three different age levels. The development of these devices was based upon the assumption that intelligence is global. The three age-level tests include the Wechsler Adult Intelligence Scale (WAIS) for use with adults over the age of sixteen, a Wechsler Intelligence Scale for Children (WISC) for use with children with ages between six and sixteen. (This test is perhaps the most widely used intelligence test in the public school system and will be the focus of more detailed discussion later in this section.) The Wechsler Pre-school and Primary Scale of Intelligence (WPPSI) was designed for use with children under the age of six. Within each of the three intelligence tests can be found measures of verbal as well as performance intelligence. From these two intelligence scales, a third full-scale intelligent quotient can be derived.

It is perhaps the feature showing verbal and performance scales that makes the WISC the most popularly used intelligence test. A revised edition of the WISC has been published, the WISC-R or the Wechsler Intelligence Test for Children—Revised, was an attempt to account for environmental influences, to test item ambiguity, and to increase the acceptable standardized responses that would encompass the broad range of ethnic variability within a school age population. It is the most widely used test and probably a test with which teachers will have some association during their career.

The results of a formal intelligence test as the WISC-R can be interpreted for program planning in a number of specific ways other than just a global measure of intellectual capacity if the test is thoroughly understood. The WISC-R is composed of 12 subtests, each being designed to measure a separate skill of cognitive functioning. These 12 tests are divided into verbal and performance categories. During the administration of the test the verbal and performance tests times are alternated. In order to avoid some misunderstanding, as well as to make better use of the WISC-R as a diagnostic tool, a detailed analysis of each subtest must be undertaken. The subtests should be considered in terms of: what they measure; what factors are involved, besides the ones being measured; and what academic areas are being influenced. Subtest scores need to be understood in terms of what they mean for a child's cognitive, social/emotional, or academic functioning. Scores viewed in this light provide a pattern of strengths and weaknesses for use in predicting, isolating or identifying more specifically those areas that may be of assistance to the teacher for selecting appropriate educational program strategies.

An in-depth discussion of normative data and the significance of raw and scaled scores is not within the scope of this chapter. It should be noted, however, that the reliability coefficients on the full-scale IQ scores utilizing a test-retest format were at or above .90. Validity correlation coefficients ranged from .60 to .73 when compared concurrently with IQ scores from the Stanford-

Binet. The theoretical average WISC-R verbal, performance, and full-scale IQ is 100, with the standard deviation for each being 15. The average WISC-R subtest scaled score is 10 with the standard deviation for each being 3. IQ scores should not be considered discrepant unless there exists at least a 15-point difference between them. Scaled scores should not be considered discrepant without at least a 3-point difference. Differences may be compared relative to the theoretical average or to the child's own individual scores.

It is most useful initially to examine the significance of a few broad or general themes in interpreting a WISC-R profile. The following themes are generally accepted as guides for interpreting the scores obtained for the WISC-R (Gustavson, 1978).

Analysis of IQ Scores[1]

I. Verbal IQ significantly above Performance IQ (15–20 points or more)

   A. Verbal IQ high (130–140) and Performance IQ average suggests academic and intellectual orientation, not much motor or performance orientation; that is, not much of a doer.

   B. Verbal IQ average or above (although this varies greatly) and Performance IQ low (80s, although this, too, may vary) suggests:

      1. Depression or depressive conditions, particularly if the performance subtests are down owing to a general slowness of the subject and verbalizations allude to self-punishment.

      2. With particularly low (7 or under) scaled scores in block design, coding, object assembly, and picture arrangement—organic brain damage in the right hemisphere is suggested; physiological immaturity; and/or poor eye-hand coordination involving the visual-motor area of the brain.

1. This discussion for the IQ scores, Verbal Subtests and Performance Subtests was adapted from J. L. Gustavson, *A Brief Analysis of the Subtests of the Wechsler Intelligence Scale for Children—Revised.* Department of Educational Psychology Semester Project, Brigham Young University, Provo, Utah, 1978. Used by permission of the author.

3. With particularly low scaled scores in digit span, coding, arithmetic, and block design—anxiety and tension states.

II. Performance IQ significantly above Verbal IQ
   A. Performance IQ average or above (although this varies greatly) and Verbal IQ slightly below average suggests:
      1. A performance-oriented doer with limited verbal ability.
      2. Acting out and/or delinquent tendencies, especially if accompanied by impulsive, aggressive, or destructive verbalizations.
      3. Marked verbal problems and motor performance strength.
      4. Organic brain damage in left cerebral hemisphere.
      5. Cultural deprivation or impoverishment.

III. Similarity between Verbal and Performance IQ
   A. Both Verbal and Performance IQ high (130+) suggests:
      1. A powerful problem solver with equal strength in most areas of problem solving.
      2. Tremendous intellectual ability and potential.
   B. Verbal and Performance IQ low (below 75) with all scale scores below 7 or 8 suggests mental retardation

IV. Wide intersubtest variability or scatter
   A. Each scaled score differing 5 or more points from each other suggests:
      1. Specific learning disability.
      2. Emotional disturbance or maladjustment.

V. Certain measures may be derived by the combination and analysis of certain subtests:
   A. Spatial—picture arrangement, block design, object assembly.
   B. Conceptual—comprehension, similarities, vocabulary.
   C. Sequencing—coding, digit span, picture arrangement.
   D. Concentration—arithmetic, digit span.
   E. Academic—information, arithmetic, vocabulary.

It should be pointed out that extremely high or low scores on any one of the subtests may be indicative of mental instability, gross emotional maladjustment, or neurological or physiological impairment. If this is suspected, further diagnostic investigation should be carried out. As a general rule, a scaled score drop in any of the verbal subtests may be the result of auditory input, memory, and/or meaning problems of a verbal output disorder. On the other hand, a drop in any of the performance subtests may be due to visual-input or visual-motor coordination problems.

Once the general themes have been considered and applied to the interpretation of the IQ scores, an analysis of each of the subtests should be made. Following is a discussion of the subtests as to the information that can be used to interpret a child's performance relation to each.

Analysis of the WISC-R Verbal Subtests[2]

Information
1. Functions measured:
    General knowledge of facts, long-term memory of factual, isolated data; range and fund of information.
2. Influencing factors:
    Education and cultural background; ambition; interests; ability to assimilate facts; mental alertness; auditory discrimination; remote auditory memory.
3. Advantages:
    Good correlation with general intelligence; avoids specialized knowledge; indication of intellectual capacity; relatively few zero scores; relatively unyielding to impairment.
4. Disadvantages:
    Penalizes those of foreign language or impoverished cultural background; variable results from one location to another; favors the better educated.
5. Validation:
    Picture completion subtest for knowledge in a visual format.
6. Unusually low scores suggest:
    Impoverished early environment including lack of formal schooling; withdrawal or repressive tendencies; possible organic impairment.
7. Unusually high scores suggest:

2. Gustavson, *A Brief Analysis—Revised.*

Intellectualizing or obsessive-compulsive tendencies, especially when verbalizations are stilted.

8. Academic implications:
   Test memory for names, dates, spelling, and abstract terms.

9. Considerations:
   Testing through multiple choice; teaching with meaning visual associative clues; teaching with manipulative experiences; language development and visualization training; auditory memory training.

Similarities

1. Functions measured:
   Ability to perceive common elements in verbally presented task and bring them into a single concept; analysis of relationships, concrete, functional and/or abstract; verbal concept formation; logical abstract reasoning.

2. Influencing factors:
   Experiential and educational opportunities; information regarding the nature or structure of objects coupled with the concept of likenesses and differences and categories for grouping; language level; ability to verbalize; auditory discrimination.

3. Advantages:
   Good correlation with general intelligence; ascertains evenness and level of intellectual functioning; easy wording but requires high quality of thought; interest appeal; qualitative scoring.

4. Disadvantages:
   Penalizes those of impoverished cultural background; penalizes poor verbalizers; susceptible to subjective interpretation in scoring.

5. Validation:
   Picture Arrangement subtest for the ability to conceptualize part-to-whole relationships with a visual format; analogies tests.

6. Unusually low scores suggest:
   Inability or impaired ability to think abstractly; concrete thought processes; poor reality testing; depression; possible organicity.

7. Unusually high scores suggest:

Intellectualizing defenses; obsessive-compulsive tendencies; with high arithmetic and high picture completion, possible paranoid trends.

8. Academic implications:
   Concept formation at all levels; use of reading and listening as a learning avenue.

9. Considerations:
   Teaching through pictogramming; learning by rote; testing of factual data—no essays; language visualization training; categorization and conceptualization training.

Arithmetic (Timed)

1. Functions measured:
   Ability to hold orally presented details and solve orally presented math problems; retention of arithmetical concepts and processes; logical reasoning and abstraction; facility with numbers.

2. Influencing factors:
   Educational and cultural background; math level at school; occupational or vocational interests and pursuits; alertness and concentration; immediate auditory memory for details; language visualization; emotional status; level of anxiety.

3. Advantages:
   Basic appeal and interest; good correlation with academic achievement and educational ability; fair correlation with total score; global rather than specific measure; easily devised and standardized.

4. Disadvantages:
   Influenced by educational achievement; not a measure of skill with numbers per se; penalizes the distractible person; correlation with total score tends to be lower at lower levels of intelligence.

5. Validation:
   Block design subtest and school math achievement testing.

6. Unusually low scores suggest:
   Poor ability to concentrate; high distractibility; poor arithmetic reasoning or lack of training in simple arithmetic skills; anxiety; short-term auditory memory disorder; delinquency, possible psychotic conditions especially when combined with low comprehension or picture arrangement; possible organic impairment.

7. Unusually high scores suggest:
Likelihood of normal adjustment; low distractibility; possible intellectualizing tendencies as in obsessive conditions; possible paranoid overalertness.
8. Academic implications:
Handling math word problems; learning from lectures; following oral directions.
9. Considerations:
Teaching and testing with a static visual format; use of associative memory clues; language visualization and auditory math skills development; number-facts recall training.

Vocabulary
1. Functions measured:
Language development; knowledge of word meanings; concept formation; verbal fluency and information.
2. Influencing factors:
Educational and cultural background; range of ideas, experiences, or interests.
3. Advantages:
Excellent index of schooling as well as of general intelligence; one of the most stable scores; correlates well with total score; no penalty for inelegance of wording.
4. Disadvantages:
Biased against educationally or culturally impoverished persons or those of foreign language background.
5. Validation:
Peabody Picture Vocabulary Test to compare receptive vocabulary versus expressive vocabulary knowledge.
6. Unusually low scores suggest:
An impoverished early environment; mental deficiency; possible organic impairment.
7. Unusually high scores suggest:
Intellectualizing or obsessive-compulsive tendencies, especially when verbalizations are stilted.
8. Academic implications:
Reading and listening comprehension in all areas; inability to communicate verbally or in writing.
9. Considerations:
Use of kinesthetic translation of language; multiple choice testing; use of charts, diagrams, and pictures in teaching and

testing; language visualization training; language memory through an auditory visual approach.

Comprehension

1. Functions measured:
   Common sense; social judgment; organization and practical application of knowledge; ability to evaluate from experience; logical reasoning; appropriate reaction to reality; pertinent, meaningful, and emotionally relevant use of facts.

2. Influencing factors:
   Social and cultural background; exposure and experiences; moral code; willingness and/or ability to respond to social rules; emotional status and maturity.

3. Advantages:
   Effective despite limited education; good correlation with total score; rich clinical data—presence of bizarre trends, perverse answers, compulsive corrections; not influenced by practice effects.

4. Disadvantages:
   Penalizes persons with impoverished cultural experience or poor verbal fluency; some sex differences; scoring standards susceptible to subjective interpretation.

5. Validation:
   Picture arrangement subtest for knowledge with a visual format.

6. Unsually low scores suggest:
   Less than adequate judgment; probability of impulsive or maladjusted behavior; obsessive-compulsive tendencies; depressive conditions; delinquent tendencies.

7. Unusually high scores suggest:
   Adequate to better than average judgment, common sense, or social competence; adequate to better than average ability to delay impulsive reaction tendencies and to behave properly or in emotionally appropriate ways in affect arousing situations; paranoid personality.

8. Academic implications:
   Study of behavioral sciences: civics, government, history, literature; learning from listening and reading.

9. Considerations:
   Rote learning; exposure to experiences to enhance understanding; use of auditory-visual format.

Digit Span

1. Functions measured:
   Ability to hold and manipulate unrelated auditorially presented digits—first forward, then backward; immediate auditory sequential memory.
2. Influencing factors:
   Attention span; concentration; level of anxiety; auditory discrimination; passive receptivity.
3. Advantages:
   Good test for lower levels of intelligence, especially in identifying mental defectives; not dependent on cultural background.
4. Disadvantages:
   Distractible persons are penalized.
5. Validation:
   Auditory memory for words; auditory memory for sentences.
6. Unusually low scores suggest:
   Likelihood of anxiety and/or tension of significant magnitudes; distractibility; possible organic, epileptic, or psychosomatic migraine conditions; short-term auditory sequential memory disorder.
7. Unusually high scores suggest:
   Good attentive processes which include low anxiety, and an easy, effortless contact with one's environment.
8. Academic implications:
   No subject matter, per se, is affected directly; if severely impaired in digit span subtest, all school success would likely suffer because of the attention factor.
9. Considerations:
   Use of simultaneous visual motor input while listening; reduce anxiety; provide visualization training.

Analysis of the WISC-R Performance Subtests[3]

Picture Completion (Timed)

1. Functions measured:
   The ability to note pertinent missing details in pictures of familiar objects; differentiating between essential and non-essential details; visual alertness and memory; appraisal of relationships.

3. Gustavson, *A Brief Analysis—Revised.*

2. Influencing factors:
   Cultural experiences; knowledge of objects and their structure or parts; figure-ground perception; visual acuity; visual memory; concentration.
3. Advantages:
   Particularly good at lower levels of intelligence; not subject to practice effects; little time to administer; nonlinguistic test of general information.
4. Disadvantages:
   Relatively restricted range of effectiveness; some sex differences; vulnerable to emotional and visual-perceptual conditions; only fair correlation with total test.
5. Validation:
   Information subtest.
6. Unusually low scores suggest:
   Emotional disturbances interfering with the ability to distinguish essential from non-essential details; poor basic perceptual and conceptual ability; poor visual concentration; anxiety.
7. Unusually high scores suggest:
   Greater than average breadth of general information; satisfactory adjusting; adequate ability to differentiate essential from non-essential details; efficiency in concentration.
8. Academic implications:
   Detail errors in all academic work.
9. Considerations:
   Use of pictograms when reading to focus on details; use of color coding, underlining, large type, uncluttered format of work papers; information development program based on visually presented data.

Picture Arrangement (Timed)
1. Functions measured:
   Ability to place pictures sequentially in a logical causal relationship; anticipation, planning, and organization; perception and synthesis of part-to-whole relationships; ability to pick out essential cues; comprehension of social situations.
2. Influencing factors:
   Cultural background; social awareness; social intelligence; visual acuity; visual-motor control.

3. Advantages:
Interesting content; broad appeal; ease of scoring; provides good clinical data—asking child to tell a story may reveal logical, fanciful, or bizarre arrangements; information or emotional content not inherent in the story.
4. Disadvantages:
Dependent to a large extent on cultural background and experience; correlates only fair with total test; vulnerable to emotional states of the subject.
5. Validation:
Similarities subtest, if Similarities score is high with a low Picture Arrangement score, the child is working by rote and not building information from the environment.
6. Unusually low scores suggest:
Likelihood of impaired ability in getting along with others; relatively poor planning in interpersonal relations; poor cultural background with lack of compolitan sophistication; possible organic impairment.
7. Unusually high scores suggest:
A socially adept, perhaps normally adjusting person; possible delinquency or psychopathy.
8. Academic implications:
Reading comprehension; listening comprehension; and the use of reading as a learning tool, especially in the social sciences.
9. Considerations:
Ask questions first, then read for the answers; provide the overview to work to; provide models and visual aids; visual-perceptual training for interpreting and organizing the environment.

Block Design (Timed)
1. Functions Measured:
Ability to analyze and to reproduce abstract designs with blocks; visual-motor integration and coordination; psychomotor speed and control; spatial or form perception, analysis, and synthesis.
2. Influencing factors:
Visual acuity; form perception; perceptual-motor coordination and speed; neurological and physiological organization; anxi-

ety and tension; flexibility; persistence; and frustration.
3. Advantages:
   Conforms to most criteria of a "good test"; correlates well
   with verbal subtests; correlates well with total score; measures creative ability to a degree.
4. Disadvantages:
   Penalizes slow methodical persons; influenced by emotional
   states or maladjustment; affected adversely by difficulties in
   visual-motor organization.
5. Validation:
   Any perceptual-motor test.
6. Unusually low scores suggest:
   Organic impairment, especially in the right hemisphere, is
   involved; likelihood of anxiety, stress, or tension; possible
   hyperactive or impulsive tendencies.
7. Unusually high scores suggest:
   Superior visual motor coordination and perceptual organization; possibly good creative ability; contraindications of organicity.
8. Academic implications:
   Math achievement with paper and pencil school arithmetic;
   affects transfer from manuscript to cursive writing.
9. Considerations:
   Use associative-manipulative approach with symbols; visual-
   perceptual training with emphasis on interpretation of abstract designs and their structure.

Object Assembly (Timed)
1. Functions measured:
   Ability to perceive and to construct from part-to-whole with
   single familiar objects in puzzle form; recognition of patterns;
   visual perception and synthesis; visual-motor integration; perceptual organization of minimal or non-meaning parts.
2. Influencing factors:
   Visual acuity; psychomotor speed and precision; visual-motor
   coordination knowledge and awareness of structure; flexibility; persistence; frustration sensory-motor feedback.
3. Advantages:
   Reveals degree to which one relies on trial and error; taps ar-
   tistic and creative ability.

4. Disadvantages:
    Vulnerable to emotional states; correlates poorly with other subtests and total score; shows great practice effects; only fair reliability.
5. Validation:
    Reading achievement pattern in school.
6. Unusually low scores suggest:
    Likelihood of anxiety or tension; possible organicity, hyperactive or impulsive tendencies; depressive tendencies.
7. Unusually high scores suggest:
    Good perceptual motor coordination; possibly good creative ability; good adjustment.
8. Academic implications:
    Ability to use a phonetic analysis approach in learning to read, especially important in first through third grades.
9. Considerations:
    Needs overview provided to work to in the form of meaningful static visual model; use manipulative, part-to-whole teaching devices; visual perceptual training related to spatial awareness, position in space, part-to-whole and interpretation of the whole form from minimal clues.

Coding (Timed)
1. Functions measured:
    The ability to copy nonmeaningful symbols for familiar digits; speed and accuracy in learning and writing symbols.
2. Influencing factors:
    Visual perception; psychomotor speed; perceptual alertness; attention; concentration; short-term visual recall; learning ability; fixation ability for keeping in place while working; understanding of the code concept; visual motor coordination; fatigue; anxiety; interest.
3. Advantages:
    Speed and accuracy serve as a good measure of intellectual ability; unfamiliar symbols reduce advantage of number-facile subjects; correlates substantially with total score.
4. Disadvantages:
    Penalizes specific visual defects and poor motor coordination; poor scores may reflect sporadic efficiency rather than intellectual limitation.

5. Validation:
   Digit pan for anxiety factor.
6. Unusually low scores suggest:
   Probability of organic impairment; anxiety, frustration, or tension.
7. Unusually high scores suggest:
   Relatively high psychomotor speed and visual-motor coordination; possibility of high rote learning ability or visual memory; relative freedom from distractibility.
8. Academic implications:
   Handwriting and copying at all grade levels.
9. Considerations:
   Pointing with finger to keep in place; card under the line of type to keep in place; large uncluttered format; structured copy work; visual-motor skills training.

Mazes

1. Functions measured:
   Planning foresight used in solving paper and pencil mazes; perceptual organization; visual motor coordination and speed.
2. Influencing factors:
   Visual perception; eye-hand coordination; attention and concentration; figure-ground perception; anxiety; motivation.
3. Advantages:
   Ease of understanding and basic appeal of the test.
4. Disadvantages:
   Vulnerable to hasty or impulsive action; low correlation with total score; penalizes motor handicapped.
5. Validation:
   Nothing noted.
6. Unusually low scores suggest:
   Poor perceptual-motor planning; impulsiveness, anxiety; control problems.
7. Unusually high scores suggest:
   Good perceptual-motor planning, organization, and speed.
8. Academic implications:
   Nothing noted.

Slosson Intelligence Test (Slosson, 1971). Another widely used intelligence test is the Slosson Intelligence Test. This test was designed by Richard Slosson following or using many of the same concepts and similar test items as the Stanford-Binet. It was designed to be given as a quick screening instrument to measure mental ability. Many practitioners find the test to be of relatively little value; however, the test was designed for teacher use in the classroom. It is a quickly administered test and can be used with children three years of age and older, including use with adults. The test has very high correlations of .90 and above with the Stanford-Binet, as well as the Wechsler scales. A discussion as to why it is held in ill-repute with many practitioners is not within the purview of this presentation; however, it may be because of the relative ease of administering and scoring the test.

As with other test scores, the score itself has little value, but a thorough understanding of the test may reveal more specific information about a person's performance relative to that test score. Due to the relative simplicity of the Slosson Intelligence Test (SIT) analysis of the tasks (item analysis) that compose the test can be easily made. One such analysis is provided in the following figure (Figure 4-1). As can be seen, the items from the test have been broken down into nine areas of performance covering arithmetic, vocabulary comprehension, verbal expression, perceptual organization, motor expression, usage, sequential memory, visual-motor integration, and general information. Once the test has been administered information beyond the test score can be obtained through an analysis of the test terms as has been done with the SIT in Figure 4-1. This analysis should yield a great deal of specific information and a person performing poorly in any one of the identified areas may be an indication of the direction the teacher should take in developing an educational program. To complete an item analysis such as this the teacher needs to first become familiar with all the test items; next to drive or specify categories that could be or seem to be inclusive of the test items. In the example, Figure 4-1, the test items were reviewed and a decision made as to the categories best reflecting all the content of the test. The last step in the analysis is to sort out each item into the category that best reflects the item's content or meaning.

The California Mental Maturity Scale (Burgermeister, Blum, and Lorge, 1972). This is a nonverbal test that was designed originally for children who were cerebral palsied and for very young or preschool age children. It is now widely used with younger children. It is a test that requires only a pointing response. This test

Figure 4-1   Item Analysis of the Slosson Intelligence

Category	Corresponding Test Item Numbers
Arithmetic	5-3, 8-8, 9-6, 10-8, 11-10, 12-2, 12-8, 13-0, 13-2, 13-4, 14-0, 14-6, 14-10, 15-2, 15-6, 16-0, 16-9, 19-0, 19-3, 19-9, 20-3, 20-9, 21-9, 22-3, 22-9, 23-3, 24-0, 24-3.
Sequential Memory	2-9, 3-0, 3-5, 3-9, 4-0, 4-5, 4-8, 4-9, 4-10, 5-0, 5-6, 7-0, 8-0, 8-8, 10-10, 12-0, 12-8.
Visual Motor	3-1, 3-6, 5-2, 7-4.
General Information	2-1, 2-2, 2-3, 2-6, 2-8, 3-2, 3-3, 3-4, 3-7, 3-8, 3-10, 4-1, 4-2, 4-3, 4-6, 4-7, 4-11, 5-4, 6-0, 6-2, 6-8, 7-6, 7-10, 8-2, 8-4, 8-6, 8-10, 9-0, 9-2, 9-4, 9-8, 9-10, 10-0, 10-2, 10-4, 10-6, 11-2, 11-6, 12-4, 12-6, 12-10, 13-8, 13-10, 14-2, 14-8, 15-0, 15-4, 15-8, 15-10, 16-3, 16-6, 17-0, 17-3, 17-6, 17-9, 19-6, 20-6, 21-3, 21-6, 22-6, 23-6.
Vocabulary Usage	2-0, 2-4, 2-7, 2-11, 3-11, 4-4, 5-10, 6-4, 6-6, 6-10, 7-2, 7-8, 11-0, 11-6, 11-8, 16-3, 16-6, 17-0, 17-3, 17-3, 17-6, 17-9, 18-9, 19-6, 20-0, 20-6, 21-0, 21-3, 21-6, 22-0, 22-6, 23-0, 23-6, 23-9, 24-6, 24-9.

takes relatively little time to administer and is good for use with nonverbal and motor impaired children.

Primary Mental Abilities Test (Thurstone and Thurstone, 1965). These tests assess children, kindergarten through 12 years of age, and can be administered in a group. Five different levels of performance are assessed by the teacher through a group administration. The areas of verbal meaning, number facility, reasoning, perceptual speed, and spatial relationships are assessed. This is a good test for the classroom teacher to use because the test items can be revealing in terms of a child's academic capabilities.

Detroit Test of Learning Aptitude (Baker and Leland, 1935). This test yields an IQ score, a mental age, and a visual profile of strengths and weaknesses. The test is composed of 19 subtests that preview eight specific mental abilities including: reasoning and comprehension, practical judgment, verbal ability, time and space relationships, number ability, auditory attentive ability, visual attentive ability, and motor ability. The test was designed for use with preschool to high school age childen.

Other Cognitive Assessment Devices. For very young children, or preschool age children, a number of measurements are available. These include the *McCarthy Scales of Children's Abilities* (McCarthy, 1972) for children two and a half to eight years of age. These tests assess general cognitive functioning as well as verbal and perceptual strengths and weaknesses. Further, memory, laterality, motor development, and quantitative skills are assessed. *Goodenough-Harris Drawing Test* (Harris, 1963) is designed to assess the approximate intellectual abilities through analysis of an individual's drawing of a person. This test is suggested for use as a "crude index" of mental development for individuals for whom no appropriate measure of mental ability is available (Gearheart and Willenberg, 1974). The *Kuhlmann-Anderson Intelligence Test* (Kuhlmann and Anderson, 1963) is a group-administered test that assesses general mental capacity and learning aptitude. This test can be easily administered, scored, and interpreted by classroom teachers. The *Leiter International Performance Scale* (Author Adaptation, Author, 1950) was designed as a test to circumvent the use of verbal constructs. The individual who is bilingual, has poor hearing, or has inadequate use of language skills can be assessed with this device. The *Vision-Up Project* (Croft and Robison, 1976) is a preschool assessment device based upon Piagetian and Gesell developmental concepts. It is used with children from birth to six years of age and assesses five levels of development: fine motor, intellectual, language, physical, self-help, and social personality areas of development. This test is broken down into subareas of performance and has been sequentially developed.

Summary

There are a number of formal tests of intelligence and cognitive abilities. It is not the intent of this discussion to identify all of them. Only those tests that are commonly used or have been found to be extensively used throughout public school systems have been identified and presented here. A review of Buro's

Mental Measurements Yearbook (7th edition) would be a helpful and necessary resource in identifying other distinct or particular measures. It is important to review that the intelligence test score is meaningless if it is not considered in conjunction with a number of other information elements which include: the child's age and grade level placement and the expectancies involved there; the environmental influences that the child has been associated with for a majority of the child's existence; the observation of social-emotional abilities and motor levels of the child on the part of the teacher. All of these are necessary elements of information that must be considered in making a sound and accurate cognitive assessment.

Can You Answer These Questions?

1. What is a mental age?
2. Given an IQ score of 85 and a CA of 12.5, what would be the mental age?
3. What are the subtests from the WISC-R that would give some indication of a child's sequencing abilities?
4. For what type of disorders in children would a wide intersubtest scatter of WISC-R scores be a possible indicator?
5. In what areas of performance may an item analysis of the Slosson reveal helpful information?
6. What are three devices used to assess the cognitive abilities of very young children?
7. Which primary elements should be included in a cognitive assessment?
8. What are some of the concerns expressed for using IQ test scores?
9. What are some of the reasons for use of IQ test scores?
10. Which of the tests discussed in this chapter was designed primarily for use by teachers?

References

Author, G. *The Author Adaptation of the Leiter International Performance Scale.* Chicago: C. H. Stoelting, 1950.

Baker, H. J., and B. Leland. *Detroit Tests of Learning Aptitude.* Indianapolis: Bobbs-Merrill, 1935.

Biehler, R. F. *Psychology Applied to Teaching.* Boston: Houghton Mifflin, 1974.

Burgemeister, B. B., L. H. Blum, and I. Lorge. *Columbia Mental Maturity Scale* (3rd ed.). New York: Harcourt Brace Jovanovich, 1972.

Croft, N., and L. Robinson. *Project Vision-Up.* Boise, Idaho: Educational Services, Inc., 1976.

Cronback, L. J., and G. C. Glaser. *Psychological Tests and Personnel Decisions* (2nd ed.). Urbana: University of Illinois Press, 1965.

Deno, E. "Use and Interpretation of Tests for Teachers," in E. Meyer (ed.), *Strategies for Teaching Exceptional Children.* Denver, Colorado: Love Publishing Co., 1972.

Gearheart, B. R., and E. P. Willenberg. *Application of Pupil Assessment Information: For Special Education Teachers.* Denver, Colorado: Love Publishing Co., 1974.

Gustavson, J. *A Brief Analysis of the Subtests of the Wechsler Intelligence Scale for Children—Revised.* Provo, Utah: Department of Educational Psychology, Brigham Young University, 1978.

Hallahan, D. P., and J. M. Kauffman. *Introduction to Learning Disabilities: A Psycho-Behavioral Approach.* Englewood Cliffs, New Jersey: Prentice-Hall, 1976.

Harris, D. *Children's Drawings as Measures of Intellectual Maturity.* New York: Harcourt Brace Jovanovich, 1963.

Kuhlmann, R., and R. G. Anderson. *Kuhlmann-Anderson Test.* Princeton, New Jersey: Personnel Press, 1963.

McCarthy, P. *Manual for the McCarthy Scales of Children's Abilities.* New York: Psychological Corporation, 1972.

Moran, M. R. *Assessment of the Exceptional Learner in the Regular Classroom.* Denver, Colorado: Love Publishing Co., 1978.

Piaget, J. *Origins of Intelligence in Children.* New York: Norton, 1963.

Sattler, J. M. "Analysis of Function of the 1960 Stanford-Binet Intelligence Scales, Form L-M." *Journal of Clinical Psychology,* 1965, 21, 173–179.

Slosson, R. *Slosson Intelligence Test for Children and Adults.* East Aurora, New York: Slosson Educational Pub., 1971.

Stellern, J., S. F. Vasa and J. Little. *Introduction to Diagnostic-Prescriptive Teaching and Programming.* Glen Ridge, New Jersey: Exceptional Press, 1976.

Terman, L., and M. Merrill. *Stanford-Binet Intelligence Scale,* 1972 Norms Edition. Boston: Houghton Mifflin, 1973.

Thurstone, L., and T. Thurstone. *Primary Mental Abilities Test.* Chicago: Science Research Associates, 1965.

Wallace, G., and S. C. Larsen. *Educational Assessment of Learning Problems: Testing for Teaching.* Boston: Allyn and Bacon, 1978.

Wechsler, D. *The Measurement of Adult Intelligence.* Baltimore: Williams and Wilkins, 1944.

Wechsler, D. *Manual for the Wechsler Adult Intelligence Scale.* New York: Psychological Corporation, 1955.

Wechsler, D. *Manual for the Wechsler Preschool and Primary Scale of Intelligence.* New York: Psychological Corporation, 1967.

Wechsler, D. *Manual for the Wechsler Intelligence Scale for Children—Revised.* New York: Psychological Corporation, 1974.

chapter

Preschool Assessment

Objectives

At the conclusion of this chapter, the reader should be able to:

1. outline the expected behaviors of a preschool child's cognitive, language, motor, and social development;
2. outline the major components of Piaget's developmental theory;
3. identify formal assessment instruments that can be used to identify educational problems in preschool children;
4. specify informal language procedures to be used to screen and identify education problems in preschool children.

Introduction

Greater emphasis is being placed on early identification of learning problems in children. There are many who feel the earlier the child's problem is identified, the greater the chances that that problem can be corrected and that even early stimulation through enrichment programs can improve a child's overall performance level in the academic areas (Elkind, 1969; Evans, 1971; Payne, Kauffman, Brown, and Demott, 1974). It is the purpose of this chapter to explore preschool assessment as it applies to formal and informal assessment techniques. Assessment will be discussed in terms of cognitive, language, motor, and social development patterns of preschool children.

There is a great deal of literature that focuses on early stimulation in the areas of language, motor, social, and cognitive development. Preschool can have dramatic effects in children, relative to these areas. However, the effects do not appear to have a lasting influence in terms of later school-related behavior (Evans, 1971). It may be that the early stimulation programs such as Head Start are utilized at the wrong times during the child's development or that they end much too soon before long-lasting effects can take place (Painter, 1968). Evans (1971) clearly indicates that the Head Start program and its related counterparts facilitated identification of mental and physical problems that may have gone unnoticed without this preschool opportunity. Kappelman (1969) found that a high incidence of neurologically impaired and emotionally disturbed problems were identified among disadvantaged children who had been initially screened in a preschool program. This was similar to the finding of Mico (1966) who found that over 75 percent of the children screened for participation in a Head Start program in Boston required further assessment of suspected problems. From these findings it appears that preschool assessment may be an important preventive measure in controlling learning problems of children.

Assessing Preschool Abilities

Preschool programs and development are usually discussed in terms of a child's cognitive, language, motor, and social development. These four components will be discussed in relationship to the expected developmental patterns of children. This information forms a basis from which expected levels of behavior can be ascertained and against which a child's present level of performance can be measured for assessment purposes.

Cognitive Development. In discussing cognitive development the literature usually focuses upon the child's ability to perform tasks involving reasoning, memory, and creative abilities. These abilities are assessed using formal tests of intelligence; however, assessing the intelligence of children using a formal diagnostic measure does not appear to be a very sound practice. A preschool child's intelligence, as measured by a standardized intelligence test, is somewhat unstable (Mussen, Gonger, and Kagen, 1969). This is especially evident when the Intelligence Quotient (IQ) scores of children two and three years of age are compared with their IQ scores at ages five and seven years. Mussen, Gonger, and Kagen (1969) report that IQs obtained at ages three and five are more highly correlated than are IQs between the ages of three and seven. Further, these authors indicate that the IQ becomes less likely to change with increasing age. This is similar to the findings of Bloom (1966) who correlated the IQs of children at ages 3 and 17 and found that there was greater change in this age category than when the intelligence measures of children age five were compared with their IQ scores at age 17. It is not uncharacteristic to see a variation of as much as 20 points between a child's early preschool IQ and a later childhood measure of intelligence (Mussen, Conger, and Kagan, 1969). In terms of children with tested IQs 70 or below, it appears these scores are more stable over time than the IQ scores obtained from children who have been tested as having normal or above normal intelligence.

A number of factors have been identified as influencing cognitive development. Bloom (1964) hypothesizes that environment has perhaps the greatest influence on development in the early years than at any other time and that deprivation within the first four years of life will have far greater consequences than deprivation in the years between 8 and 17. An important concept in this discussion is to point out that the child's cognitive or intellectual ability in the early years cannot be a predictor of the child's future academic or school-related success; and to ensure that the child reaches a maximum level of cognitive development, he or she should be given early stimulation through environmentally enriched experiences.

Perhaps the most reviewed developmental theorist in the literature on cognitive development is Jean Piaget. Because of his contributions in this area, his work will be summarized as representing expected levels of cognitive development in preschool-age children. The question of how one determines the present level of the child's cognitive development can be answered through a study of the stages of development outlined by Piaget. There are four major stages in Piaget's schema of cognitive development: the sensory motor, the preoperational, the concrete, and the formal stages of development (see Figure 5-1).

The *sensory motor stage*, which occurs first in the child's life and lasts until approximately two years of age, is characterized by six substages (see Figure 5-1). During this stage the child's primary behavior is first of a reflexive organism, eventually progressing to one of a more organized behavioral system. Marshall (1975) states that from the behavior of a three- or four-month-old fetus it is obvious that the brain is "capable of organizing quite complicated responses to stimuli at this age" (p. 43), such as opening its mouth, turning its head sideways, or moving its arms and legs, and early reflexive behaviors including sucking and blinking. The infant moves through the sensory motor stage to the invention of new means of obtaining new ends. The child progresses to a higher functional level involving the conscious manipulation of objects—for instance, using the bottom drawer in a cupboard to be able to reach and to obtain a piece of bread resting on top of the cupboard (Simpkins, 1976).

The *preoperational stage* is that stage of cognitive development that occurs between the ages of two and seven years and involves the child making judgments primarily based on perceptual cues that are dealt with one variable at a time. Therefore, the child's reasoning is characterized as egocentric. Things are as they appear to the child within the particular time and place that they occur or are viewed. There is a lack of consistency in the child's judgments since they may change when one variable changes. For example, Simpkins (1976) points out that a young child of about three will ask for a glass of milk. The mother finds the carton almost empty but pours the remains into a large glass; the

Figure 5-1   Piaget's Stages of Development (Selected from Dr. Kathrine Simpkins's instructional materials, Department of Educational Psychology, Brigham Young University. Used by permission of Dr. Simpkins).

Sensory-Motor (approximately birth to 2 years)

Development from a state of reflex activity to an organized sensory-motor action system.
   a. Reflexive (0–1 month)
      Simple reflex activity; example—kicking.
   b. Primary Circular Reaction (1–4.5 months)
      Reflexive behavior elaborated and coordinated; example—a thing grasped becomes something to suck.
   c. Secondary Circular Reaction (4.5–9 months)
   d. Coordination of Secondary Schema (9–12 months)
   e. Tertiary Circular Reactions (12–18 months)
      Discovers new ways to obtain desired goal; example—pulls pillow nearer in order to get music box resting on it.
   f. Invention of New Means Through Mental Combinations (18–24 months)
      Invents new ways and means; example—uses stick to reach desired object.

Preoperational (approximately 2 to 7 years)

Perceptually oriented; makes judgments in terms of how things appear; generally deals with only one variable expression; speech is repetitious; frequent egocentric monologues.
   a. Preconceptual (2–4 years)
      Capable of deferred imitation and of verbal expression; speech is repetitious; frequent egocentric monologues.
   b. Intuitive (4–7 years)
      Speech becomes socialized; reasoning is egocentric; example—"to the right" means to *the child's* right.

Concrete Operations (approximately 7 to 11 years)

Mobile and systematic thought organizes and classifies information. Can follow successive changes through various types of detours and reversals. Operations are tied to action; they are concrete rather than abstract.

Formal Operations (generally achieved after age 11)

Ability to think abstractly, formulate hypotheses, engage in hypothetico-deductive reasoning, and check solutions. Thought now directs observations.

milk only partially fills the glass. The child begins to fuss, explaining that the desired glass is not full. The mother explains that there is no more milk, but there is no quieting the child. Using Piagetian concepts at this time, the mother would pour the milk from the partially filled large glass into a smaller glass, filling the smaller glass to the brim. The child at this point should be satisfied in that the child has received a full glass of milk. In this case, only the height of the milk in the glass is a relevant variable to the child, not the actual volume of content. It is these two areas of development, sensory motor and preoperational, that are of most concern in developing an understanding of the preschool youngster. If these expected levels of behavior are understood, the child's ultimate behavior patterns can be more thoroughly analyzed and deficient patterns can be identified.

The remaining two stages, concrete operations and formal operations, occur between the ages of 7 and 12 years of age. In the *concrete operational stage* (7 years to 12 years), logical thinking begins to emerge. The child is able to go through a series of transformations, detours, and other changes to obtain a successful solution. No longer will this child be fooled by the size of a drinking glass. The child now knows that a change of size or shape of containers will not change the amount of milk. Observations are now tied to the concrete observable reality of the situation. An example of concrete operational functioning is seen in the child's attempt to classify large, medium, and small circles into groups. Initially, the grouping may be done on the basis of shape, but the reality of the various pieces creates a beginning awareness of the simultaneity of two criteria, size and shape. Concepts of the shape and size of the pieces develop so that the child is now able to sort on the basis of these two criteria. The child can group them into large circles, large squares, medium circles, medium squares, small circles, etc. This development suggests that the child's underlying structure for classification has been extended to include classification by two criteria simultaneously.

In the *formal operation stage*, which occurs around 12 years of age and carries the child into adulthood, the child begins to perform abstract reasoning involving processes similar to the scientific method in that a problem can be defined, hypothesis formulated, and methodologies specified as to what should be done about the problem. The child engages in hypothetical deductive reasoning, carries out systematic experimentation, can form conclusions based upon that experimentation, and can check these conclusions against existing criteria (Simpkins, 1976).

Language Development. This area involves the analysis of the child's language abilities to include the application and use of phonemes, morphemes, syntax, semantics, as well as the fluency, vocabulary, and discrimination skills necessary to perform adequate language functions. At one time it was felt that a child's language acquisition could be measured by the number of words in a child's vocabulary (Lefrançois, 1973). The child's active vocabulary in conjunction with the passable vocabulary was a better measure of the child's overall language skills.

Language is one of the chief measuring devices in assessing cognitive development. It would be difficult to discuss cognitive capacity without also discussing the child's language abilities. Figure 5-2 outlines the language acquisition abilities of children from approximately 12 weeks to 4 years of age.

Language acquisition or development usually follows a pattern of babbling that follows crying. Roots of language are found in a child's babbling. Up to six months of age, the babbling appears to be somewhat unstructured or unsystematic. It has been reported (Lefrançois, 1973) that the child begins babbling with a preponderance of vowel sounds followed by simpler consonants. After six months of age the babbling becomes more structured and apparently purposeful. It is difficult to determine at just what exact moment in time the child's controlled babbling is associated with an understanding of the sounds elicited. Somewhere close to the *first year of age* the meaning of sounds to the child can be determined with the occurrence of "mama" and "dada." This is usually one of the first occasions in which the child meaningfully uses language to describe an object. This does not mean that a child can attach meaning only to one or two words. The child has demonstrated up to this time an understanding of words by responding appropriately to them; "come to mama," "pick up your toy," or other similar examples demonstrate that the child understands and can respond to language appropriately.

Just prior to the *second year* of development the child's language is composed primarily of one- or two-syllable words and the

Figure 5-2   Expected Language and Motor Development Patterns of Infants

Approximate Age of Clearance	Language	Motor
0–4 months	Crying differential beings; front vowels k, l, g.	Supports head when in prone position; weight is on elbows; sits with props.
4 months	Cooing and chuckling; one-syllable sounds.	
6–12 months	Babbling—playing with sounds 1. Reflexive sounds (crying) 2. Repeats self (babbling) 3. Repeats others (echolalia).	Stands holding on; picks up small items with thumb and finger tips; creeps; pulls to standing position; walks when held by one hand; mouthing of objects almost stopped.
12–18 months	A few first words (which are mostly nouns)— "mama," "dada"; follows simple commands; responds to "no."	Sits on child's chair; creeps downstairs backward; difficulty building tower of 3 cubes; walking is stiff and tentative.
18–24 months	Vocabulary 20–200 words; points to named objects; comprehends simple questions; 2-word phrases.	Can run but falls in sudden turns; can quickly alternate between sitting and stance; walks stairs up and down, one foot at a time.
24–30 months	300–400 words; 2–3 word phrases.	Jumps with both feet; stands on one foot for short period; jumps from chair; good hand and finger coordination; builds tower of six or more cubes.
30–36 months	Fastest increase in vocabulary (300–1000 words); 3–4 word sentences.	
36–40 months	Vocabulary of more than 1500 words; well-formed sentences	Runs smoothly and can accelerate and decelerate with ease; can make sharp and fast curves without difficulty; walks stairs by alternating feet; can ride a tricycle; jumps over rope; hops on right foot; catches ball in arms; walks line.

child's verbal vocabulary is at best a simple object-word association. At approximately the *end of the second year and beginning of the third year*, the child begins to construct simple sentences that again communicate meaning. During the *third year* of development, the child's acquisition of language is greatly enhanced. At this stage of development the child's vocabulary increases as well as the amount of words used within a sentence. The sophistication of language usage reveals that the child has an understanding of syntax and semantics. By the onset of the *fourth year* the child's language skills are well established. The child has an active use of approximately 2,500 words with usage of that active vocabulary deviating slightly from the adult norm.

Language development is immensely influenced by the environmental situation in which the child is placed. To some professionals the quality of the child's early environment, in terms of fostering language acquisition, is the most important external factor affecting the rate of that development (Carroll, 1960; Mussen, Conger, and Kagan, 1969). A stimulating language environment that offers good models together with a variety of novel and rewarding verbal interchanges would enhance the learning and cognitive development of the child (Mussen, Conger, and Kagan, 1969). It has been demonstrated that preschool children from institutions where they were neither highly motivated nor encouraged to speak frequently also demonstrate handicaps in other areas of language development including the correction of speech and the intelligent use of language (Goldfard, 1945; Mussen, Conger, and Kagan, 1969). Assessing language and cognitive development in preschool children cannot be done successfully without taking into consideration the environmental background of the child.

Motor Development. Lenneberg (1967) indicates that there is a strong relationship between development of motor capability and the acquisition of language and that this relationship is almost inseparable. In their study of the acquisition of language and motor skills of mongoloid children ages 2 to 22 years Lenneberg, Nicholes, and Rosenberger (1964) found that there were parallels between crawling and babbling and talking and walking. Figure 5-2 illustrates this relationship between motor development and language acquisition. Further, the figure outlines nicely the motor development stages related to their occurrence by age (Lenneberg, 1967).

Shirley (1933), through a longitudinal study, identified the motor development patterns of infants as being able to raise the chin at *one month*, raise the chest and head at *two months*, to reach for an object in *three months*, sit with a support at *four months*, while at the *fifth* month being able to grasp an object. During the *seventh and eighth months* the child sits alone and can stand with help, the *ninth through the eleventh months* the child can stand while holding on to furniture, begins to creep, and can walk when led. The *twelfth through the fourteenth months* are characterized by the child pulling on an object to stand up, demonstrating an ability to ascend and descend stairs, and standing alone. By the *fifteenth month* the child should be able to walk unassisted.

It should be noted that the components of motor development outside of physical growth include the child's perceptual and sensory capabilities. The child's perceptual ability appears related to the maturational or physical growth level of the child. A child of four years of age will have a great discrepancy in the perception of an object or happening when compared to that of a ten year old. This discrepancy is due in part to the child's learned behavior or experiential background. In other words, the four-year-old child has not had the same experiences or opportunities to learn the same amount of material as has a ten year old. Obviously, the higher the maturational level, the greater the child's perceptual abilities should be.

To determine if a child has a perceptual deficit, it is necessary to consider the maturational or physical growth level of a child in conjunction with the experiential background of that child. Knowing the expected or normal growth and development patterns would be helpful in making that determination.

Social/Emotional Development. It appears that the elements of cognition, language, and motor development are interwoven and seemingly inseparable from this last area of development. Social/emotional development is dependent upon the other three areas. This section can best begin with a statement by Lefrançois (1973) in which he indicates that making any statements about the child's emotions is at best tentative because emotions are subjec-

Figure 5-3   Social/Emotional Development of Preschool Children

	Birth to About 3 Years of Age	From 2 Through 6 Years of Age
Personal Independence	A very dependent being; beginning self-awareness	Adjusting to less private attention; becoming independent physically (while remaining strongly dependent emotionally)
Social/emotional Development	Developing affection	Giving affection
	Developing of rudimentary social interaction skills (smile techniques)	Beginning to interact with agemates
		Awareness of being a member of a social unit (family)
	Adjusting to expectations of others	Developing ability to be obedient to authority
		Developing self discipline in absence of adult leadership or authority
		Differentiating between male adult and female adult roles
	Adjusting to adult feelings and demands	Changing behavior on the basis of changes in physical capabilities
	Adjusting to adult cleanliness demands	

tive responses not easily observed and the situations in which emotions can be evoked are such that to an adult they may be emotion-producing, while to a child they may not be.

The social/emotional area has had a great deal of attention directed toward it in an attempt to identify the stages that a child experiences in developing a mature social/emotional level of behavior. Figure 5-3 provides an outline of the anticipated social or emotional behaviors of children as they would occur at a particular age level.

It must be pointed out that all the behaviors mentioned above are merely indications of expected levels of behavior and are illustrative of what usually and characteristically occurs within an age level relative to each of the developmental areas mentioned. In educational assessment of preschool children, the teacher should be able to make more accurate judgments of a child's performance as well as the predictors of potential future learning problems if there is an understanding of the growth and development patterns and expected levels of behavior. A judgment that is made concerning the potential problems in the child should be made in consideration of not only the expected growth and development patterns but also the child's experimental and environmental background.

Preschool Attainment Record (Doll, 1967). This device is completed by the child's parent or an adult confidant who is aware of the child's overall development. The parent or confidant is interviewed to collect information relative to eight categories of development: ambulation, manipulation, rapport, communication, responsibility, information, ideation, and creativity. The raw data are then translated into a language-age equivalent that illustrates the relative school readiness of the child. This device was designed for use with children from six months to seven years of age.

The Denver Developmental Screening Test (Frankenburg, Dodds, and Vandal, 1970). This is an individually administered, norm-referenced measure designed to identify behavior problems in children. Its intended use is for children from birth to six years of age. This device is broken down into four areas of development: the social, fine motor, language, and gross motor. The raw score data are interpreted into a developmental level or an estimate of development in each of the four areas that is indicative of either normal or delayed development.

Test of Basic Experiences (Moss, 1972). The intended purpose of this test is to assess the child's experiences and preparedness in completing projected school tasks. The test can be administered to a small group of children (it is recommended that ratio of the group not exceed six children to one test proctor). The test is composed of two parts: the first part assesses the child's understanding of language, math, science, and social studies at a preschool or kindergarten level; the second level assesses the same areas at a kindergarten to first-grade level. Raw score data are translated into percentile rankings and standard scores from which a child's relative development can be measured against others of the same age.

The Boehm Test of Basic Concepts (Boehm, 1971). This test is a measure of a child's understanding of those concepts considered necessary for achieving in the primary grades. It is a group test that is norm-referenced. There are alternate forms for this test, which are considered to be equivalent in difficulty. Each of the forms contains two levels of concepts that range from simple to more complex. The child responds to a series of pictures and corresponding statements read by the teacher and then is to mark an answer on the record booklet provided. Essentially, the child is identifying a picture that appropriately represents the statement read. Raw scores are translated into percentile equivalents, giving an indication of how the child would score in relationship to kindergarten, first-, and second-grade children. Even though the test is norm-referenced, its most obvious use is in the identification of the child's ability to perform or not perform the tasks comprising the test, and it should be used only as a screening device for identifying the concept development of children relative to their understanding of space, quantity, and time.

Preschool Inventory—Revised Edition (Caldwell, 1970). This is an individually administered inventory designed to identify the readiness skills of children three to six years of age. This inventory provides information concerning the child's understanding of personal information, social role, numbers, colors, and geometric forms. Even though raw scores can be translated into percentile rankings, it is suggested that the use of this test be directed by the content; that is, the items comprising the inventory are such that a great deal of information concerning the child's understanding of self, others, and basic academic concepts can be ascertained. If the percentiles are to be used, they should be used with caution and only as a guide in determining if a potential problem does exist in one of the tested areas.

Evanston Early Identification Scale (Landsman and Dillard, 1967). This scale can be administered either individually or to a group. The test is primarily used with children between five and six years of age. The primary purpose of the test is to identify high risk children or those children who have a high probability of failing in school. The child simply draws a person and, based upon point values assigned to the component parts of the person drawn, the child is then classified as either high risk (a child with a higher probability of complete failure), middle risk (indicating that the child may have some difficulty in school), or low risk (in which there are few, if any, problems expected to be encountered by the child in completing school-related tasks). This scale, at best, should be considered a gross screening instrument and should not be used as the sole means of determining the existence or nonexistence of problems in children. It can be used, the author feels, as a very valuable, quick means of identifying children on which further or more extensive diagnosis should be completed to determine their problem areas.

Project Vision-Up (Robinson and Croft, 1976). The *Project Vision-Up* is a developmental scale that is designed for use with children from birth through six years of age in the areas of fine motor, intellectual, language, physical, self-help, and personality development. The survey consists of several items within each of these major areas that are arranged sequentially in order of difficulty. The device is designed to be completed individually with a parent or an adult confidant who is well aware of the child's developmental progression. The survey was designed to be used in conjunction with an extensive curriculum package that includes materials and instructional strategies for use in remediating, correcting, or teaching specific kinds of skills for each of the major categories mentioned above. Figure 5-4 illustrates the major and sub areas of development assessed through the Project Vision-Up survey. The survey is criterion-referenced.

The child is assessed in relationship to each major area and a determination is made as to the behaviors that can be manifest in relation to each of the major areas. Identification of subsequent behaviors that then need to be learned is completed. The unique feature of this survey is the corresponding instructional materials. Each of the items that comprise the survey corresponds to an instructional strategy. Each instructional strategy is designed for use by a parent in the home, utilizing materials and aids that in most cases can be found within the home environment (that is, eating utensils, string, pieces of carpet, bowls, brooms, chairs, and the like). Figure 5-5 is an illustration of a sample of the survey items with their corresponding instructional strategies and materials.

Figure 5-4   Project Vision-Up Major Areas and Sub-areas of Development. (Each of the sub-areas is further broken down into behaviors that are sequenced in difficulty from birth to six years of age.)

Major Areas	Sub-areas
Fine Motor Development	Hand use
	Visual-motor
	Object manipulation
	Pounding
	Wrist rotation
	Finger use
Intellectual Development	Object permanence
	Environmental events
	Object in space
	Self in space
	Operational causality
	Sensory discrimination
	Seriation
	Body image
	Immediate memory
	Number
	Classification
	Length
	Time
	Weight
	Substance
	Science
Language Development	Preverbal behavior
	Spontaneous speech
	Vocabulary
	Articulation
	Sentence structure
	Language experience
	Description
Physical Development	Head control
	Sitting
	Creeping, crawling
	Arm control
	Walking
	Rolling
	Standing
	Climbing
	Kicking

Figure 5-4 Project Vision-Up Major Areas and Sub-areas of Development. (Each of the sub-areas is further broken down into behaviors that are sequenced in difficulty from birth to six years of age.) (*Continued*)

Major Areas	Sub-areas
	Running
	Jumping, hopping
	Pedalling
	Skipping
Self-help	Eating
	Dressing
	Sleeping
	Toileting
	Mobility
	Grooming
Social-personal	Play
	Social interaction
	Behavioral adjustment

From Croft and Robinson, 1977. Used by permission of the publisher.

Figure 5-5 Behavioral Description and Programming Activities (From the Project Vision-Up (Croft and Robinson, 1976). Used with permission of the authors.)

FINE MOTOR

GRASP REFLEX PREDOMINATES
Description of Behavior: When the child receives stimulation in his palm, he grasps the stimulus object.

Indications of a Disability: If the child is unable to grasp an object or if his hand is too tense or rigid to do so, further evaluation is indicated. If disability is diagnosed, follow the clinician's recommendations.

Programming Activities:
1. Open the child's palm and run a soft object across it. Repeat, using other soft objects, such as a feather duster, soft brush, towel, cloth, and soft toy.
2. Place your finger in the child's palm and close the palm around your finger.
3. Open and close the child's hand manually.

4. Place small objects in the child's palm and gently close his hand around them. Hold his hand around them.
5. Place an ice chip in the child's hand and gently close his hand around it.

Materials: Soft objects such as a feather duster, soft brush, towel, cloth, soft toy; various small objects; ice chip

HANDS BEGINNING TO BE FISTED

Description of Behavior: The child on occasion holds hands in a fisted position.

Indication of a Disability: If the child's hand will not make a fist, or if it is extremely difficult to release the hand from the first position, further evaluation is indicated.

Programming Activities:
1. Repeat activities for Card No. 1FMO3W*: Grasp Reflex predominates.
2. Close the child's hands and gently rub the child's fist.

Materials: Various small objects; soft objects such as a feather duster, soft brush, cloth, soft toy; ice chip

HANDS REMAIN FISTED

Description of Behavior: Most of the time the child maintains the fisted position with his hands.

Indication of a Disability: If the child's hand will not make a fist, or if it is extremely difficult to release the hand from the first position, further evaluation is indicated.

Programming Activities:
1. Repeat activities for Card No. 2FMO3W*: Hands Beginning To Be Fisted.
2. Allow the child to keep his hands in a fisted position.

Materials: Various objects as listed on Card No. 2FMO3W*

GRASP REFLEX STILL PRESENT

Description of Behavior: On most occasions when the child is stimulated in the area of his palm he still responds with the grasp reflex.

Indications of a Disability: If after two or three months the child is still unable to grasp an object, if his hand is too tense or rigid to do so, if his hand will not make a fist, or if it is extremely difficult to release the hand from the original or fisted position, further evaluation is necessary.

Programming Activities:
1. Open the child's palm and run a soft object across the child's palm. Repeat, using various soft objects.
2. Place your finger in the child's palm and close the palm around your finger.
3. Open and close the child's hand manually.

Figure 5-5   Behavioral Description and Programming Activities (From the Project Vision-Up (Robinson and Croft, 1976). Used with permission of the authors.) (*Continued*)

FINE MOTOR

4. Place small objects in the child's palm and gently close his hand around them. Hold his hand around them.
5. Place an ice chip in the child's palm and gently close his hand around it.
6. Allow the child to grasp items without assistance. Be careful the child does not get any small object in his mouth.

Materials: Soft objects, various small objects, ice chip

TURNS EYES TO RED LIGHT

Description of Behavior: The child responds to the presence of a red light in his visual field by turning his eyes in the direction of the light source.

Indication of Disability: If the child makes little or no response to the light stimulus, further evaluation is indicated.

Programming Activities:

1. Hold a flashlight with a red filter in front of the child's face, and make various movements with the light. Observe to determine if the child moves his eyes in response to the movements made by the light.
2. Repeat Item 1 above, on various occasions. It will help to darken the room before the session begins. Experiment with the period of time the child will respond to the light's movements, but do not fatigue him.
3. If the child does not respond in any way, or if the response to the light's movements is limited, increase the brightness of the light until the child makes some response. Try using Christmas tree lights or luau lights. If the child makes no response to any light, attempt the use of a photo flashbulb to gain his attention.

Materials: Flashlight with red lens cover, Christmas tree lights, luau lights, photo flash system

REGARDS DANGLING OBJECT

Description of Behavior: When presented with an object directly in his visual field, the child fixates his attention on it.

Indication of Disability: Lack of response to either visual or auditory stimulus indicates the need for further evaluation.

Programming Activities:

1. Place the child on his back. Dangle a bright-colored object or hold a red lens over a flashlight and display it in the child's view. Make adjustments concerning room and the distance the object is held from the child. On most occasions a distance of two or three feet will be sufficient.

2. When the child focuses on the object, move it a few inches to the left and let him follow it. Repeat, moving the object to the right.
3. Tie a mobile across the child's crib or playpen, or, if the child has impaired vision, fashion an object from miniature Christmas tree lights and suspend it across his crib. This will help the child to focus and practice using his eyes as the objects move and attract his attention.
4. Hold a rattle (if needed, attach a light to the rattle) about one foot above the child's face. Stand behind the child's head so that you are out of his line of sight. When you are sure the child sees the rattle, move it in a slow circle around the child's head so that he can keep it in his line of sight by just moving his eyes without moving his head.

Materials: Mobile, lights as needed, flashlight with red lens, stimulus object, rattle

FOLLOWS OBJECT TO MIDLINE
Description of Behavior: When presented with a stimulus object directly in his visual field, the child is able to follow the object to the center of his body.

Indications of Disability: If the child makes little or no response to the light stimulus, further evaluation is indicated.

Programming Activities:
1. Place the child on his back and turn his head to the side. Shake a rattle in the child's line of vision about a foot from his face. (If needed, a light can be attached to the rattle and the room darkened.) When he focuses on the object, move it slowly toward the child's midline.
2. Repeat Item 1 above, turning the child's head to the opposite side.
3. Repeat activities from Card No. 6FM1*: Regards Dangling Object.

Materials: Lighted rattle, items from Card No. 6FM1*

---

* Refer to other instructional materials found in *Project-Vision-Up*.

Informal Assessment Methods

The teacher, armed with the information concerning the expected growth and development patterns of children in terms of cognitive, language, motor, and social-emotional development, should be able to construct a very comprehensive checklist of preschool behaviors. Further, if the school tasks are clearly understood by the teacher and the school curriculum thoroughly scrutinized to determine the expected school behaviors, then the prerequisite behaviors needed to successfully complete each school task can be identified.

This information can be used to construct a preschool inventory of academically related tasks. Utilizing a scale such as the Project Vision-Up (Croft and Robinson, 1976) also provides clues as to the type of information that can be included in the development of an informal device to assess preschool readiness. Figure 5-6 is an example of an informal preschool screening device that was developed to ascertain information concerning a child's performance relative to some specifically identified school-related tasks.

Figure 5-6   Example of a Teacher-Made Preschool Readiness Checklist (From Shea-Kelly, 1978. Used with permission of the authors.)

Shea-Kelly Early Childhood Evaluation of Learning Readiness Score Sheet

Name _____   Present Date _____
Address_____   Birth Date _____
School_____   Teacher_____
Age or CA_____   Grade_____   Examiner _____

	Yes	No
I. Verbal self-awareness: (Ask directly)		
A. Knows name:		
1. First name only	____	____
2. Full name	____	____
B. Knows birthdate:		
1. Month	____	____
2. Day	____	____
3. Year	____	____
4. Age	____	____
C. Knows address:		
1. House number	____	____
2. Street name	____	____
3. City	____	____
4. State	____	____

	Yes	No
II. Concept development: (Use stimulus cards 1–8. Ask, "What color is this?")		
A. Knows colors:		
1. Red	____	____
2. Yellow	____	____
3. Green	____	____
4. Blue	____	____
5. Purple	____	____
6. Brown	____	____
7. Black	____	____
8. Orange	____	____

B. Counts 1 to 13: (Circle correct response)
   1 2 3 4 5 6 7 8 9 10 11 12 13
C. Understands number concepts:
   1. Show me 4 fingers   ____ ____
   2. Show me 7 fingers   ____ ____
   3. Draw me 5 balls   ____ ____
   4. Draw me 9 balls   ____ ____
D. Recognizes coins: (Use stimulus cards 9–12.
   Ask, "What do we call this?": If subject says,
   "Money," say, "Yes, but what is its name?")
   1. Penny   ____ ____
   2. Nickel   ____ ____
   3. Dime   ____ ____
   4. Quarter   ____ ____
E. Knows alphabet: (Ask child to say the alphabet. Underline all consecutive correct responses.)
   Sing   Say
   a b c d e f g h i j k l m n o p q r s t u v w x y z

III. Awareness of body parts: (Examiner points to
     parts in E, F, G, H.)   Yes   No
     A. Touch your head   ____ ____
     B. Touch your foot   ____ ____
     C. Touch your ear   ____ ____
     D. Touch your knee   ____ ____
     E. What do we call this? (eye)   ____ ____
     F. What do we call this? (neck)   ____ ____
     G. What do we call this? (hand)   ____ ____
     H. What do we call this? (shoulder)   ____ ____

IV. Awareness of left and right:
    A. Point to your left hand   ____ ____
    B. Pull your right ear   ____ ____
    C. Point to your right eye   ____ ____
    D. Point to your left foot   ____ ____

V. Auditory discrimination:
   A. Recognizes rhythmic beats as same or differ-
      ent: (Tap pencil on table at rate of 2 per sec-
      ond. Do one demonstration of a "same" pat-
      tern and one of a "different" pattern.)
      1. / /   / /   ____ ____
      2. /   / /   ____ ____
      3. / /   / / /   ____ ____
      4. / / /   / / /   ____ ____

Figure 5-6   Example of a Teacher-Made Preschool Readiness Checklist (From Shea-Kelly, 1978. Used with permission of the authors.) *(Continued)*

Shea-Kelly Early Childhood Evaluation of Learning Readiness Score Sheet

---

	Yes	No
B. Reproduces patterned taps: (Ask child to copy your pattern.)		
1. /	___	___
2. / / / /	___	___
3. / / / / / /	___	___
4. / / /	___	___

C. Recognizes pairs of words, read to him, as the same or different. (Ask child to sit facing away from examiner and indicate if the words are the same or different. Give example of child's name.)

	Same	Diff.
1. red red	___	___
2. some come	___	___
3. rib rum	___	___
4. clay clay	___	___
5. hit hat	___	___
6. big big	___	___

	Yes	No
VI. Auditory memory:		
A. Repeats series of syllables and words read to him. (Read words at 1 per second. Read sentence at 2 words per second.)		
1. shim clung	___	___
2. bug ship because	___	___
3. The dog chased the cat up the tree.	___	___
B. Repeats series of numbers read to him. Say at a rate of 2 per second.)		
1. 4, 7	___	___
2. 2, 8, 1	___	___
3. 9, 3, 6, 5	___	___
C. Follows directions in sequential order. (Give instructions once only.)		
1. Stand up. Pick up your pencil. Sit down.	___	___
2. Put the pencil on the table. Stand up. Turn around. Sit down.	___	___

VII. Auditory blending:
   A. Blends isolated sounds and syllables into words. (Say the sounds at a rate of 2 per second. Demonstration item—"What am I talking about? c : at")

	Yes	No
1. s·ee	——	——
2. sh·o·p	——	——
3. gr·a·ss	——	——
4. st·e·p	——	——
5. c·ar	——	——

VIII. Motor coordination: (Ask child to perform the task. Examiner may demonstrate.)

	Adeq.	Inadeq.	Demo.
A. Stands on one foot and maintains balance	——	——	——
B. Jumps	——	——	——
C. Skips	——	——	——
D. Walks heel to toe on a straight line 5 ft. long	——	——	——
E. Pencil grasp (Note on subtest X.)	——	——	——

IX. Visual motor: (Use answer sheet.)

	Yes	No
A. Trace ⟲	——	——
B. Trace ✗	——	——
C. Trace ⊏⊐	——	——
D. Copy △	——	——
E. Copy ∨∨	——	——
F. Copy D	——	——

X. Visual discrimination:

	Yes	No
A. Matches pictures of identical objects. (Show stimulus cards 10–13.)		
1. Sweater	——	——
2. Top	——	——
3. Chair	——	——
4. Tree	——	——
B. Recognizes letters that are exactly alike. (Use stimulus cards 14–17.)		
1. H	——	——
2. B	——	——
3. C	——	——
4. P	——	——
C. Distinguishes letters that are exactly alike. (Use stimulus cards 18–19.)		
1. (b)	——	——
2. (f)	——	——
D. Recognizes words that are exactly alike. (Use stimulus cards 20–21.)		
1. (hot)	——	——
2. (jar)	——	——

Figure 5-6 Example of a Teacher-Made Preschool Readiness Checklist (From Shea-Kelly, 1978. Used with permission of the authors.) (*Continued*)

Shea-Kelly Early Childhood Evaluation of Learning Readiness Score Sheet

---

			Yes	No
E.	Distinguishes words that are exactly alike.			
	1. (tag)		——	——
	2. (den)		——	——
XI.	Visual memory:			
	A.	Locates shape or letter after seeing stimulus for 3 seconds. (Example—Say, "See this?" [Show 3 seconds and remove] "Find one here." Slide cover paper down page to expose row correspoding to stimulus. Use stimulus cards 22–27.)		
		1.○	——	——
		2.▯	——	——
		3.△	——	——
		4.√	——	——
		5.ß	——	——
		6. ΡΟΡ	——	——
XII.	Comments			

It should be noted at this time that the teacher is in the best position to make a prediction of preschool success. Haring and Ridgeway (1967) indicate that teachers are very good at identifying or predicting those children who will eventually have difficulty with school tasks. This is similar to the finding of Keogh and Smith (1970) who found that there is a significant relationship between the teacher's rating of a child and the child's actual achievement on academically related tasks. It can be concluded that teachers of preschool children, usually kindergarten, Head Start, or nursery schools are in a very good position to determine which children who are going to have difficulty in future academic tasks and can begin prescribing educational programs to correct those problems.

The identification of the child's problem or potential problem must be based upon an understanding of the principles underlying growth and development that are well documented in the literature. In making an assessment of preschool abilities, the teacher should, as a minimum, review the material available in this chapter in relationship to developmental expectancy levels for the different areas mentioned as well as the suggested formal measures that have been included as a reference for screening and identifying the readiness of children for performing successfully within the school environment.

Preschool assessment that results in the identification of potential problems should not end there, but should be the initial information used to identify, develop, and implement instructional programs for correcting those problems.

Can You Answer These Questions?

1. What are the expected behaviors of preschool children's language and motor abilities?
2. How stable is a preschooler's tested intelligence, especially if the child's age is under four years?
3. What are the developmental stages of Jean Piaget? Outline them.
4. What are three formal assessment devices for use in determining developmental readiness for school?
5. Which of the formal assessment devices presented is strictly criterion reference?
6. What is the value of the criterion reference device identified in question #5?
7. What are the steps you would use in conducting a preschool assessment?
8. How valuable is a teacher's assessment of a child's readiness for school?

References

Boehm, A. E. *Boehm Test of Basic Concepts.* New York: Psychological Corporation, 1971.

Bloom, B. *Stability and Change in Human Characteristics.* New York: John Wiley and Sons, 1964.

Caldwell, B. *Preschool Inventory Revised Edition.* Princeton, New Jersey: Educational Testing Service, 1970.

Carroll, J. B. "Language Development." In C. W. Harris (ed.), *Encyclopedia of Educational Research.* New York: Macmillan, 1960.

Doll, E. *Preschool Attainment Record.* Circle Paines, Minnesota: American Guidance Service, 1967.

Elkind, D. "Preschool Education: Enrichment or Instruction?" *Childhood Education,* 1969, 46, 321–328.

Evans, E. D. *Contemporary Influences in Early Childhood Education.* New York: Holt, Rinehart and Winston, 1971.

Frankenburg, W. K., J. D. Dodds, and A. W. Fandal. *Denver Developmental Screening Test.* Denver, Colorado: Ladora Project and Publishing Foundation, 1970.

Goldfarb, W. "Psychological Privation in Infancy and Subsequent Adjustment." *American Journal Psychiat.,* 1945, 15, 247–255.

Haring, N., and R. Ridgeway. "Early Identification of Children in Learning Disabilities." *Exceptional Children,* 1967, 33, 387–395.

Kappelman, M. M. "A Study of Learning Disorders among Disadvantaged Children." *Journal of Learning Disabilities,* 1969, 2, 262–268.

Keogh, B. K., and C. Smith. "Early Identification of Educationally High Potential and High-Risk Children." *Journal of School Psychology,* 1970, 8, 285–290.

Landsman, M., and H. Dillard. *Evanston Early Identification Scale.* Chicago: Follett, 1967.

Lefrançois, G. R. "Jean Piaget's Developmental Model: Equilibration-through-adaptation." *Alberta Journal of Educational Research,* 1967, 13, 161–171.

Lefrançois, G. R. *Of Children: An Introduction to Child Development.* Belmont, California: Wadsworth Publishing Company, 1973.

Lenneberg, E. H. *Biological Foundations of Language*. New York: John Wiley and Sons, 1967.

Lenneberg, E. H., I. A. Nichols, and E. F. Rosenberger. "Primitive Stages of Language Development in Mongolism." In *Disorders of Communication*, Vol. XLII: Research Publications, A.R.N.M.D. Baltimore, Maryland: Williams and Williams, 1964.

Marshall, W. A. "The Child as a Mirror of his Brain's Development." In J. Sants and H. J. Burcher (eds.), *Developmental Psychology*. Baltimore, Maryland: Penguin Books, 1975.

Mico, P. R. "A Look at the Health of Boston's Project Head Start Children." *Journal of School Health*, 1966, 36, 241, 244.

Moss, M. H. *Test of Basic Experiences*. Monterey, California: CTA/McGraw-Hill, 1972.

Mussen, P. H., J. J. Conger, and J. Kagan. *Child Development and Personality*. New York: Harper and Row, 1969.

Painter, G. *Infant Education*. San Rafael, California: Dimensions Publishing Company, 1968.

Payne, J. S., J. M. Kauffman, G. B. Brown, and R. M. Demott. *Exceptional Children in Focus: Incidents, Concepts, and Issues in Special Education*. Columbus, Ohio: Charles E. Merrill, 1974.

Robinson, L., and N. Croft. *Project Vision-Up*. Boise, Idaho: Educational Products Training Foundation, 1976.

Shirley, M. M. *The First Two Years: A Study of 25 Babies*. Institute of Child Welfare Monographs, Series No. 6. Minneapolis, Minnesota: University of Minnesota Press, 1933.

Simpkins, K. *Exploding a Myth: Not To See Is To Understand Also*. Paper presented at the Sixth Annual Jean Piaget Society Symposium. Philadelphia, Pennsylvania, June 12, 1976.

6

Reading Assessment Principles

Objectives

1. Identify and define essential components of the reading process.
2. Identify formal and informal procedures for assessing reading skill development.

Fundamentals of Reading

The importance of reading in the total educational program cannot be overstated. A child's success in school is dependent upon his ability to read. Reading skills are fundamental to every curriculum area. This fact led the National Advisory Committee on Dyslexia and Related Disorders (1969) to conclude that the problem of reading failure was the "most serious educational program confronting the nation" (Lerner, 1976).

If this problem is to be solved, teachers must develop the understanding necessary to analyze the reading area in depth and take necessary remedial action to correct reading problems. The useless statement, "Johnny has a reading problem," must be converted to identification of the specific skill areas that underlie Johnny's reading difficulties.

In order to assess reading difficulties, an understanding of the elements that compose the reading process is essential. Understanding the process will enable the teacher to conduct a task analysis as well as assess the child's development in relation to the tasks involved. Since various reading authorities categorize and label stages of reading development using a wide variety of terms, the author has attempted to identify and present terms and concepts that appear to be most commonly used throughout the reading literature. The primary purpose of this chapter is to acquaint teachers with those reading terms and concepts that are basic to the reading process.

Reading Definition

A definition of reading may vary from "word calling" to "the meaningful interpretation of printed symbols in light of the reader's own background of experience" (Hammill and Bartell, 1975). Within most definitions two major components dominate: word recognition and comprehension. Harris and Sipay (1975) emphatically stated, "It can hardly be overemphasized that *meaningful response* is the very heart of the reading process" (p. 6).

Reading is based on the development of sequentially ordered skills and is a highly complex process. Development of skills on a higher level will be hampered if reading readiness skills are not mastered. Each reading problem has highly individual causes and multiple, varied roots. Many children have a problem in only one specific area of reading. If this one area can be isolated, remediation techniques can be used to correct the problem.

Reading Readiness

Before formal reading instruction is begun, the child should successfully complete the developmental stages of reading readiness. Many reading problems are created by beginning formal instruction too soon.

Two essential skills involved in reading readiness are perception and discrimination. Perception refers to the child's ability to organize and interpret the information received from the senses. Skills of discrimination allow the child to differentiate between the different stimuli received by those senses. Adequate development of each of these skills is a prerequisite to successful reading.

Vocabulary and background of experience are also of vital importance. Many children who enter school are not able to relate to words and concepts that were not part of their background. This is especially true if a cultural difference exists between the school and the home (Harris and Sipay, 1975). Before formal reading instruction begins, an adequate speaking vocabulary must be developed and experiences must be provided that will give the child a frame of reference for the words and concepts he or she will encounter in the reading program.

Another essential element of reading readiness involves developing the understanding that "reading is talk written down" (Fry, 1972). If a child cannot develop this association, the child will be attempting to decode symbols that are meaningless to him. A summary of reading readiness skills that teachers should become familiar with is found in Figure 6-1.

Formal Reading Instruction

After successful completion of the readiness stage, formal instruction is begun. Usually it proceeds in the following order: letter identification, word identification, word attack, comprehension, and higher level skills.

Figure 6-1   Reading Readiness Skills

Physical Factors
1. ability to concentrate
2. attention span
3. general health
4. muscular coordination
5. normal vision and hearing
6. ability to use classroom equipment (scissors, crayons, paste, chalk)

Auditory and Memory Factors
1. ability to hear likeness and difference in speech sounds
2. listen with comprehension
3. ability to recall story
4. ability to recall sequence
5. ability to answer questions
6. ability to discriminate sounds of varying pitch and loudness

Interest in Learning to Read
1. has he been read to
2. stimulation and motivation
3. educational background of parents
4. family size (smaller indicates greater interaction between parent and child)
5. desire to read-develop motives
6. appreciation for stories and poetry
7. likes to look at pictures

Intelligence Factors
1. ability to deal with abstracts. Concepts such as yesterday, some, tall
2. knowledge of opposites
3. ability to predict outcomes
4. ability to distinguish relationship between things
5. ability to make interpretations beyond what is seen
6. ability to differentiate between what is real and what is imaginary

Visual and Motor Factors
1. ability to see likenesses and differences in visual forms
2. good binocular acuity—near and far
3. ability to shift focus
4. eye-hand coordination
5. ability to copy patterns
6. ability to put puzzles together
7. ability to see differences in size and shape
8. left-to-right sequence and top-to-bottom sequence
9. lateral dominance

Language Ability
1. meanings of words
2. vocabulary
3. enunciate words correctly
4. use of complete sentences
5. familiar with structure of English language
6. express self with clarity and fluency
7. speech defect (stammer or stutter)
8. relate ideas and concepts to words

Social Factors
1. experience success in working with others
2. ability to share materials
3. able to lead or follow
4. experiencing dramatic play as a natural way of using language

Background Experience
1. ability to relate to classroom materials
2. previous experience
3. adequate background in the language used in the school
4. socioeconomic status

Letter Identification. Accurate knowledge of the letters of the alphabet is one of the strongest predictors of success in reading. Once the letters are known, the child can use them in word recognition activities (Stellern, Vasa, and Little, 1976).

Word Identification. One of the initial steps in teaching reading is the development of a large number of words that the child recognizes instantly. This step enables the child to read without hesitation and forms a frame of reference for word attack skills. Meaning is facilitated in reading when the child does not have to analyze each word.

Word Attack. After an adequate sight word vocabulary has been developed, the child is taught initial code-breaking skills. These skills require the association of the printed letters (graphemes) with the speech sounds (phonemes) they represent. They enable the child to decode unfamiliar words and form the basis for independence in reading.

The child is taught to study the whole structure of a small word. Then larger words are analyzed in terms of their component parts (prefixes, suffixes, root words, etc.). Once recognition and meaning of each of the parts are obtained, the entire word can be synthesized from those parts. Skills of syllabication and accent are emphasized at this stage. Syllabication skills facilitate the process of breaking a large word into meaningful units. Accent aids the child in determining the appropriate sound for each vowel.

Association clues are taught next. Picture clues, context clues, and similarities in word sound or structure are examples of clues that can help a child relate a known word to an unknown stimulus. That stimulus may be auditory or visual. When faced with the unknown visual stimulus "book," the child may decode it by pairing his recognition of the letter "b" with the word's similarity to the known word "look."

Comprehension. Reading without meaning is "word calling." Many factors affect comprehension. A fundamental prerequisite to adequate comprehension is a reference point to which the child can attach encountered words. "Bank" will either be read as a place to deposit money or the ground on either side of a river. Each child's realm of experience will determine the frame of reference used in comprehension of words.

Age is another important factor in comprehension. As the child matures, so will the child's thought processes. The child will read with more comprehension as he or she learns to think on a more diversified plane.

Purposes for reading will also determine how materials will be read. Reading for the main idea, to predict outcomes, to follow directions, to find sequences, or to form conclusions will be different than reading for entertainment.

Further, interest and motivation are major factors to consider. Comprehension will increase when materials are meaningful and of interest to the reader.

Higher Level Skills. If reading is to become functional, formal instruction must include the development of skills for locating, organizing, and remembering information. These skills include:

1. using the library, card catalogue, and readers' guide;
2. outlining;
3. note-taking (both from lectures and printed materials);
4. summarizing.

Learning to read critically, to obtain abstract concepts from reading materials, and to select appropriate reading materials are also essential for meaningful reading experiences.

Categorizing Reading Instruction

Categorizing reading instruction generally includes three levels of reading ability: the independent, instructional, and frustration levels. Familiarity with the qualifying characteristics of each of these levels is necessary to understand the reading assessment process fully.

Independent Level. At the independent level the child reads material with comfort and complete mastery of concepts, vocabulary, and sentence structure. The child's comprehension is 90 to 96 percent of the material read. No more than one word recognition error per 100 words is made at the independent level.

Instructional Level. Level at which the child can function adequately *with supervision of the teacher.* Comprehension is 75 percent or better. The child does not make more than five word recognition errors in one hundred words.

Frustration Level. This is a level at which the reader is frustrated by the difficulty of the material. The child's comprehension is 50 percent or less, with frequent reading errors and emotional symptoms occurring.

Very simply stated, at the (1) independent level, the child reads well alone; (2) instructional level, the child reads well with help; and (3) frustration level, the child reads half (or less) of the material.

The development and mastery of reading readiness skills, followed by the successful development of those skills necessary for formal reading proficiency, is essential to train efficient readers. The heart of the assessment process is determining the point at which this sequential development was not mastered.

Process of Reading Assessment

The process of reading assessment contains several elements. These include assessment at the readiness level, assessment of word analysis skills, and analysis of higher competencies of reading. Each of the elements will be discussed in the following section along with formal and informal devices for use within each.

Assessment at the Readiness Level

Assessment at this stage often consists of predicting the probable success of formal reading instruction. Most of the procedures used are informal and attempt to establish whether prerequisite reading skills have been successfully developed. Predictive sources of information frequently used include school records, parent interviews, and reading readiness checklists.

School Records. Information regarding a child's family background (size of family, socioeconomic factors, primary language), general health, school attendance, and mobility of family, as well as previous achievement and intelligence test performance and previous school grades can be accumulated by an examination of the child's school file. Patterns of problems in reading may be developing as the school file grows. One particular interest to reading teachers would be indications of a conflict in language between the home and the school.

Parent Interviews. An interview with the parents can provide information regarding a child's exposure to reading in the home, possible reading problems noted by the parent, and information regarding the history of reading problems in the family. Parental problems with the language of the school can be noted.

Readiness Checklists. These checklists are available in many forms. Figure 6-2 is an example of the type of checklist used to determine readiness. Teacher-constructed checklists often rank-order skills and are used as a guide in writing the child's instructional program.

A readiness assessment device can be constructed by converting the table of readiness factors (Figure 6-1) into a checklist for each child. Each item could be stated as an instructional or a behavioral objective. Specific deficiencies noted on the checklist can provide the basis for remediation. Formal readiness assessment devices are listed in Figure 6-3.

Figure 6-2 Readiness Checklist

This readiness checklist is devised to become a part of the child's cumulative file and is to be used in conferences with parents as the occasion arises. Specific skills are listed not as standards but as guides in areas of concern.

Check if Child Is at Average Performance for His or Her Level

I. General Health

_____ A. Is regular in attendance

_____ B. Participates in work and play activities

_____ C. Completes tasks without undue fatigue

_____ D. Has no known visual difficulties

_____ E. Has no known hearing difficulties

_____ F. Is not hyperactive

_____ G. Has no known history of serious physical illness

II. Movement Patterns and Muscular Coordination

A. Large muscles and balance—standing, walking, skipping

_____ 1. Stands on one foot (10 seconds)

_____ 2. Stands on each foot alternately, *with eyes closed*

_____ 3. Walks on toes without touching heels

_____ 4. Walks along a board 2″ x 4″ x 12′

_____ 5. Skips using feet alternately

    B. Specific small movement patterns (visuo-motor skills)
_____ 1. Neatly cuts out pictures with scissors, following lines, angles, and curves
_____ 2. Manuscripts correctly own name
_____ 3. Ties a shoe lace in a loop bow
_____ 4. Draws a house (with windows, door, and chimney, without copy)
_____ 5. Fastens small buttons, press studs, and hooks and eyes
_____ 6. Copies a circle, square, triangle, and divided rectangle
_____ 7. Copies pattern designs
_____ 8. Draws a person (metropolitan readiness)
    C. Left-to-right orientation
_____ 1. Identifies left and right
_____ 2. Observes pictures in a rightward progression
_____ 3. In games, uses left and right sides of body appropriately

III. Auditory Skills
    A. General auditory awareness
_____ 1. Has good auditory imagery
_____ 2. Has awareness of relationship of reading to listening
_____ 3. Can devise stories from familiar sounds presented in sequence.
        4. Has ability to recognize significance of sound in his environment
    B. Specific aural skills related to reading
_____ 1. Recognizes that words are sounds put together
        2. Can hear likenesses and differences in
_____   a. Word beginnings
_____   b. Word endings
_____   c. Medial positions
_____ 3. Can locate specific sounds in word patterns
_____ 4. Can identify rhyming words
    C. General language listening skills
_____ 1. Can listen to a story for a specific purpose
_____ 2. Can follow oral directions for carrying out the work at first grade level

IV. Visual Skills
_____ A. Sees likenesses and differences in geometric and word shapes
_____ B. Sees *details* on geometric and word patterns
_____ C. Can discriminate among the colors
_____ D. Can observe pictures and work on study pages in an orderly fashion (e.g., on independent seatwork activities does not "jump about" in performance)

Figure 6-2   Readiness Checklist (*Continued*)

V. Speech and Language
- A. Speech
  - _____ 1. Can articulate clearly
  - _____ 2. Has a clear pattern in speech
  - _____ 3. Is free of such difficulties as stuttering, lisping
  - _____ 4. Has adequate voice quality
- B. Language
  - _____ 1. Has adequate English vocabulary (defines in terms of *use,* generally)
  - _____ 2. Speaks in sentences of average complexity and length
  - _____ 3. Uses simple quantitative and space concepts such as counting objects, recognizing *middle*
  - _____ 4. Can organize information into simple classifications (name all the animals you know)
  - 5. Has ability to tell stories from pictures by
    - _____ a. Naming objects in the picture
    - _____ b. Describing what is happening
    - _____ c. Interpreting (using imagination, telling what will happen next, using inferences)
  - _____ 6. Contributes to chart stories
  - _____ 7. Can tell simple stories, repeat nursery rhymes, etc.
  - _____ 8. Is familiar with well-known children's stories such as *Little Red Riding Hood*
  - _____ 9. Participates in classroom conversations or discussions

VI. Personal Independence
- _____ A. Can tell own full name and address
- _____ B. Knows age and birthdate
- _____ C. Knows names of parents and where they work
- _____ D. Tidies work table
- _____ E. Washes hands and takes care of personal needs
- _____ F. Takes turns when playing or working with other children
- _____ G. Enters into group play with other children, with or without adult supervision
- _____ H. Can work on simple tasks without adult supervision for periods of 10 to 15 minutes (minimum)
- _____ I. Shows minimum fears in the school situation

VII. Readiness Test Scores and Comments

Sight Word and Vocabulary Assessment

At this stage assessment involves the determination of the number of sight words instantly recognized by the child. This is frequently determined by the use of a prepared list of words from the basal reading series. Word lists similar to the Dolch Basic Sight Vocabulary or the Ayres List are also used to determine whether an adequate sight vocabulary exists. For vocabulary assessment beyond the sight word level, the San Diego Quick Assessment Tests (LaPray and Ross, 1969) or Fry's Instant Words (Fry, 1972) can be used.

Assessment of Word Analysis Skills

At this stage assessment involves determining whether the child correctly identifies letters, associates the correct sound with the correct letter, and is able to blend the sounds to form a recognizable word. The Roswell-Chall Diagnostic Reading Test of Word Analysis Skills (Roswell and Chall, 1959) analyzes single consonant sounds, consonant combinations, short vowels, rule of silent E, vowel combinations, and syllabication. It is an individual test and easy to administer, score, and interpret.

Assessment of Higher Competencies

Assessment at this level is performance-based. Teachers at the intermediate and high school levels are most often concerned with reading at this level as it includes having students demonstrate an ability to use library resources, the dictionary, encyclopedias, and other reference materials. A checklist of these skills is prepared as an assessment device for those skills the teacher feels are necessary. Having students demonstrate the skills of using the card catalogue, demonstrate an understanding of the referencing system used to catalogue and shelve books, or find a journal reference and the article itself is a way of assessing on the basis of actual performance.

Achievement and Group Placement Assessment

These areas are also components of reading assessment. Frequently a reading program involves a pretest at the beginning of the school year and a posttest at the end to enable a teacher to measure individual progress. Different but equal forms of the same test are sometimes used for this purpose. An increase of one grade level or improvement of nine months or higher on the posttest is the desired result of a reading program. There are many tests designed with different but equal forms for use in pre- and post-testing. These are illustrated in Figure 6-3.

Assessment has been discussed in terms of evaluating competency in individual skill areas from readiness to higher order competencies. The purpose of this procedure has been to develop an understanding that progressive assessment is a necessary and vital part of the reading program.

Formal Assessment Devices

Instruments that can be used to complete each of the kinds of assessment noted above are summarized in the following chart (Figure 6-3).

Informal Reading Assessment Devices

Teachers have many sources of information regarding a child's reading performance that can be examined for determining problem areas. These sources include the school records and parent interviews already mentioned. Other sources are interest inventories, daily schedules, teacher observation, and reading skills checklists.

Interest Inventories and Daily Schedules. An examination of the child's reading interests, hobbies, and free-time activities can indicate how much enjoyment is obtained from reading and how much time is spent in voluntary reading or activities related to reading.

Teacher Observation. This is one of the most valuable sources of assessment information. To be most effective, observations should be structured in the following manner.

1. Provide the child with a one-page selection from a basal reader to his reading level.
2. Listen to the child read. If desired, rate can be timed.
3. Using a checklist, evaluate his performance as to the types and kinds of reading errors made. For example, does the child omit letters and words, reverse words, transpose letters, substitute, or apply adequate word attack skills?

Reading Checklists.   These may be constructed by the teacher to suit individual needs or chosen from many available which list specific strengths and weaknesses in reading skills. Obviously the teacher must be familiar with the content of the checklist in order to know what behaviors to evaluate.

The checklist becomes a permanent record of performance and can also be used as a basis for remediation and a comparative measure of progress.

Three examples of checklists follow. The first measures development under six categories. Use of this list will provide for very specific diagnosis of skills or problem areas. Check any appropriate statement and then convert the statement into an instructional objective for each child.

The second checklist provides a measure of general reading habits, oral reading performance, and reading comprehension. By noting the behaviors that are typical of an individual child's reading performance, the teacher can determine whether or not a reading problem may exist and if formal assessment needs to be carried out. The areas needing further assessment will also be indicated by the scored checklist.

The third checklist details the behaviors that can indicate weaknesses in specified reading skill areas, including instructional and reading readiness weaknesses as well as skill deficits in the child. The behaviors examined by this checklist are further developed according to possible causes and remediation strategies in the remediation section.

Figure 6-3 Formal Assessment Devices For Screening and Specific Reading Diagnosis

Purposes	Name				Grade Levels	Time to Admin	Indiv or Group
					3–9	30 min.	Group

Content of Test

Purposes	Name	Content of Test
1. Overall screening of reading achievement	The Nelson Reading Test 1962	2 forms A & B —175 items—100 to measure vocabulary, 75 to measure reading comprehension —IBM answer sheets or self marking answer sheets —reusable test booklets —class record sheet

Informat Provided about Student's Reading Skills

—vocabulary and passage comprehension
—3 comprehension questions per paragraph to test
   —general signification
   —knowledge of detailed information
   —ability to predict outcomes
3 normed scores—raw scores, percentile ranks, grade equivalent

Advantages

—national norms manual
—provides some information regarding gross interpretation of scores for program planning reliability .88–.93
—reusable test booklets

Disadvantages

—does not provide diagnostic interpretation of student's problems

Content of Test			
PIAT Peabody Individual Achievement Test 1971	2 subtests related to reading: 1—reading recognition 84 items ranging from reading readiness skills to high school skills 2—reading comprehension—66 items, 2 pages per item	K–12	10–15 min.	Indiv

Informat Provided about Student's Reading Skills

raw scores, grade or age equivalents
—percentile ranks, standard scores
—a profile of the student's performance is provided on protocol using above scores

Advantages

detailed administration and scoring
reliability—reading rec .89, reading comp .64
—easily administered and scored (manual)

Disadvantages

—finding the different subtests can be confusing due to set up of Easel-kits (3 subtests in one volume)

How to Use Diagnostically

—as a screening device—to pinpoint those students needing more intensive assessment
—note wrong response on the reading recognition subtest to check for problems with sight words or phonetic skills

Figure 6-3 Formal Assessment Devices For Screening and Specific Reading Diagnosis (*Continued*)

Purposes	Name	Content of Test	Grade Levels	Time to Admin	Indiv or Group
	WRAT Wide Range Achievement Test 1965	2 parts: a pre-reading and reading: —reading subtest —recognizing and naming letters and pronouncing words	Level 1 5–0 to 11–11 Level 2 12–0 to Adult		Indiv

Informat Provided about Student's Reading Skills

—provides raw score, grades equivalents, percentiles, standard basic letter and word recognition skills

Advantages

reliability .98–.99

How to Use Diagnostically

—analyze errors for specific patterns of weakness. Use to determine if student may be having problems. If so, use a more indepth assessment measure

		Content of Test			
	Metropolitan Achievement Tests 1971	1) Word Knowledge—(Vocabulary) 2) Reading—(Read passage and select correct answer)	Elementary (grades 3 & 4)	50 min.	Group

Informat Provided about Student's Reading Skills

—level of achievement in word knowledge and reading
—expression of scores in terms of stanines, percentile ranks and grade equivalents

Advantages

—quick screening device

Disadvantages

—standardized on a group of pupils somewhat above average in mental ability

How to Use Diagnostically

—determine if student's vocabulary needs to be improved
—analyze comprehension errors, subtest 2
—Reading, to understand how he is comprehending what he reads

Content of Test

Iowa Tests of Basic Skills 1956	Listening Vocabulary Word Analysis Pictures Sentences Stories Spelling Capitalization Punctuation Usage Maps Graph and tables References (2 Math subtests)	1.7–9	4 hrs. 20 min. (administered over 5 days)	Group

Figure 6-3 Formal Assessment Devices For Screening and Specific Reading Diagnosis (*Continued*)

Purposes	Name		Grade Levels	Time to Admin	Indiv or Group
		Informat Provided about Student's Reading Skills			
		raw-scores, grade equivalents, percentile ranks, stanines —behavior on the part of the pupils that is called for in the ITBS coincides as nearly as possible with the behavior required in real life situations			
		Advantages			
		broad spectrum of skills is assessed			
		Disadvantages			
		No information on standardization, reliability or validity			
		How to Use Diagnostically			
		assesses listening skills, vocabulary, word analysis, reading comprehension, language skills, work study skills			
		Content of Test			

2. Specific diagnosis of reading skills	Woodcock Reading Mastery Tests 1974	—easel kit of test items, protocol, manual
		—5 subtests:
		  word identification
		  letter identification
		  word attack
		  word comprehension
		  passage comprehension
		—two alternate forms A & B
			K–12	20–30 min.	Indiv

Informat Provided about Student's Reading Skills

—raw scores, grade equivalents, age scores, percentile ranks, standard scores in each area, plus total reading scores

—provides grade equivalent scores for independent, instruction and frustrational level for each subtest

—a mastery score which predicts the student's relative success with different levels of reading tasks

—also SES adjusted norms and norms for boys and girls

Advantages

Can be used in classroom to:
a) measure individual reading growth
b) detect reading problems
c) group for instruction
d) evaluate curriculum and programs
e) for accountability

—also for clinical and research use

—can be administered by classroom personnel with minimal training

Disadvantages

no implications for instruction or remediation

How to Use Diagnostically

—write down phonetically any incorrect responses students make. Then analyze each of errors for specific patterns—e.g., reversals, inadequate knowledge of long or short, vowels, unknown phonics generalizations, etc.

Figure 6-3 Formal Assessment Devices For Screening and Specific Reading Diagnosis (*Continued*)

Purposes	Name		Grade Levels	Time to Admin	Indiv or Group
		Content of Test			
	Stanford Diagnostic Reading Test	—two levels (I and II) with 2 forms (W and X) at each level	Level 1 Grade 2–middle of Grade 4 Level II Later part of Grade 4 to middle of Grade 8	No info.	Group

Informat Provided about Student's Reading Skills

—to identify needed areas of instruction at the beginning of a school term
—areas tested:

Level 1
reading comprehension
vocabulary
auditory discrimination
syllabication
beginning and ending sounds
blending
sound discrimination

Level II
reading comprehension (literal & inferential)
vocabulary
syllabication
sound discrimination
blending
rate of reading

Advantages

—for use by classroom teacher
—easily scored
—level II can be used with poorly performing high school students

How to Use Diagnostically

analyze:
  reading comprehension
  vocabulary
  word analysis

Content of Test

No info.   Indiv

Gates–
McKillop
Reading
Diagnostic
Tests 1962

8 subtests
a) oral reading
b) flash presentation of words
c) untimed presentation of words
d) flash presentation of phrases
e) knowledge of words parts (blending, letter sounds, capital and lowercase letters)
f) recognizing the visual form of sounds in nonsense words
g) auditory blending
h) supplementary tests
  —spelling
  —oral vocabulary
  —syllabication
  —auditory discrimination

Purposes	Name	Grade Levels	Time to Admin	Indiv or Group

Informat Provided about Student's Reading Skills

—raw scores; grade score tables convert raw scores into grade score norms, which may be rated as High, Medium, Low or Very Low as compared with pupils actual grade; interpretive tables in which raw scores are converted directly to ratings of Normal, Low or Very Low, compare the pupil's ability in a given aspect of reading with his general reading ability

Advantages

—2 forms, Form 1 and Form 2
—a comprehensive test of a write variety of reading skills

Disadvantages

requires a long time to administer
does not provide an adequate measure of reading comprehension
no reliability or validity data provided

How to Use Diagnostically

analysis of oral reading
word analysis skills
auditory discrimination
spelling skills
word recognition skills

Content of Test

Durrell Analysis of Reading Difficulty	Primarily for Grades 3-6	30-90 min.	Indiv

—oral reading
—silent reading
—listening comprehension
—word recognition and word analysis
—letters (naming letters, identifying name letters, matching letters)
—visual memory of word forms

Informat Provided about Student's Reading Skills

—grade equivalent normed scores
—a checklist of instructional needs
—a checklist of reading difficulties in the oral and silent reading areas, word recognition and word analysis
—child's imagery abilities
—reading speed

Advantages

—administration procedures are clearly defined and straightforward
—provides a thorough diagnosis of initial and primary reading skills
—manual provides some suggestions for informal tests

Disadvantages

no information on reliability and validity

How to Use Diagnostically

analysis of:
reading comprehension
oral reading
word analysis
word and letter recognition

Figure 6-3 Formal Assessment Devices For Screening and Specific Reading Diagnosis (*Continued*)

Purposes	Name	Content of Test	Grade Levels	Time to Admin	Indiv or Group
Screening Tests for Identifying Children with Specific Language Disability		—tests visual copying, memory and discrimination —3 group auditory tests —one individual audit tests	Levels for grades 1–2, 2–3, 3–4, 5–6	50 min.	Group

Informat Provided about Student's Reading Skills

—used to locate children who have, are likely to develop disabilities in reading, spelling and handwriting
1) problems of direct or confused recall
2) problems with direction or sequencing
3) motor development or kinesthic memory or visual-motor coordination
4) modality integration
5) problems in direction, spatial organization and handwriting

Advantages

in-depth analysis of modalities

Disadvantages

difficult scoring techniques

How to Use Diagnostically

analyze to determine who manifests perceptual motor behavior that is indicative of potential interference with adequate development in reading, writing, and spelling

		Content of Test			
3. Determine Group Placement	Sucher–Allred Reading Placement Inventory 1973 (similar to Varoli & Gilmore)	1. word-recognition test of 12 graded lists 2. 12 graded passages for oral reading	Primarily 9th grade	20 min.	Indiv

Informat Provided about Student's Reading Skills

—identifies students' independent, instructional, and frustrational levels
—identifies common word recognition and comprehension errors in oral reading
—groups students for reading instruction

Advantages

5 kinds of comprehension questions—main idea, facts, sequence, interference, critical thinking
manual contains good description of 3 reading levels
easy to administer and score

How to Use Dignostically

elaborate error marking system to allow for error pattern analysis of oral reading errors

Figure 6-3 Formal Assessment Devices For Screening and Specific Reading Diagnosis (*Continued*)

Purposes	Name	Content of Test	Grade Levels	Time to Admin	Indiv or Group
	Gates-MacGinitie Reading Tests 1965	speed and accuracy word comprehension passage comprehension	K-12	60-75 min.	Group or Indiv

Informat Provided about Student's Reading Skills

1) Readiness—8 subtest for K-1 grade scores, percentiles, standard scores
2) Primary A—Vocabulary, comprehension (grade 1)
   B—Vocabulary, comprehension (grade 2)
   C—Vocabulary, comprehension (grade 3)
   CS—Speed and accuracy (grades 2,3)

   Survey D, F & G speed, vocal and comprehension Grades 4-6, 7-9 (10-12)

Advantages

good reliability
—easy to administer

How to Use Diagnostically

as a screening and grouping tool
How scores in one or more areas should be followed up by individual diagnostic testing

Content of Test

					Normal 45 min. Indiv

4. Assess reading comprehension

Spache Diagnostic Reading Scales 1972

3 word recognition lists
22 reading passages to establish oral reading, silent reading and listening comprehension
8 supplementary phonics tests in the areas of
—consonant sound
—vowel sounds
—consonant blends and diagraphs
—syllables
—blending
—letter sounds, initial consonant substitution
—auditory discrimination

Normal I.Q. 1–6 grade
Retarded Grades 1–12

Informat Provided about Student's Reading Skills

—normative data
word recognition, word analysis skills, instructional reading level, measured comprehension, independent reading level, potential level
—specific phonics skills (through the supplementary tests)

Advantages

reliability ranges from .84–.96
—use of supplementary phonics test can provide good diagnosis of word attack skills

Disadvantages

—difficulty in determining reading levels

How to Use Diagnostically

—supplementary phonics tests to analyze word attack skills

Figure 6-3 Formal Assessment Devices For Screening and Specific Reading Diagnosis (*Continued*)

Purposes	Name	Content of Test	Grade Levels	Time to Admin	Indiv or Group
	PIAT	**Content of Test** Reading comprehension subtest **Informat Provided about Student's Reading Skills** a good measure of passage comprehension **Advantages** —can be used with handicapped as only a pointing response is required **Disadvantages** —method of response does not provide information regarding use of context clues due to poor word attack.	K–adult	untimed	Indiv
	Gray Oral Reading Tests 1967	**Content of Test** 13 graded reading passages in each form —examiner's record book —4 forms, A, B, C & D (Bobbs-Merrill Company, Inc.) **Informat Provided about Student's Reading Skills** accuracy and rate combined in one score separate norms for boys and girls types of errors noted: 1. aid 2. gross mispronunciation 3. partial mispronunciation 4. omission 5. insertion 6. substitution 7. repetition 8. inversion —a measure of oral reading achievement —normed grade equivalents —no measure of silent reading	1–12		Indiv

	Advantages
	reliability .86

Disadvantages

limited analysis of skills

How to Use Diagnostically

note what errors the student makes the same on easy and difficult paragraphs

Content of Test

			7 to college	40–45 min.	Group

5. Assess word attack skills	Calif. Phonics Survey 1963	75 items divided into 5 test exercises

1. vowels
   a. long-short vowel confusion
   b. other vowel confusion
2. consonants
   a. confusion with blends and diagraphs
   b. consonant-vowel reversals
3. configuration
4. endings
5. negatives, opposites, sight words
6. rigidity

tape; computerized answer sheet, test booklet

Informat Provided about Student's Reading Skills

—individual or group level of phonics ability

4 raw score cutting off points to separate students with problems from students with adequate skills

—eight diagnostic scores to reveal specific problems

Purposes	Name		Grade Levels	Time to Admin	Indiv or Group

Advantages

—can be administered to a group
—provides a profile and keys to interpret it—to use for remedial starting point
—provides a tape to guarantee proper and clear enunciation of stimulus words
—2 forms for retesting reliability .92

Disadvantages

—requires clear and accurate pronunciation of test items. Use of tape can overcome this

How to Use Diagnostically

diagnose word attack skills
—uses reading and listening to reveal reversals, confusions of blends and vowels

Content of Test

Roswell-Chall
Diagnostic
Test of
Word-Analysis
Skills

Informat Provided about Student's Reading Skills

test knowledge of phonics rules: silent " e," consonants, short vowels, consonant and vowel diagraphs syllabication

How to Use Diagnostically

diagnose word attack skills

Content of Test

		K–12	10–15 min.	Indiv

6. Assess Word Recognition Skills

PIAT Peabody Individual Achievement Test 1970

2 subtest related to reading:
1—reading recognition 84 items ranging from reading readiness skills to high school skills
2—reading comprehension—66 items, 2 pages per item

Informat Provided about Student's Reading Skills

raw scores, grade or age equivalents
—percentile ranks, standard scores
—a profile the student's performance is provided on protocol using above score

Advantages

detailed administration and scoring
reliability—reading rec .89, reading comp .64

Disadvantages

—finding the different subtests can be confusing due to set up of Easel-kits (3 subtests in on volume)

How to Use Diagnostically

—as a screening device —to pinpoint those students needing more intensive assessment
—note wrong response on the reading recognition subtest to check for problems with sight words or phonetic skills

Figure 6-3 Formal Assessment Devices For Screening and Specific Reading Diagnosis (*Continued*)

Purposes	Name	Grade Levels	Time to Admin	Indiv or Group
	Content of Test			
	SORT Slosson Oral Reading Test 1963	1–12		Indiv

Informat Provided about Student's Reading Skills

recognition of words presented in recognition
—does not measure word attack or comprehension

Content of Test

	WRAT Wide Range Achievement Test 1965	Level 1 5–0 to 11–11 Level 2 12–0 to Adult		Indiv

2 parts: a pre-reading and reading:
—reading subtest
—recognizing and name letters and pronouncing words

Informat Provided about Student's Reading Skills

—provides raw score, grades equivalents, percentiles, standard
—basic letter and word recognition skills

Advantages

reliability .98–.99

How to Use Diagnostically

—analysis errors for specific patterns of weakness. Use to determine if student may be having problems. If so, use a more in-depth assessment measure

Checklist Number 1
Checklist of Reading Difficulties

Name_____ Age_____ Date_____
School _____ Teacher_____

ORAL READING:
____Evidence of emotional tension
____Strained, high-pitched voice
____Monotonous tone
____Volume too loud or too soft
____Poor enunciation
____Word by word reading
____Incorrect phrasing
____Eye-voice span too short
____Oral Accuracy Errors:
____Hesitations
____Refusals
____Omissions
____Repetitions
____Mispronunciations
____Ignore punctuation
____Substitutions
____Additions
____Inadequate oral comprehension
____Low oral reading rate

SILENT READING:
____Knowledge of latter names
____Use of context clues
____Phonic analysis
____Single consonants
____Consonant blends
____Silent consonants
____Short vowels
____Vowel blends
____Vowel diagraphs
____Phonic rules
____Sound blending ability
____Structural Analysis
____Inflectional endings
____Compounds
____Common prefixes
____Common suffixes
____Roots
____Auditory-visual recognition of syllables
____Syllabication rules
____Use of Dictionary

VOCABULARY DEVELOPMENT:
____Inadequate sight vocabulary
____Inadequate meaning vocabulary

COMPREHENSION SKILLS:
____Recall of factual detail
____Main idea of paragraphs
____Sequence of idea and events
____Following directions
____Making inferences
____Critical, evaluative reading

READING RATE:
____Lack of flexibility in rate
____Low silent reading rate
____Scanning
____Skimming
____Finger pointing
____Head movements

STUDY SKILLS:
____SQ3R
____Notemaking-class
____Test taking
____Reading maps and globes
____Reading charts, tables & graphs
____Using the card catalogue
____Using the encyclopedia
____Using several reference books
____Using the *Reader's Guide to Periodical Literature*
____Research report writing
____Proofreading
____Outlining

Developed by Northern Arizona University, College of Education. University Reading Program, Dr. John Rambeau, Instructor.

Checklist Number 2
Checklist of Oral Reading Problems

Student _____ Teacher_____
Grade _____ School _____
Date _____ Current reading program_____

I. General Reading Habits:
____holds book too close
____holds book too far away
____tries to avoid reading
____frowns, appears tense in reading situation
____avoidance of materials requiring reading
____uses finger or marker as guide
____poor attention span
    ____unable to sit down
    ____easily distracted
____squints, rubs eyes, covers one eye when reading
____easily loses place when reading
____shows marked head movements when reading

II. Oral Reading Performance
____inappropriate vocal expression
    ____reads in a loud voice
    ____reads in a soft voice
    ____reads in a strained, high-pitched voice
    ____little or no intonation
____repetitions: ____words
                  ____phrases
                  ____whole lines
____reversals: ____words
                  ____letters within words
____adds words
____omits words
____inadequate sight vocabulary
____inadequate word analysis skills:
    ____will not try difficult words
    ____spells out unfamiliar words
    ____cannot blend sounds into words
    ____does not know names of letters
    ____does not know sounds of letters
    ____does not know vowels
    ____does not know consonants
    ____ignores endings of words
____guesses at unknown words
____ignores word or phrasing errors
____reads in a slow word-by-word manner

_____reads too quickly
_____ignores punctuation

III. Reading Comprehension:
_____cannot recall basic facts
_____cannot sequence recall of facts
_____answers questions by experiential background, not the reading content
_____cannot make inferences
_____cannot draw conclusions
_____does not use new vocabulary in responses
_____cannot answer questions about new vocabulary
_____guesses
_____answers appropriate and in great detail.

IV. Other observations:

Checklist Number 3
Checklist for Reading Problems

Name_____School_____
Grade _____Teacher_____
Date _____

Reading Problem	Behavior Clues	Frequently	Often	Seldom	Never
A. *Deficit Tool Skills:*					
Inadequate vocabulary (listening, speaking)	low comprehension difficulty in oral and written self-expression lacks ability to interpret implications misunderstands "obvious" facts lower capability lower self-concept slow reading rate.				
Faulty eye movement	regressions reversals				

	Frequently	Often	Seldom	Never
Checklist Number 3 (*Continued*) *Checklist for Reading Problems*				

Reading Problem	Behavior Clues	Frequently	Often	Seldom	Never
A. *Deficit Tool Skills:*					
Narrow perceptual span	reads words from different line inaccurate reading lip movement slow reading rate word-by-word reading makes regressions lacks comprehension reads with hesitancy "loses place" has reversals				
Short memory span	lacks comprehension inability to remember words poor memory for visual materials remembers only short sentences day dreams difficulty in following directions disinterested				
Reversals	confusion of word poor spelling avoidance of writing emotion				
Letter confusions	reversals low comprehension anxiety ineffective word analysis ineffective oral reading avoidance of reading				

Reading Problem	Behavior Clues	Frequently	Often	Seldom	Never
B. *Fluency Problems:* Word-by-word reading	poor comprehension poor expression in oral reading poor silent reading rate indifferent to reading				
Lip movement and sub-vocalization	slow reading poor comprehension word-by-word reading				
Unsatisfactory silent reading rate	low comprehension lack of enjoyment in reading slow in completing assignments inadequate study methods				
Fails to use context clues	limited reading vocabulary low comprehension slow reading indifference to reading				
C. *Comprehension Problems:* Ineffective comprehension	passive reading does not answer questions lack of interest poor concentration inexpressive oral reading cannot follow continuity of story tense and inattentive lacks organization				
D. *Word Attack Problems:* Omitting word endings or beginnings	poor oral reading misunderstands what is read weakened word recognition				

Checklist Number 3 (*Continued*) *Checklist for Reading Problems*					

Reading Problem	Behavior Clues	Frequently	Often	Seldom	Never
D. *Word Attack Problems* Inability to analyze words phonetically	poor spelling poor word perception stagnate vocabulary				
Difficulty in syllabication	poor spelling inability to perceive words stagnate vocabulary				
E. *Emotional/ Environmental Factors:* Emotional instability	reading disability lowered energy level behavior problems lacks stick-to-it-iveness excitable or passive personality lower concept of self				
Lack of interest	inattention unsatisfactory work in school behavior problems easily annoyed carelessness				
Extrinsic rather than intrinsic motivation	lack of sustained involvement in reading development of dependence lack of purposeful learning				
Regressions	poor oral reading lower comprehension				
Improper grouping	child unable to progress at own rate				

Reading Problem	Behavior Clues	Frequently	Often	Seldom	Never
Instructional	feeling of failure lowered self-concept lack of interest reading failure—lowered self-concept lack of progress emotion-tensions public relations needless disabilities				
Unsuitable reading materials	reading failure disinterested readers lack of appropriate progress				

Conclusion

This chapter has discussed the nature of the reading process and identified formal and informal reading assessment devices. In the next chapter, the assessment principles discussed in Chapter 1 will be applied to the reading process.

Can You Answer These Questions?

1. What are the essential elements of the reading process?
2. Can you define the following terms and concepts:
   a. reading;
   b. perception;
   c. discrimination;
   d. letter and word identification;
   e. word attack;
   f. comprehension;
   g. sight word.

3. What are the categories of reading instruction?
4. What are five formal instruments for assessing reading performance?
5. Can you name four informal procedures or techniques that could be used to assess reading performance?

References

Brown, G. M., and A. B. Cottrel. *California Phonics Survey.* Monterey, California: California Test Bureau, 1963.

Dunn, L. M., and F. C. Markwardt. *Peabody Individual Achievement Test.* Circle Pines, Minnesota: American Guidance Service, 1970.

Durost, W., H. Bixler, W. Wrightstone, B. Prescott, and I. Balow. *Metropolitan Achievement Tests.* New York: Harcourt Brace Jovanovich, 1971.

Durrell, D. D. *Durrell Analysis of Reading Difficulty.* New York: Harcourt Brace Jovanovich, 1955.

Fry, Edward B. *Reading Instruction for Classroom and Clinic.* New York: McGraw-Hill Book Company, 1972, pp. 58–69.

Gates, A. I., and W. MacGinitie. *Gates-MacGinitie Reading Tests.* New York: Teachers College Press, Columbia University, 1965.

Gates, A. I., and A. S. McKillop. *Gates-McKillop Reading Diagnostic Tests.* New York: Bureau of Publications, Teachers College Press, Columbia University, 1962.

Gilmore, J. W. *Gilmore Oral Reading Test* (new edition). New York: Harcourt Brace Jovanovich, 1968.

Gray, W. S., and H. M. Robinson (eds.). *Gray Oral Reading Test.* Indianapolis: Bobbs-Merrill, 1967.

Greene, H. A., A. N. Jorgansin, and V. H. Kelly. *Iowa Silent Reading Tests.* New York: Harcourt Brace Jovanovich, 1956.

Hammil, D. D., and N. R. Bartel. "Teaching Children with Reading Problems," in *Teaching Children with Learning Problems.* Boston: Allyn and Bacon, 1975, pp. 15–59.

Harris, A. J., and E. R. Sipay. *How to Increase Reading Ability*. New York: McKay, 1975.

Jastak, J. F., and S. R. Jastak. *Wide Range Achievement Tests*. Wilmington, Delaware: Guidance Associates, 1965.

Karlsen, B., R. Madden, and E. F. Gardner. *Stanford Diagnostic Reading Tests*. New York: Harcourt Brace Jovanovich, 1971.

LaPray, M., and R. Ross. "The Graded Word List: Quick Gauge of Reading Ability." *Journal of Reading*, 1969, 12, 305–307.

Lerner, Janet W. "Teaching Strategies: Reading." *Children with Learning Disabilities*. Boston: Houghton Mifflin, 1976, pp. 234–252.

National Advisory Committee on Dyslexia and Related Disorders. *Report to the Secretary of the Department of Health, Education and Welfare*, August, 1969.

Nelson, M. F., and C. E. Denny. *The Nelson Reading Test*. Boston: Houghton Mifflin, 1962.

Roswell, F. C., and J. S. Chall. *Roswell-Chall Diagnostic Test of Word Analysis Skills*. New York: Essay Press, 1959.

Slingerland, B. H. *Slingerland Screening Tests for Identifying Children with Specific Language Disabilities* (2nd ed.). Cambridge, Massachusetts: Educators Publishing Service, 1970.

Slosson, R. L. *Slosson Oral Reading Test*. East Aurora, New York: Slosson Educational Publications, 1963.

Spache, G. D. *Diagnostic Reading Scales*. Monterey, California: California Test Bureau, 1972.

Stellern, J., S. F. Vasa, and J. Little. *Introduction to Diagnostic Prescriptive Teaching and Programming*. Glen Ridge, New Jersey: Exceptional Press, 1976.

Sucher, F., and R. A. Allred. *Sucher-Allred Reading Placement Inventory*. Oklahoma City, Oklahoma: The Economy Co., 1973.

Woodcock, R. W. *Woodcock Reading Mastery Tests*. Circle Pines, Minnesota: American Guidance Service, 1974.

chapter

Conducting a Reading Assessment

Objectives

At the conclusion of this chapter the reader should be able to:

1. conduct a discrepancy analysis of a child's reading performance on an intra- and inter-individual basis;
2. identify the relationship of capacity in this analysis;
3. identify the major tasks involved in the reading process;
4. identify specific subtask areas and analyze performance in relation to subtask;
5. identify specific factors that can influence reading performance.

Discrepancy Analysis

In the previous chapter the reading process was reviewed and formal and informal reading assessment measures introduced. During this chapter an application of the principles of assessment discussed in Chapter 1 will be made of the reading process.

As previously discussed, the first assessment principle is recognition and identification of a problem. This is accomplished using a discrepancy analysis and by conducting both an intra-individual and an inter-individual comparison. Consider the following example of a discrepancy analysis.

Shawn is a twelve-year-old boy in the third month of the sixth grade (6.3). From the results of several recent tests (California Mental Maturity Scale resulted in a MA of 13.5, Wechsler Intelligence Scale for Children—Revised, IQ = 115) and observations by the teacher of Shawn's overall school performance, the teacher concludes that Shawn's expected level of performance should be at the level of a thirteen- to fourteen-year-old child in the academic areas. Utilizing the WISC-R IQ score, a mental age is computed.

$$MA = \frac{IQ}{CA} \times 100 \qquad MA = \frac{115}{12.0} \times 100 = 13.8$$

After carefully considering all the information about Shawn, including the WISC-R and CMMS data, the teacher decides that Shawn's expected academic performance level should be comparable to that of a child of 13.5 years of age.

To establish Shawn's grade expectancy, five is subtracted from the expected level of performance to establish a grade expectancy of 8.5. In other words, it has been determined that Shawn should be capable of completing academic tasks at about the 8.5 grade level.

His performance on the Sucher-Allred Reading Diagnostic Test (1974) placed his overall reading score at 6.2. Does Shawn have a reading problem? Inter-individually (Shawn's performance against that of his peers), there is a discrepancy of only a month.

grade level placement   6.3
reading performance level   6.2
                                        .1

However, on an intra-individual basis, Shawn's reading performance could be considered as being problematic.

level of capacity	8.5
actual achievement	6.2
discrepancy	2.3

A discrepancy of over two years is indicative of a problem, and, in comparison with Shawn's overall academic abilities, this reading problem should be considered serious.

The above example illustrates the importance of conducting both kinds of comparisons. Frequently, a child's performance, is only compared to grade level placement. If no gross discrepancy is evident between grade placement and actual performance, the fact that Shawn is capable of much better work is ignored. Shawn has a reading problem. *Grade level achievement is not the goal of effective reading instruction. Achievement to the individual's capability level is.* Figure 7-1 illustrates Shawn's performance in profile form.

To reinforce the principle that *no valid* comparison between chronological age and grade placement can be made until level of expected performance has been determined, the following example is presented.

James is in the third month of the fourth grade. His chronological age is 10.4. His MA, determined by a Slosson Intelligence Test, is 8.5. Other performance indications such as quality of completed assignments, apparent inability to complete tasks at grade level, leads the teacher to place James's expected level of performance at approximately the 9.0 age level of difficulty. Academic grade level expectancy is then determined to be at about the fourth grade. James's scores on the subtests of the Woodcock Reading Mastery Tests were as follows.

Letter Identification	5.0
Word Identification	4.2
Word Attack	4.4
Word Comprehension	4.0
Passage Comprehension	3.6
Total Reading	4.2

Figure 7-1 Shawn's Performance Profile Comparing Grade Placement (GP) and Actual Performance (AP) With His Grade Expectancy (GE) as Computed from His Expected Level of Performance

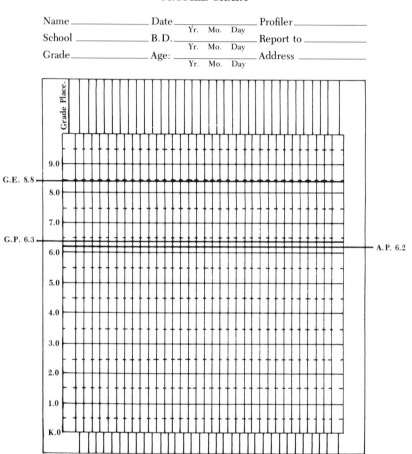

PROFILE CHART

Name _____ Date _____ Profiler _____
                          Yr.   Mo.   Day
School _____ B.D. _____ Report to _____
                          Yr.   Mo.   Day
Grade _____ Age: _____ Address _____
                          Yr.   Mo.   Day

Figure 7-2 James' Performance Profile Comparing Grade Placement (GP) and Actual Performance (AP) With His Grade Expectancy (GE) as Computed from His Expected Level of Performance

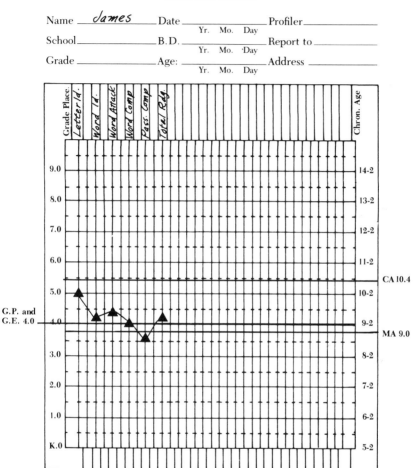

This information is shown on Figure 7-2. Does James have a reading problem? Is it serious?

By comparing expected to actual performance levels (intra-individual comparison), it can be determined that he does not have a reading problem. James is achieving at or above his expected level of performance, which could be owing to his being highly motivated and/or having developed compensatory behaviors that enable him to achieve above this estimated level. By comparing James's performance to that of his peers (inter-individual comparison), it can be determined that he is not performing at his grade placement level. However, he is certainly performing within the expectancy level of ability:

Examine Figure 7-3. Does Susan have a reading problem?

Figure 7-3 Susan's Performance Profile Comparing Grade Placement (GP) and Actual Performance (AP) With Her Grade Expectancy (GE) as Computed from Her Expected Level of Performance

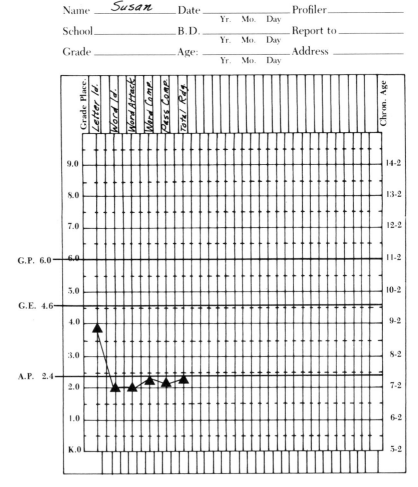

On an intra-comparative basis, Susan's expected level of performance has been determined to be at the 4.6 grade level. She is performing at a 2.4 grade level. Inter-comparatively the grade placement of her peers is 6.0. By either method of discrepancy analysis, Susan's reading problem is a serious one.

Task and Behavioral Analysis

Once it has been determined that a problem does exist, the problem is analyzed in terms of requirements to complete the task and the child's behavior in relation to the task. In reading, the subtasks have been identified as:

1. reading readiness;
2. letter recognition;
3. word recognition;
4. word attack;
5. comprehension.

Because the Woodcock Reading Mastery Test (Woodcock, 1974) assesses all of these tasks and further breaks them into subtask areas, it will be used as the basis for analysis. Figure 7-4 presents a sample of "test results interpretation." The three reading grade levels generated by the Woodcock (easy reading level, 96%; reading grade score, 90%; and failing reading level, 75%) correspond to the independent, instructional, and frustration levels discussed earlier. As most teachers focus on a child's instructional level, these scores are usually the ones reported in an evaluation.

Figure 7-5 presents in profile form the same information as found in Figure 7-4.

Behavior Analysis in Relation to the Task

A unique feature of the Woodcock Reading Mastery Test (1974) is a percentage measurement of behavior in relation to task. In Figure 7-4, the vertical line is grade level placement. The percentage figures represent the grade level of mastery of each task. Did the child perform the task? In Figure 7-4, the student has

Figure 7-4 Woodcock's Interpretation of Test Results Illustrating (1) Reading Subtasks Related to This Test and (2) Percentage of 6.0 Grade Level Placement

INTERPRETATION OF TEST RESULTS/FORM B
SUMMARY OF SCORES

TEST	RAW SCORES AND MASTERY SCORES			READING GRADE LEVELS AND RELATIVE MASTERY						
	Raw Score	(MS) Mastery Score TABLE 1		(E) Easy Reading Level TABLE 1	Relative Mastery at E	(R) Reading Grade Score TABLE 1	Relative Mastery at R	(F) Failure Reading Level TABLE 1	Relative Mastery at F
Letter Identification ... (45)	42	160		3.1	96%	3.8	90%	4.8	75%
Word Identification .. (150)	53	115		1.9	96%	2.0	90%	2.3	75%
Word Attack .... (50)	10	83		1.7	96%	2.0	90%	2.7	75%
Word Comprehension . (70)	14	64		1.8	96%	2.2	90%	2.8	75%
Passage Comprehension . (85)	14	64		1.8	96%	2.1	90%	2.5	75%
(Total) 486									
TOTAL READING[2] .... (Total ÷ 5)	97			2.1	96%	2.4	90%	2.7	75%

Reading subtasks — MASTERY PROFILE — Percentage of 6.0 Grade Level Placement

Reading readiness — Letter Identification
Letter Recognition — Word Identification
Word Attack — Word Attack
Word Recognition — Word Comprehension
Comprehension — Passage Comprehension
TOTAL READING

not performed the five tasks successfully. We have progressed from "The child has a reading problem" to identification of the main areas of difficulty. In Figure 7-5, using the total reading grade score of 2.9, each subtest can be identified as to relative strengths and weaknesses. In this profile the subtests for word identification (2.5), word attack (2.5), and passage comprehension (2.0) are below the grade score 2.9. This information more specifically pinpoints problem areas. The subtasks of each test can be

Figure 7-5   Woodcock Subtest Reading Grade Level Scores in Relationship to Total Reading (2.9 grade)

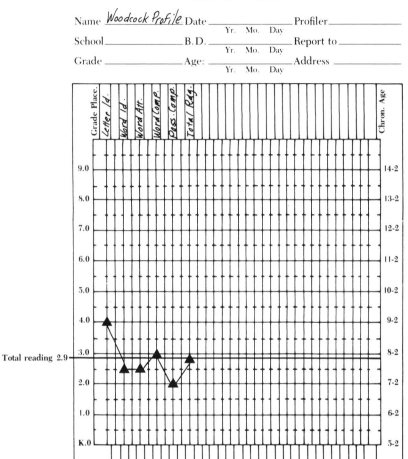

further analyzed to provide an even more accurate basis for writing instructional objectives to correct identified reading problems.

Letter identification (Figure 7-6) illustrates that Simon did not perform the behavior of identifying the upper case letters I, L, and Q. This information provides a more exact basis for remediation.

Figure 7-6 Simon's Letter Identification Errors

Letter Identification Test

RESPONSES: (Incorrect responses may be recorded following the printed answers)

1 ＿X	11 ＿U	21 ＿W	31 ＿A	41 ＿x
2 ＿B	12 ＿r	22 ＿v	32 ＿q	42 ＿J
3 ＿S	13 ＿G	23 ＿g	33 ＿k	43 ＿I
4 ＿i	14 ＿y	24 ＿t	34 ＿Y	44 ＿z
5 ＿C	15 ＿L	25 ＿N	35 ＿L	45 ＿Q
6 ＿Z	16 ＿n	26 ＿a	36 ＿n	
7 ＿K	17 ＿a	27 ＿m	37 ＿p	
8 ＿m	18 ＿j	28 ＿d	38 ＿S	
9 ＿T	19 ＿H	29 ＿w	39 ＿V	
10 ＿p	20 ＿R	30 ＿e	40 ＿r	

RAW SCORE __42__

Diagnostic Interpretation of Errors:

for Simon

Implications for Instructions:

I, 2, Q

Word identification (see Figure 7-7) illustrates that Simon did not perform the behavior of identifying the following words: water, mitten, bear, etc. These words, in addition to words from basal lists at second grade level, become a more exact basis for remediation.

During the word attack test, the child's incorrect response is written on the test form. The teacher is able to analyze the incorrect responses and diagnose which subtasks of word attack are not being performed. In Figure 7-8 notice that the teacher is able to progress from "word attack skills three years below grade level placement" to the following statements:

1. reversals of letters in final position.

Figure 7-7 Simon's Word Identification Errors (all words with a "0" by them)

WORD IDENTIFICATION TEST

RESPONSES: (Incorrect responses may be recorded following the printed answers) *Simon*

1 ____ is	31 _0_ mitten	61 _I_ listen
2 ____ come	32 _I_ duck	62 _I_ paper
3 ____ the	33 _I_ name	63 _I_ until
4 ____ look	34 _I_ sit	64 _0_ peace
5 ____ up	35 _0_ bear	65 _0_ remember
6 ____ big	36 _I_ farm	66 _I_ strange
7 ____ down	37 _I_ night	67 _0_ angry
8 ____ that	38 _0_ could	68 _I_ while
9 ____ she	39 _I_ food	69 _I_ watch
10 ____ on	40 _I_ high	70 _0_ leap
11 ____ my	41 _0_ walk	71 _0_ quick
12 ____ jump	42 _I_ told	72 _0_ crash
13 ____ something	43 _I_ street	73 _0_ body
14 ____ at	44 _0_ much	74 _0_ piece
15 ____ book	45 _I_ still	75 ____ public
16 ____ him	46 _0_ pony	76 ____ brought
17 ____ of	47 _I_ love	77 ____ busy
18 ____ work	48 _I_ morning	78 ____ surface
19 ____ what	49 _I_ ship	79 ____ groan
20 ____ rabbit	50 _0_ surprise	80 ____ gravy
21 ____ out	51 _0_ wife	81 ____ comfort
22 ____ was	52 _0_ most	82 ____ engine
23 ____ man	53 _I_ better	83 ____ soapy
24 _I_ be	54 _I_ city	84 ____ human
25 _I_ as	55 _I_ always	85 ____ design
26 _I_ fly	56 _0_ found	86 ____ crime
27 _I_ away	57 _I_ learn	87 ____ warning
28 _I_ cake	58 _0_ once	88 ____ zigzag
29 _0_ water	59 _I_ front	89 ____ twilight
30 _I_ sheep	60 _0_ meaning	90 ____ produce

---

2. insertion of letters in medial and final positions.
3. inadequate knowledge of short and long vowel sounds.

These statements provide a specific basis developing instructional objectives.

Figure 7-8 Simon's Analysis of Word Attack Skills

WORD ATTACK TEST
RESPONSES: (Incorrect responses may be recorded following the printed answers)

1 _/_ din
2 _O_ mam *man*
3 _/_ gis
4 _/_ unn
5 _/_ shif
6 _/_ oft *ought*
7 _/_ poe
8 _O_ en *net*
9 _O_ dod *trod*
10 _O_ fet *flet*

11 _/_ cug
12 _O_ hend *head*
13 _/_ unhip
14 _O_ plip *plib*
15 _/_ ful's
16 _O_ gog *God*
17 _/_ ef
18 _/_ pand
19 _O_ weaf *leaf*
20 _O_ twem *tearl*

21 _O_ futt *full*
22 _O_ plad *play*
23 _O_ fime *flam*
24 ___ knop
25 ___ jinnest
26 ___ depine
27 ___ reest
28 ___ fabe
29 ___ femty
30 ___ overclan

31 ___ lel
32 ___ baim
33 ___ tadding
34 ___ vitnap
35 ___ scority
36 ___ dinlo
37 ___ troil
38 ___ shobly
39 ___ mistrans
40 ___ gaked

41 ___ febmifsack
42 ___ snikgof
43 ___ odlud
44 ___ zeepstol
45 ___ antilobby
46 ___ ufwut
47 ___ ipdan
48 ___ pelnidlun
49 ___ wifyep
50 ___ hopdalhup

Diagnostic
Interpretation
of Errors:

insertions
reversals
silent E rule

Subvocalizes

Implications for
Instruction:

SIMON

Word and Passage Comprehension

Examination of incorrect responses made by the child can reveal what specific subtasks of comprehension are not adequately developed. Specific problem areas include decoding skills, use of picture and context clues, grammatic closure, vocabulary development, and short-term memory. Specific analysis of the child's behavior will provide a basis for remediation. Does the child spend so much time analyzing a new word that meaning of the sentence is forgotten? Does the child rely heavily on picture and context clues? Does the child understand meanings of words at his level? Can the child classify and categorize material? Each behavior analyzed in relation to the task provides a basis for an instructional objective.

In a formal reading test, each item is an example of a skill required for reading. In order to provide adequate remediation, the teacher must be able to determine what skill each item measures. For example, if the child pronounces hide incorrectly (hīdē), this may be indicative of the child's not knowing the silent *e* rule.

Item Analysis

To help determine which specific skill the child needs further instruction in, an item analysis of the Woodcock is presented. This is an example of how any test can be analyzed into more functional information for the teacher. An item analysis is an attempt to determine the specific functions the test is composed of. Once the functions are identified, the teacher has only to locate those areas of failure to get a better idea of what remediation strategies to employ.

Figure 7-9 shows the skills tested in the word identification and word attack sections. Circling each item missed can reveal patterns of breakdown in specific areas.

Figure 7-10 presents a similar task breakdown for the letter identification subtest of the Woodcock. Again, circling incorrect responses can reveal patterns of skill deficiencies.

Performance in relation to the task can also be measured using checklists. The items on the list identify the task. As the item is either checked or not checked, it establishes mastery or lack of mastery of the task. Figure 7-11 presents a list from which the checked items form a basis for remediation objectives. This example is taken from the Durrell Analysis of Reading Difficulty (1955).

Figure 7-9 Woodcock Reading Mastery Tests—Word Identification and Word Attack Decoding Analysis

Instructions: Circle the number of any items read incorrectly by the student.

| Word Identification | | Word Attack | | Reading Skill Being Assessed |
Form A	Form B	Form A	Form B	
2, 3, 5, 19*, 22, 23, 25, 32, 34, 41, 42, 44*, 45, 49*.	16, 19, 23, 27*, 28*, 29, 34, 38*, 39, 45*.	1, 2, 3*, 5, 6, 7, 8, 9*, 10, 11, 12, 13*, 17, 19*, 21, 22*, 23, 24*, 25*, 29*, 32*, 35*, 40*, 42*, 43*, 44*, 45*, 46*, 47*, 48*, 49*, 50*.	1, 2, 3, 5, 8, 9, 10, 11*, 12, 15, 16, 17, 18, 20*, 21*, 24, 29*, 31, 33*, 34, 42*, 43*, 46*, 47*, 48*, 49*, 50*.	Short vowel; formed by a single vowel in a medial position: consonant, vowel, consonant (CVC). Form closed syllables because they end with a consonant.
9, 24, 26, 28, 33, 46*.	20, 30, 31*, 42, 45*.	4*, 18, 26*, 28*, 30*, 36*, 38*.	7, 23*, 26*, 28*, 32, 40*.	Long vowel; sounds "the same as the alphabet letter name of the vowel." Open syllables formed because they end with a vowel.
43*, 50*.	4, 26*.	15, 16, 24*, 27*, 28*, 49*.	14, 20*, 22, 35*, 37*, 39*, 42*.	Consonant blends: a combination of two or three consonant letters blended in such a way that each letter in the blend keeps its own identity. They are not divided when separating a word into syllables.
19*, 30*, 37*, 40*, 44*, 48, 49*.	19, 23, 24, 26*, 36, 38*.	9*, 22*, 32*.	38*, 41*.	Consonant digraphs: a combination of two consonant letters representing one phoneme or speech sound that is not a blend. They are not divided when separating a word into syllables.

Concept				
Silent consonants: those consonants which, when combined with specific other letters, are not pronounced.	6, 24.	19*.		37*, 40*, 50*.
Final "e": in words with a vowel-consonant-e pattern (VCE), the vowel frequently (60% of the time) has the long sound while the "e" is silent.	23*, 26*, 28*, 40*.	18, 26*, 28*, 36*, 38*.	8, 21, 32, 40, 43*.	28, 33.
Vowels modified by "r": vowels followed by the letter "r" are neither long nor short, but the sound is modified by the letter "r" (85% of the time).			17, 41*.	18, 36, 48, 50.
Vowel digraphs: a combination of two vowels representing one sound that is not a blend.	5, 27, 32, 44, 19*.	20, 30*, 33, 34, 14*.	13, 28*, 37, 47, 48, 26*.	4, 15, 39.
Schwa sound: the vowel sound in an unaccented syllable.	4, 11*, 13*, 21*, 25*, 30, 35*, 43*, 48*, 50*.	3*, 13*, 25*, 31*, 35*, 36*, 38*, 42*, 43*, 44*, 47*.		20*, 31*.
Two consonants (UC-CV): if the initial vowel is followed by two consonants, divide the word between the two consonants (80% of the time true).	25*, 29*, 33*, 34, 36, 41*, 42*, 43*, 44, 45*, 46*, 47*.	25*, 27*, 29*, 32*, 35*, 36*, 38*, 39*, 40*, 42*, 43*, 44*.	22, 27*, 49*.	
Consonant-Le (C-13) endings: if a word ends in "le," the consonant preceding the "le" begins the last syllable.		41*.	6*, 49*.	13.
Prefixes and suffixes: prefixes and suffixes usually form a separate syllable.	13*, 25*, 26*, 30*, 33*, 38*, 39*, 40, 45*.	4*, 27*, 31*, 32*, 36*, 38*, 41*, 47*.	33*, 41*, 43*, 44.	

Figure 7-9 (Continued)

	Word Identification		Word Attack		Reading Skill Being Assessed
	Form A	Form B	Form A	Form B	
	11, 26, 46*.	10, 27*, 28*, 30, 31*.	25*.	29*, 35*, 45*.	The final "y" sound: in one-syllable words, has the sound of a long "i"; in multisyllable words, has the long "e" sound.
	20*, 31*.	3, 6*, 27*, 31*, 50.	13*, 14*, 32*, 39*.	25*, 33*, 45*.	Double consonant: if two identical consonants are in a word, the syllable before the double consonant is usually accented.
	1, 2, 3, 4, 5, 6, 7, 8, 9, 10, 11, 12, 14, 16, 17, 18, 19, 21, 22, 23, 24, 25, 26, 27, 29, 38, 41, 58.	1, 2, 3, 4, 5, 6, 7, 8, 9, 10, 11, 12, 13, 14, 15, 16, 17, 19, 21, 22, 24, 25, 26, 27, 28, 30, 31, 32, 34, 35, 38.			Dolch Sight Word List (200)

*These items are repeated in other boxes for that subtest. Examine rule before circling number.

Figure 7-10   Letter Identification Test

Form A	Form B	Skill Being Tested
20, 24, 25, 26, 27, 29, 30, 31, 33, 34, 35, 36, 37, 38, 39, 40, 41, 42, 43, 44, 45.	14, 22, 26, 27, 28, 29, 30, 32, 34, 36, 37, 38, 39, 40, 41, 42, 43, 44, 45.	Cursive letters
1, 2, 3, 4, 5, 6, 7, 8, 9, 10, 11, 12, 13, 14, 15, 16, 17, 18, 19, 21, 22, 23, 28, 32.	1, 2, 3, 4, 5, 6, 7, 8, 9, 10, 11, 12, 13, 15, 16, 17, 18, 19, 20, 21, 23, 24, 25, 31, 33, 35.	Printed letters
1, 2, 3, 5, 6, 7, 9, 11, 13, 15, 19, 20, 21, 25, 31, 34, 35.	2, 4, 6, 8, 9, 10, 11, 12, 13, 14, 16, 18, 22, 24.	Upper case letters
4, 8, 10, 12, 14, 16, 17, 18, 22, 23, 24, 26, 27, 28, 29, 30, 32, 33.	7, 15, 17, 19, 20, 21, 23, 25.	Lower case letters

Analysis of Factors Affecting the Problem

Process analysis attempts to establish the method in which the task is to be learned. Good reading instruction attempts to provide for maximum learning by teaching a variety of methods for learning the tasks. Modality factors are considered. Strengths and weaknesses in this area should be evaluated to determine how well the child processes information through sensory channels. These factors are discussed in more detail in Chapter 11.

Another factor to consider is the child's understanding of the task. Consider the example of sound blending. Does the child understand that the isolated sounds are combined to form a word? Can the child match the phoneme with its appropriate grapheme? Other factors that must be taken into consideration include:

1. the social-emotional makeup of the child;
2. motivation;
3. physical conditions;
4. environmental conditions.

Figure 7-11   A Checklist of Instruction Needs for Simon (From Durrell Analysis of Reading Difficulty (1955))

Non-Reader or Pre-primer Level	Primary Grade Reading Level	Intermediate Grade Reading Level
Needs help in:	*Needs help in:*	*Needs help in:*
1. Listening comprehension and speech	1. Listening comprehension and speech	1. Listening comprehension and speech
___ Understanding of material heard	___ Understanding of material heard	___ Understanding of material heard
___ Speech and spoken vocabulary	___ Speech and spoken vocabulary	___ Speech and oral expression
		2. Word analysis abilities and spelling
2. Visual perception of word elements	2. Word analysis abilities	___ Visual analysis of words
___ Visual memory of words	___ Visual memory of words	___ Auditory analysis of words
___ Giving names of letters	✓ Auditory analysis of words	✓ Solving words by sounding syllables
___ Identifying letters named	✓ Solving words by sounding	___ Sounding syllables, word parts
___ Matching letters	___ Sounds of blends, phonograms	___ Meaning from context
___ Copying letters	___ Use of context clues	___ Attack on unfamiliar words
	___ Remembering new words taught	___ Spelling ability
3. Auditory perception of word elements		___ Accuracy of copy Speed of writing
___ Initial or final blends	3. Oral reading abilities	___ Dictionary skills: Location, pronunciation, meaning
___ Initial or final single sounds	___ Oral reading practice	
___ Learning sounds taught	___ Comprehension in oral reading	___ _____
4. Phonic abilities	✓ Phrasing (Eye-voice span)	
___ Solving words	✓ Errors on easy words	3. Oral reading abilities
___ Sounding words	✓ Addition or omission of words	___ Oral reading practice
___ Sounds of blends—phonograms	✓ Repetition of words or phrases	___ Comprehension in oral reading
___ Sounds of individual letters	___ Ignoring punctuation	___ Phrasing (Eye-voice span)
5. Learning rate	___ Ignoring word errors	___ Expression in reading Speech skills
___ Remembering words taught	___ Attack on unfamiliar words	___ Speed of oral reading
___ Use of context clues	___ Expression in reading	___ Security in oral reading
6. Reading interest and effort	___ Speech, voice, enunciation	___ Word and phrase meaning
___ Attention and persistence	___ Security in oral reading	
___ Self-directed work	___ _____	
7. Other		
___ _____	4. Silent reading and recall	4. Silent reading and recall
___ _____	___ Level of silent reading	___ Level of silent reading
___ _____	___ Comprehension in silent reading	___ Comprehension in silent reading
___ _____	___ Attention and persistence	___ Unaided oral recall
	___ Unaided oral recall	___ Unaided written recall
	___ Recall on questions	___ Recall on questions
	___ Speed of silent reading	___ Attention and persistence
	___ Phrasing (Eye movements)	___ Word and phrase meaning difficulties
	✓ Lip movements and whispering	___ Sentence complexity difficulties
	___ Head movements Frowning	___ Imagery in silent reading
	___ Imagery in silent reading	___ _____
	✓ Position of book Posture	5. Speeded reading abilities
	___ _____	___ Speed of reading (Eye movements)
	___ _____	

Non-Reader or Pre-primer Level	Primary Grade Reading Level	Intermediate Grade Reading Level
Needs help in:	*Needs help in:* 5. Reading interest and effort ____ Attention and persistence ____ Voluntary reading ____ Self-directed work Workbooks	*Needs help in:* ____ Speed of work in content subjects ____ Skimming and locating information 6. Study abilities ____ Reading details, directions, arithmetic ____ Organization and subordination of ideas ____ Elaborative thinking in reading ____ Critical reading ____ Use of table of contents References 7. Reading interest and effort ____ Voluntary reading ____ Variety of reading ____ Self-directed work

These areas identify specific questions to be answered. Is the child's attitude toward reading negative because of previous experiences? Is the child healthy? Did the child eat breakfast? Can the child see and hear well enough? Is there too much noise outside the room that is distracting?

Even the time scheduled for reading instruction is important. The child will not perform as well at 2:30 as at 9:00. A child who has not had breakfast may perform better after lunch. Every factor that affects performance should be studied in order to identify those that will most efficiently correct the problem areas.

Synthesis of Results

The final steps in the assessment process are the synthesis of results into a program plan and continual evaluation of the program. To illustrate application of the process in the reading area, a sample of program planning ideas that can be generated by an observation checklist is presented in Figure 7-12. These were taken from the work of Dunn (1977) in training reading teachers at Brigham Young University.

Figure 7-12   Program Planning in Reading (Used by permission of Dr. James Dunn, Department of Elementary Education, Brigham Young University)

Inability to Use Context Clues for Decoding

Behavior Exhibited	Possible Causes	Possible Remedies
Limited listening-speaking vocabulary	Lacks language facility	Build conceptual language background
Low comprehension	Lack of conceptual background	Build language facility
Slow reading	Reading on frustrational level	Build letter-sound association
Lack of interest in reading	Lack of motivation	Instruction should be appropriate.
	Lack of phonic training	(The reader does not guess.)
		Completion of sentences—oral—written
	Inadequate instruction in vocabulary	Provide material within language experience
		Use tape recorder with key words omitted.
		Ask three questions and provide appropriate instruction when student cannot answer:
		1. What kind of word is it?
		2. What are some words that would make sense?
		3. Which has the right phonic elements?

Difficulty in Decoding Words Phonically

Behavior Exhibited	Possible Causes	Possible Remedies
Poor spelling	Lacks auditory acuity, discrimination, association, or sequential memory	Auditory training: Gross: sounds of environment likenesses-differences
Poor word perception	Unable to blend sounds (phonemes)	Refined: tone, pattern sequence figure-ground, closure phonemes, synthesizing
Stagnate vocabulary	Comes from noisy environment	Hear precise speech
Word guessing	Inadequate or premature instruction	Use familiar words in phonic analysis
		Avoid distorted sounds c = /kŭ/ −/sŭ/ r = /ĕr/
		Student visually see words sequenced (use of phonic respellings by teacher)

Difficulty in Decoding Words Phonically

Behavior Exhibited	Possible Causes	Possible Remedies
		Small group instruction in quiet area
		Teach sequential steps for analyzing an unfamiliar word through use of error avoidance strategy.

Confusion in Letter Knowledge

Behavior Exhibited	Possible Cause	Possible Remedies
Reversals	Visual disability	Check auditory and visual acuity
Anxiety in writing and reading	Hearing disability (acuity-figure ground)	Auditory and visual discrimination training
Ineffective word analysis	Carelessness	Small group instruction at chalkboard in initial teaching
Ineffective oral reading	Neurological development	Easily confused letters taught separately
Avoidance of writing	Inadequate instruction (improper pacing)	Appropriate training in phonics by use of error avoidance strategy for mastery
Poor spelling		Kinesthetic-tactile training

Difficulty in Structural Analysis

Behavior Exhibited	Possible Causes	Possible Remedies
Poor spelling	Auditory acuity and discrimination	Precise speech—separate words in spoken language
Inability in word perception	Lack of hearing precise speech	
Stagnate vocabulary	Inadequate instruction	Training in visual and auditory discrimination
Word guessing	Lack of understanding of what a syllable is	Differentiating between words or similar sounds (minimal pairs—pen, pin)
	Teacher insecurity in personal knowledge resulting in avoidance	Recognition and Synthesizing elements of word (phonemic, syllabic, morphemic)
		Build memory of word form
		Teach common affixes
		Adequate listening-speaking vocabulary
		Use of directed inquiry strategy in visual clues for syllabicating
		Provide sequential procedure in analyzing unfamiliar words

Figure 7-12   Program Planning in Reading (*Continued*)

Difficulty in Comprehending

Behavior Exhibited	Possible Causes	Possible Remedies
Inappropriate answers to questions	Lack of experiential background	Build conceptual background
Distractability	Inadequate vocabulary—sight and meaning	Develop sensory imagery (T.V. syndrome)
Inexpressive oral reading	Lacks sentence sense	Set purpose (develop self purposing)
Inability to follow directions	Reading at frustration level	Develop "testing does not teach" philosophy
Tense and inattentive	Inadequate study skills	Teach processes of thinking through a questioning strategy
Lacks organization in completing tasks	Inadequate method of study	(open, focusing, interpretive, capstone, apply)
Avoidance of reading	Overemphasis on oral reading	Build appropriate vocabulary
	Overemphasis on testing—poor instruction	Proper placement in material and environment (non-judgmental)
	Reading without purpose set	Teach to interpret organization of content material (total—paragraph)
	Inadequate word analysis	Teach method of study O.A.R.W.E.T.—S.Q.R.R.
	Anxiety	Increase silent reading rate by less emphasis on oral reading
	Round robin reading	Teach purpose of punctuation marks
	Teaching isolated words in lists	Teach paraphrasing
	Overuse of flash cards	Increase word recognition
	Judgmental acceptance of answers	Teach expressive oral reading
		Teach outlining skills
		Provide options in assignments

Lip Movement and Subvocalization in Silent Reading

Behavior Exhibited	Possible Causes	Possible Remedies
Low reading rate	Overemphasis on phonics	No round robin reading
Poor comprehension	Overemphasis on oral reading	Less emphasis on oral reading
Word by word reading	Overemphasis on reading with expression	Phrase reading exercises
Movement of lips in silent reading	Auditory learner	Proper placement—easy material
	Improper placement	Proper initial instruction (silent reading early in program)
	Insufficient sight vocabulary	Do not overemphasize phonics
		Put something in mouth
		Literature program

Ineffective Eye-voice Span in Oral Reading

Behavior Exhibited	Possible Cause	Possible Remedies
Slow reading rate	Visual problems	Initial instruction emphasize thought units
Regressions in oral reading	Improper placement	Reduce size of print
Inadequate comprehension	Inappropriate instruction	Read silently before oral reading
Reads with hesitancy	Inadequate sight vocabulary	Easier material (placement)
Loses place in reading	Fatigue	Planned developmental physical education program
	Has not learned to read in thought units	Analytical approach to reading when appropriate
		Use tachistoscope activities
		Use direct instruction techniques

Limited Visual or Auditory Memory

Behavior Exhibited	Possible Causes	Possible Remedies
Lacks comprehension	Lack of experiential background	Build experiential background
Inconsistency in remembering sight vocabulary	Instruction appealing to only one sense	Build memory in areas of interest
Poor visual-sequential memory	Task not valued (disinterest)	Do errands—carry messages
Remembers only short sequences	Emotional interference	Peek box activities
Inattentive	Anxiety	Retell stories within experiential background
Difficulty in following instructions		Games of concentration, matching
		Dramatizations, songs, nursery rhymes
		Tachistoscopic activities
		Visual and auditory memory exercises
		Adjust length of work periods
		Have work in supportive environment
		Recognize causes of anxiety and avoid situations where possible
		Use error utilization strategies

Figure 7-12   Program Planning in Reading *(Continued)*

Inappropriate Reading Materials

Behavior Exhibited	Possible Causes	Possible Remedies
Reading failure	Ignoring the needs of the child	Language experience approach
Disinterested readers	Lack of knowledge in selection	Inform administrators—have plan
Lack of appropriate progress	Finance	Discover interests of students
Avoidance behavior	Inappropriate criteria in selection	Work with parents—have plan
	Super salesman	Use of public library
	Lack of total school program	Use of bookmobile
		Inservice training in literature
	Inappropriate instructional design	Projects
	Insufficient research	
	Public relations	
	Value system	

Difficulty in Tracking Line of Print

Behavior Exhibited	Possible Causes	Possible Remedies
Regressions	Lack of binocularity	Teach reading mechanics of left to right and use marker above line
Reads words from different line	Introductory instruction (charts with hand movement for return sweep)	Developmental physical education program
Inaccurate reading	Too many eye fixations	Easier materials
	Inappropriate format of print	Rate practices
	Neurological development	Reduce size of print (increase space between lines)
	Sight vocabulary	Increase word recognition vocabulary
	Reading at frustrational level	
	Reading words rather than meaning	Occular pursuit activities
		Tachistoscope activities
	Faulty clues in word analysis	Use direct instruction techniques

Habit of Reading Word By Word

Behavior Exhibited	Possible Causes	Possible Remedies
Poor comprehension	Improper placement	Increase word recognition vocabulary
Poor expression in oral reading	Emphasis on oral reading	Proper placement
Poor silent reading rate	Stress on word perfect oral reading	Less emphasis on oral reading
Indifference to reading	Inadequate sight vocabulary	Read silently before oral reading
	Phrase reading not taught	Teach phrasing
	Narrow perceptual span	Eliminate lip movement and subvocalization
	Inadequate instruction	Interesting materials
	Emphasis on words rather than meaning	Choral reading—dramatizations—puppetry
	Inability to associate ideas	Rate pacers
		Echo reading
	Faulty eye movement	
	Round robin reading	Omit round robin reading
		Tachistoscope activities

Reversals of Letters and/or Words

Behavior Exhibited	Possible Causes	Possible Remedies
Confusion of word	Neurological development	Planned developmental physical education program
Poor spelling	Lack left to right direction	Kinesthetic—tactile training
		Use of typewriter in written expression
Avoidance of writing	Vision	
Emotion	Visual sequential memory problem	Color coding
		Arrows giving direction
	Mixed dominance	Change from manuscript to cursive writing
	Inadequate instruction	
	Lack of mastery of phonics (letter sound—association)	Proper initial instruction (mastery of letter recognition) (sequential introduction of letters)
		Comparisons
		Use error avoidance strategy
		Provide immediate feedback

Figure 7-12   Program Planning in Reading (*Continued*)

Regressions in Oral Reading

Behavior Exhibited	Possible Causes	Possible Remedies
Poor oral reading	Inadequate sight vocabulary	Proper placement
Slow reading rate	Inadequate word analysis	Contextual clues
	Interruptions when reading orally	Marker on top of line rather than below
	Inappropriate placement	Choral reading
	Inadequate listening-speaking vocabulary	Music (familiar tune, new words)
	Confusion in meaning	Read silently before orally
	Eye movement in tracking line	Build oral language facility
	Round robin reading	Build word analysis skills
		Self-evaluation of taped reading
		Do not interrupt when a word is mispronounced when reading orally.
		Use error utilization techniques
		Omit round robin reading

Lack of Interest

Behavior Exhibited	Possible Causes	Possible Remedies
Off task behavior	Lack of success experiences	Proper placement
Inconsistent errors in work	Inappropriate material—topic, level	Vary teaching strategies
Behavior problems	Reading not important in life	Trust students
Apparent carelessness in meeting assignments	Conceptual background	Broaden child's conceptual background
Tardiness	Vision—hearing	Use creative independent activities
	Relevancy (value)	Use learning centers
	Lack of stimulation in classroom	Have varied materials (level-content)

Lack of Interest

Behavior Exhibited	Possible Causes	Possible Remedies
	Anxiety	Encourage pursuit of interests and provide sharing time (small group)
	Lack of appropriate instructional strategies	Use extending interests portion of lesson manuals
	Teacher domination of learning environment	Broaden options for students to accomplish goals
	Lack of options in completing assignments	Maximize involvement of students in decision making
	Reinforcement not valued by learner	Use pupil-pupil team learning
	Stress on competition	

Unsatisfactory Silent Reading Rate

Behavior Exhibited	Possible Causes	Possible Remedies
Low comprehension	Emphasis on oral reading—read every word	Less emphasis on oral reading
		Increase word recognition
Lack of enjoyment in reading	Overemphasis on phonics	Increase word analysis skills
		Eliminate lip movement and subvocalization
Slow in completing assignments	Subvocalization and/or lip movement	Set purposes
Skipping pages to compete with neighbor	Narrow perceptual span	Teach to adjust rate according to material
	Inadequate sight vocabulary	Lessons on skimming and scanning
		Keep personal progress chart
	Lack of purpose	Proper placement (easy materials)
	Word by word reader —lacks phrasing	Rate pacer (marker above line reading)
	Reading at frustrational level	Visual pursuit activities
	Lack of instruction and application in easy material	Read under time constraints (specific lessons)
		Tachistoscope activities
	Anxiety	Recognize that comprehension will suffer in initial stages of increasing rate
	General slowness in all responding	Lots of easy reading (literature program)
	Round robin reading	Omit round robin reading

Figure 7-12   Program Planning in Reading (*Continued*)

Inadequate Listening, Speaking Vocabulary

Behavior Exhibited	Possible Causes	Possible Remedies
Low comprehension	Home vocabulary differs from school	Provide vivid and varied experience
Difficulty in self-expression (oral, written)	Speech and learning problems	Dramatization of new vocabulary
Misunderstands "obvious" facts	Adults in life who do not listen	Oral discussion of experiences
	Passive interaction with adults—peers	Use of Visual materials (posters)
Lower capability	Meager environment	Place in environment where words are used
Lower self-concept	Inadequate word analysis	Build word analysis skills
Slow reading rate	Inadequate instruction	Label objects
Slower learning rate	Avoidance of dictionary	Read to the groups or class
		Encourage personal dictionaries
		Language lessons in descriptive words
		Develop key concepts before reading new topics
		Use and encourage students to use new words
		Develop other ways to say it (said)
		Build vocabulary of content areas
		Greater emphasis on an oral environment in school

Inadequate Motivation

Behavior Exhibited	Possible Causes	Possible Remedies
Lack of sustained involvement in learning	Lack of teacher application of principles of motivation	Success in academic experiences
		Student aware of personal progress
Development of dependence	Relevancy of task	Assignments should be challenging but within ability to do
		Be encouraging and supportive
Lack of purposeful learning	Assignments without setting purpose(s)	Balance recreational and information reading
	Lack of short-and long-term goal setting	Start with interests of child
	Lack of appropriate use of open-ended or differentiated assignments	
	Teacher domination of content	Disequilibrium in learning tasks
	Lack of success experiences	Set purpose(s)
	Assignments outside of value system	Vary instructional strategies
	Lack of educational tradition in the home	Utilize error utilization lessons
	Inadequate self-concept	Use pupil-pupil team learning
	Reinforcement not used or is not valued by learner	
	Stress on competition	

Omits Beginnings or Endings of Words

Behavior Exhibited	Possible Causes	Possible Remedies
Poor oral reading	Live in noisy environment	Compare pronunciation with meaning
Misunderstands what is read	Personal speech patterns	Self-evaluation of taped reading
Weakened word recognition	Lack of word analysis skills	Choral reading
	Defective auditory-visual discrimination	Echo reading
		Hear precise speech
		Compare oral to written symbol
		Kinesthetic-tactile activities

Figure 7-12 Program Planning in Reading (*Continued*)

Ineffective Teaching

Behavior Exhibited	Possible Causes	Possible Remedies
Reading failure —lowered self-concept	Premature instruction Inadequate information about child	Gain personal knowledge (content and techniques) Self-evaluation
Lack of progress Emotion—tensions	Lack of training-education for teachers	Careful selection of materials
Needless disabilities Lack of initiative	Overemphasis on single word analysis skill to exclusion of others	Organization (planning, record keeping, content) Motivational techniques
	Time schedules	Create a need for reading
	Self-concept of teacher	Create positive learning climate
	Inappropriate materials	Have conviction and be enthused
	Teacher is not informed concerning instructional design of selected approach to instruction	Trust the student Utilize teaching moment Use appropriate reinforcers
	Selection of one method for all pupils	Provide immediate and appropriate feedback
	Lack of total school program	Maximize on task activities View self as problem solver
	Lack of application of principles of motivation	Schedule individual conferences
	Working climate-feeling tone	
	Rationalization of failures	
	Overreacting to problems	

Emotional Handicaps

Behavior Exhibited	Possible Causes	Possible Remedies
Reading disability	Problems over which he has little or no control (peers, parent, or teacher)	Avoid premature instruction
Lowered energy level		Provide appropriate pacing in learning
Behavior problems	Lack of success	Provide appropriate degree of structure
Lack stick-to-it-iv-ness and with-it-ness	Too much pressure from lack of organization and management system	Discover and capitalize on talents
		Proper placement
Excitable or passive personality	Premature instruction	Know tolerance point of individuals
Lower self-concept	Frustrational level in reading placement	Be positive and supportive in relationships
	Inappropriate expectations	Provide academic and social success experience
	Overdependency	Be consistent in expectations
	Nagging	Have honorable releases for frustration
	Reading disabilities	
	Minimal neurological disfunction	Planned developmental physical education program
	Stress on competition	Use error utilization strategy
		Use pupil-pupil team learning
		Schedule individual conference

Inappropriate Grouping Patterns

Behavior Exhibited	Possible Causes	Possible Remedies
Child unable to progress at own rate	Use of standardized test scores	Develop personal skill to diagnose
Feeling of failure	Assuming all children's needs are the same	Utilize varied evaluation techniques
Lowered self-concept	Lack of record keeping	Record keeping system
Lack of interest	Time	Have flexible grouping (need, interest)
	Inadequate planning	Be an observer and recorder
	Lack of training for teacher	Develop specific and varied strategies for teaching
	Inflexibility in groups	
	Inappropriate materials	Secure appropriate materials
	Lack of observational skills	Develop management system
		Use pupil-pupil team learning
	Lack of informal and diagnostic techniques	Use principles of planning

Conclusion

In this chapter the process required for specific analysis of a reading problem has been presented. The basic purpose has been to provide the teacher with a beginning place from which to develop reading instruction. Examples have been presented to illustrate how the teacher can take the general statement, "The child has a reading problem" and develop a more specific understanding of that problem. For example, the reading problem appears to be directly related to a lack of word attack skills and specifically the child cannot perform the following tasks:

1. sound blend;
2. apply the final *e* rule;
3. recognize the blend—bl.

This process enables the teacher to plan instruction at a more meaningful and necessary level for the child having a "reading problem."

Can You Answer These Questions?

1. Given the following data, can you conduct a discrepancy analysis?
   WISC-R full scale IQ 102
   Woodcock Reading Mastery

LI 4.3	CA 9.8
WI 2.0	Grade placement 4.5
WA 1.8	
WC 1.8	
PC 2.4	
TR 2.4	

2. What subtasks are involved in the reading process?
3. Given the following example, what are the subtask areas that should be the basis for remediation?
4. What specific factors can influence reading performance?
5. How would you define item analysis?

Example 7-1

LETTER IDENTIFICATION TEST

RESPONSES: (Incorrect responses may be recorded following the printed answers)

1 ✓ X	11 ✓ U	21 ✓ W	31 ✓ A	41 ✓ x
2 ✓ B	12 ✓ r	22 ✓ v	32 ✓ q	42 ✓ J
3 ✓ S	13 ✓ G	23 ✓ g	33 ✓ k	43 _O_ I
4 ✓ i	14 ✓ y	24 ✓ t	34 ✓ Y	44 ✓ z
5 ✓ C	15 ✓ L	25 ✓ N	35 ✓ L	45 _O_ Q
6 ✓ Z	16 ✓ n	26 ✓ a	36 ✓ n	
7 ✓ K	17 ✓ a	27 ✓ m	37 ✓ p	
8 ✓ m	18 ✓ j	28 ✓ d	38 _O_ S	
9 ✓ T	19 ✓ H	29 ✓ w	39 _O_ V	
10 ✓ p	20 ✓ R	30 ✓ e	40 _O_ r	

RAW SCORE _40_

Example 7-2

WORD ATTACK TEST

RESPONSES: (Incorrect responses may be recorded following the printed answers)

1 ✓ ift	31 ___ telequik	Diagnostic
2 ✓ bim	32 ___ shenning	Interpretation
3 ✓ ut	33 ___ quib	of Errors:
4 ✓ rayed	34 ___ laip	
5 ✓ kak	35 ___ fubwit	
6 _O_ maft _maf_	36 ___ pertome	
7 _O_ nen _net_	37 ___ sloy	
8 _O_ ab _Ad_	38 ___ subcrote	
9 _O_ tash _tis_	39 ___ pipped	
10 ✓ wip's	40 ___ etbom	
11 _O_ ziz _zip_	41 ___ polybendable	Implications for
12 _O_ ott _of_	42 ___ dinlan	Instruction:
13 ✓ nudd	43 ___ eldop	
14 _O_ weet _wet_	44 ___ wubfambif	
15 ✓ plen	45 ___ wotfob	
16 ✓ twib _crib_	46 ___ cigbet	
17 _O_ beb _bad_	47 ___ conration	
18 _O_ rejune _Affjut_	48 ___ biftel	
19 _O_ knap _knap_	49 ___ bafmotbem	RAW
20 _O_ ain _ain't_	50 ___ nolhod	SCORE _8_

References

Dunn, J. W. *Course Syllabus for Introduction to Reading— Department of Elementary Education, Brigham Young University.* Provo, Utah: Brigham Young University Press, 1977.

Durrell, D. D. *Durrell Analysis of Reading Difficulty.* New York: Harcourt Brace Jovanovich, 1955.

Sucher, F. and R. A. Allred. *Sucher–Allred Reading Placement Inventory.* Oklahoma City, Oklahoma: The Economy Company, 1973.

Woodcock, R. W. *Woodcock Reading Mastery Tests.* Circle Pines, Minnesota: American Guidance Service, 1974.

chapter

8

Spelling Assessment

Objectives

At the conclusion of this chapter, the reader should be able to:

1. identify the steps to be followed in conducting a spelling assessment;
2. specify expected spelling behaviors of children at specified age or grade levels;
3. detail the component parts of a spelling assessment;
4. conduct a phonic or structural analysis;
5. identify common spelling rules and errors;
6. specify formal and informal procedures and devices for use in conducting a spelling assessment.

Introduction

Spelling is a vital communication tool that is used throughout a person's life. It should be considered a major part of the child's total educational program. Assessment in spelling is usually completed for two reasons: (1) to determine the child's achievement level and (2) to determine the child's overall deficiencies or difficulties in completing the spelling task successfully. Unfortunately, to determine achievement appears to be of greatest concern to the teacher; knowing the child's achievement level alone does very little for the proper selection and development of instructional strategies to increase the child's spelling performance. The latter reason is sometimes avoided owing to the teacher's lack of understanding of the component parts comprising the spelling process. This chapter will focus on determining the child's spelling achievement level as well as providing information that will assist the teacher in analyzing the child's understanding and application of the components of the spelling process. Greater emphasis will be given to the latter throughout this chapter.

Conducting a Spelling Assessment

The assessment of the child's spelling abilities has to be based upon an understanding of those component parts that comprise the overall spelling task. That understanding includes being able to identify the skills needed by children to spell effectively, as well as an understanding of the skills needed by the teacher to analyze the child's spelling performance. The skills of primary importance to the child in successfully completing the spelling task include:

1. the necessary visual and auditory capabilities to process the visual and verbal information involved in spelling—adequate visual and auditory acuity;

2. the ability to discriminate between different sets of auditory and visual stimuli, as well as combinations of both types of stimuli—ability to discriminate visually between "b" and "d" and to auditorily discriminate between sounds that have minimal contrasts such as "fat" and "cat";

3. a memory capacity for the receipt, storage, and retrieval of both written and auditory stimuli;

4. the ability to demonstrate functional motor skills for writing that involve eye and hand coordination as well as fine-motor manipulations of the fingers;
5. the ability to enunciate and pronounce words adequately enough so that distortions will not result in spelling error;
6. some understanding of the rules of spelling that cover consistent letter sound patterns for consonants, vowels, digraphs, and blends, and the rules that govern syllables, and the common inconsistencies that are found within these rules; not necessarily the ability to state the rules but to show or demonstrate functional application of the rules;
7. the ability to apply information from above for making self-correction of spelling errors.

Skills of the teacher in making a proper assessment of the child's ability should include:

1. having some idea of the components of language that apply to spelling which include phonemes, morphemes, graphemes, and syllables;
2. being aware of the most common rules that are applied within the English language to the structure of words;
3. being able to specify the inconsistencies that are common to those rules;
4. having an understanding of the sequence in which spelling skills develop in children—what the expected spelling behaviors of children are and at what ages of development they occur;
5. being familiar with phonic and structural analysis of words.

Components of Spelling Assessment

Letter-sound relationships, or grapheme-phoneme relationships, are essential to understanding how words are constructed and eventually spelled. The *phoneme* is the smallest unit of sound while the *grapheme* is the graphic or letter representation of that sound. Phonemes are usually thought of in terms of vowels and consonants. The consonant grapheme-phoneme relationships are consistent throughout the English language (Ruddell, 1974). There are some exceptions to this, however, in that the letters of "c," "g," "s," and "z" can represent more than one sound. For example, "can" has a "k" sound while "center" has a "c" sound. Figure 8-1 provides a listing of the grapheme-

Figure 8-1 Phoneme-Grapheme Relationships (Adapted from Ruddell, 1974)

Sound or Phoneme	Letter or Grapheme	Sample	Sound or Phoneme	Letter or Grapheme	Sample
b	b	*b*at	n	ng	si*ng*er
k	c	*c*an		n	dri*n*k
	k	*k*itten	p	p	pi*p*er
	ck	pa*ck*er		pp	su*pp*er
	ch	*ch*asm	r	r	*r*ain
	qu	opa*qu*e		rr	hu*rr*y
s	s	*s*it		wr	*wr*eck
	ss	pa*ss*er		rh	*rh*etoric
	c	*c*ity	s	sh	*sh*ip
	ps	*ps*alm		s	*s*ure
c	ch	*ch*ip		ci	spe*ci*ous
	c	*c*ello		ce	o*ce*an
d	d	*d*oll		ss	pa*ss*ion
f	f	hei*f*er		ti	na*ti*on
	ff	cu*ff*	t	t	hi*t*
	ph	*ph*oto		tt	si*tt*er
	gh	rou*gh*		pt	recei*pt*
g	g	ti*g*er		bt	de*bt*or
	gh	*gh*etto	θ	th	pa*th*
	gg	bi*gg*er	ð	th	*th*en
j	g	*g*ym	v	v	wa*v*e
	j	*j*ump	w	w	*w*ork
	dg	le*dg*er	ks	x	bo*x*
h	h	*h*ouse	y	y	Saw*y*er
	wh	*wh*o	z	z	bla*z*er
l	l	meta*l*		s	lo*s*er
	l	fi*ll*ing		zz	no*zz*le
m	m	*m*an	ž	z	a*z*ure
	mb	co*mb*er		s	mea*s*ure
	mm	su*mm*er		si	delu*si*on
n	n	*n*ight			
	nn	si*nn*er			
	gn	*gn*aw			
	kn	*kn*it			

phoneme relationships common in English usage. The vowel grapheme-phoneme relationships are more complex and Figure 8-2 provides a relationship between long and short vowels and their corresponding grapheme-phoneme relationships.

Figure 8-2   Grapheme—Phoneme Vowel Configurations

Vowel		Sample	Vowel		Sample
ă	a	*a*pple	ī	i.e	b*i*te
ā	a	l*a*te		uy	b*uy*
	ai	b*ai*t		ie	fl*ie*s
	ea	br*ea*k		ai	*ai*sle
	ei	r*ei*n	ŏ	o	h*o*t
ĕ	e	m*e*n	ō	o.e	h*o*me
	ea	h*ea*d		oa	b*oa*t
	eo	l*eo*pard		ow	sh*ow*
	ai	s*ai*d		o	g*o*
	ie	fr*ie*nd		ew	s*ew*
ē	e.e	P*e*te	ŭ	u	b*u*s
	e	b*e*		oo	bl*oo*d
	ea	b*ea*t	ū	ou	en*ou*gh
	ee	b*ee*t		u.e	m*u*le
	ei	rec*ei*ve		ew	f*ew*
	ie	bel*ie*f			
ĭ	i	b*i*t			
	ui	b*ui*ld			
	y	h*y*mn			
	u	b*u*sy			

Syllables include an understanding of compound words, prefixes, suffixes, and root words. Syllables are those meaningful units of language that are composed of phonemes and which allow for changes to be made in the structure of words. In this sense, morphemes and syllables can be considered synonymous in their meaning. Phonemes and morphemes are discussed in Chapter 9 of this text in more detail.

Spelling Rules. The use of forming grapheme-phoneme combinations as well as syllables in analyzing the structure of a word is based on several common rules. Before discussing these rules it must be stated that the literature contains a great deal of controversy concerning the rules, and the research appears not very definitive because of the inconsistencies found throughout the English language. The rules reported below seem to appear most consistently in the spelling literature and are reported here as representing those rules that are most commonly accepted. The list is not conclusive, and the reader is referred to the bibliographic section at the end of this chapter for more detailed references to these rules. The rules will be discussed in terms of developing an understanding of grapheme-phoneme relationships for long and short vowels, consonants, and consonant-blends. These rules are discussed by Ruddell (1974) and have been found by the author to be representative of other professionals in the area of spelling, including Hildreth, 1955; Hanna, Hanna, Hodge, and Rudorf, 1966; Hanna, Hodges, and Hanna, 1971; Horn, 1954; and others. The rules include the following.

1. A long vowel sound is made when the vowel is followed by a consonant and a final "e"—like, bike.
2. The long vowel sound is given when it is followed by a consonant which is followed by "l" or "r"—zebra.
3. A long vowel sound is given at the end of a short word with an open syllable—go.
4. Short vowel sounds are usually found when only a single vowel is found at the beginning or in the medial position of a word—bed, egg.
5. The short vowel sound is given when it is found before a consonant group such as "pp" or "dd"—saddle, supper.
6. Long and short vowel sounds are sometimes spelled with a "y"— very—while the long "i" sound is also spelled with a "y"—sky; "a" is sometimes spelled "ay"—hay, say, lay—while the long "o" sound is spelled "ow" in some words—slow.

Consonants and their grapheme-phoneme relationships are, as has been stated, somewhat more consistent than vowels. A review of Figure 8-1 should be helpful in making an analysis in developing an understanding of the consonant sound symbol relationships. However, some consonants and consonant blends are governed by rules. These include the following:

1. The letter "c" has an "s" sound when followed by an "e," "i," or "y"—city, ice—and a "k" sound in other letter patterns—cut, come.
2. The letter "g" represents the letter "j" sound when followed by the letters "e," "i," or "y"—gym, gem.
3. Words spelled with the "ph" consonant digraph and pronounced "f" are usually constructed of a vowel following that initial consonant digraph—pheasant, phantom. Also the "f" sound is provided

or is given when the consonant digraph "ph" follows an "s"— sphere.

Other common rules include:

1. Plurals are formed in most nouns by adding "s" to the singular— cat, cats.
2. If a noun ends in "s," "sh," "x," or "ch," a plural is formed by adding "es"—buses, churches, boxes.
3. A noun ending in "y" but preceded by a consonant is changed to a plural by dropping the "y" and adding "ies"—lady, ladies.
4. Words that end in "y" with the "y" being preceded by a vowel, do not change—boy, boys.
5. The letter "i" is followed by "e" except after "c"; exceptions to the rule are either and neither.

Phonic and Structural Analyses. Hunt, Hadsell, Hannum, and Johnson (1963) indicate that spelling is affected by the child's ability to make a phonic as well as a structural analysis of words. In other words, the phonemes as well as the roots, prefixes, and suffixes of words and the rules that govern each must be understood and applied in the spelling task. *Phonic analysis* requires an understanding of the rules for vowels and consonants discussed above. In doing a phonic analysis, the silent letters contained within a word must be identified. This will help in determining long and short vowel sounds. The syllables that comprise a word should be identified and the vowel or vowel-like sounds contained within each should be determined. The consonants "c," "g," or "s" must be considered to determine whether they are hard or soft sounds. In *structural analysis*, the word has to be analyzed in terms of whether it is a compound word or a root word being used to form the word. Prefixes and suffixes are then analyzed. Finally, the letters within the word are identified, and the syllables of the word broken down and set apart.

Spelling Errors. Horn (1954) indicates that spelling errors are made more frequently on familiar rather than strange words. The literature on spelling identifies a number of common spelling errors. An attempt has been made to summarize these in the following discussion. These errors appear to be those that most commonly occur in the spelling performance of children:

1. Errors involving vowels usually include the silent vowel rules and vowels represented by different symbols—"ai," "ay," and "eigh."
2. common reversals of "ei" for "ie" and errors with the application of diphthongs, such as "ai," "ay," "oi," and "ow"
3. Errors related to the different consonant sounds that can be given by "c," "g," and "s"—"sity" for city
4. reversals of digraphs and blends
5. adding additional consonants in words
6. omissions of both initial, medial, and ending sounds
7. substituting words, such as "from" for "form"
8. evidence of not understanding auditory stimuli, which shows up in confusing "b"s for "d"s, "n"s for "m"s, etc.
9. a poor knowledge of spelling demons
10. poor and laborious handwriting
11. evidence that the word was mispronounced or enunciated incorrectly by the child
12. spelling words as they sound and definite evidence that the child has very little grapheme-phoneme understanding.

Figure 8-3 is an illustration of errors that are commonly made by children.

Spelling Demons. There are some words, a great number of them, that do not lend themselves to analysis either in a phonic or structural sense. These are words to which none of the rules discussed previously seem to fit. It appears, however, that more than not the rules discussed above do fit in some way to most all of the words in the English language. There are some words, usually identified as demons, that seem to pose a spelling problem to children. The list in Figure 8-4 contains those that are commonly associated with spelling problems according to grade level. As can be seen from this list, many of the rules discussed previously, if understood, could be applied in correcting the spelling errors. However, some words do not lend themselves to this and must be learned perhaps through rote or repetitive exercise and usage.

Discrepancy Analysis

In order to conduct a discrepancy analysis, a teacher must be aware of what to expect of a child in terms of spelling behaviors.

Figure 8-3   Common Spelling Errors (From Anderson, 1964)

Error	Correct	Problem Description
acurate	accurate	Failure to double the letter
docter	doctor	Variations in word endings
laffing	laughing	Sounds represented by different symbols
horse	hoarse	Meaning not understood
athalete	athlete	Incorrect pronunciation
ate	eight	Meaning not understood
bying	buying	Silent vowel
non	none	Silent vowel—spelling as it sounds
opn	open	Silent (almost) vowel
Wensday	Wednesday	Spelling as it sounds—silent consonant
beyoutey	beauty	Different spellings with same vowel sounds
exampull	example	Sounds represented by different symbols
cents	sense	Meaning not understood
except	accept	Meaning not understood
askt	asked	Spelling exactly as it sounds
berrys	berries	Different spellings with same vowel sounds
dissturb	disturb	Doubling consonants
preevent	prevent	Addition of vowel
acke	ache	Different spellings with same consonant sound
bucher	butcher	Silent consonant
allright	all right	Trying an unknown word, unchecked guess

Skills requisite to spelling appropriately include recognizing the letters of the alphabet, being able to hear and distinguish letter sounds of words, and hearing and seeing similarities in word sounds. A child must be able to pronounce words correctly and have some idea of letter sound associations that can be used in alphabetizing and classifying words. These behaviors are usually *pre-spelling skills* and are found in the preschool and first grade activities. Formal spelling is not usually taught until the second grade and continues through the eighth grade; however, many authors (Ruddell, 1974; Horn, 1954; Hunt et al., 1963; and others) point out that formal spelling and the analysis thereof takes place continually throughout the child's school program.

During the *second grade*, the single-letter consonants are taught as well as double-letter consonant sounds such as "th," "ch," and "ng." Children are also introduced in the second grade to long and short vowels, as well as the endings such as "ed" and

Figure 8-4   Spelling Demons

Primary Grades	Intermediate Grades	Upper Grades (including college)
Across	Answer	Acquaint
Among	Believe	All right
Coming	Dining	Believe
Doesn't	Pleasant	Decision
Don't	Receive	Grammar
Friend	Saturday	Necessary
Getting	Sentence	Occasion
Having	Afraid	Occur
Surprise	All right	Questionnaire
Their	Beginning	Receive
There	Disappoint	Recommend
Woman	Favorite	Studying
	Finally	Their
	Together	There
	Tries	They're
	Till	Tries
	Were	Weather
	We're	Whether
	Sincerely	Writing
	Teachers	
	Shining	
	Shiny	

"er." At the *intermediate grade levels*, plurals and singulars are introduced and the beginning of syllabication is taught. The use of syllabication, prefixes, suffixes, and root words, as well as continual exposure to vowels and consonants and their increasing complexities, are introduced to the intermediate-aged child. The writing, speech, and listening skills of the child are also taken into consideration in determining the maturational readiness of the child to participate successfully in the spelling task. These follow the same maturational levels of development discussed in previous chapters. Being aware of the expected spelling behaviors will allow the teacher to make a better determination as to what the child should be performing in comparison with the child's actual performance.

Formal Methods of Spelling Assessment

As was mentioned at the beginning of this chapter, assessment is usually conducted for two reasons: achievement determination and identification of the child's actual spelling skills. In conducting a formal spelling assessment, achievement can usually be obtained through the application of a standardized test. Figure 8-5 summarizes those tests that are discussed elsewhere in this text that have a spelling subtest resulting in an achievement test score for spelling. With the exception of the Wide Range Achievement Test (WRAT) (Jastak and Jastak, 1966), the tests mentioned in Figure 8-5 require the child to select an appropriately spelled word from a list of misspelled words (for example, Paly, Play, Plai, Pay). The WRAT requires the child to listen to a word and then, from that dictation, write the word. This dictated approach allows for a more thorough analysis of the child's spelling difficulties. However, in the case of all the achievement tests and the result of the achievement score, little diagnostic help as to the child's spelling difficulties can be determined. It is only through an analysis of the child's actual spelling performance that specific areas of difficulty can be identified for instructional purposes. So, the normative data available from each of these tests should be carefully reviewed and a determination made as to their relative validity and reliability (much of the reliability and validity information is available in the discussion of each of the tests found in different chapters of this text) and especially so when the validity of the test data is in question. All of the tests mentioned and most of those that are available to measure achievement have been validated through an analysis of the content. The teacher is, therefore, encouraged to become acquainted with the reliability and validity data available on each of the tests mentioned to determine if the achievement score obtained by the child in spelling is an accurate measure of how the child performs in relationship to normative group to which the score is being compared.

There are few tests designed specifically for the diagnosis of spelling difficulties. However, two that the author feels are representative of those that are available include the Webster Diagnostic Spelling Test (1978) and the Test of Written Spelling (Larsen and Hammill, 1976). The Webster Diagnostic Spelling Test is a

Figure 8-5 Tests for Use in Generating a Standardized Achievement Spelling Score

---

Peabody Individual Achievement Test (PIAT)
Wide Range Achievement Test (WRAT)
Metropolitan Achievement Test (MAT)
Stanford Achievement Test (SAT)
Iowa Test of Basic Skills (ITBS)

---

test to assess the child's spelling abilities from grades two through eight. The test is designed to assess phonic and structural analysis skills, to determine the child's understanding of long and short vowels, to assess the final "y" and the "c," "g," and "s" sounds, and to determine understanding of suffixes, prefixes, root words, and compound words. The test score obtained by the child can then be applied to a graph to determine percentile ranking for the individual child in relation to grade level. The Test of Written Spelling is a test that analyzes the child's written spelling performance from a dictated word list. The words are then analyzed to determine types of errors made by the child. The test is primarily designed to generate an estimate of the child's spelling ability or level that can be helpful in assisting the teacher in identifying specific spelling deficiencies.

Informal Assessment of Spelling

Perhaps the best tool available to the teacher in assessing spelling performance is the teacher's understanding of the spelling task. If the intent of the teacher is to determine the child's spelling difficulties for helping in the development or selection of instructional spelling programs, then a child's performance must be analyzed in terms of the spelling behaviors, concepts, and rules mentioned earlier and throughout this chapter. The rules governing vowels, consonants, and syllables must be understood. The teacher must also have some idea as to the approximate time when these concepts, from their simple to complex development, are understood by the child. With this information a more thorough assessment of the child's spelling performance can be made, an assessment that will result in a more direct application in instructional planning for the child.

An *informal spelling inventory* (ISI) can be constructed by the teacher to assist in diagnosing spelling behaviors of children. An ISI can be designed to specifically assess areas of interest (vowels, syllables, and the like) or to observe the occurrence of specific spelling errors. Moran (1978) outlines an eight-step procedure for conducting an informal assessment of spelling behaviors. The procedure includes the following.

1. Select 20 words which have been read successfully on the informal reading inventory. Words should be selected from the independent reading level, if it has been established. If not, items can be drawn from the words recognized correctly at the instructional reading level.

2. Selection should be made so that a variety of initial and final consonants, blends, and vowel combinations are represented. A balance also should be sought between words which are phonetic for spelling and those which contain silent consonants or diphthongs. Approximately half the words selected should be those which are irregular in spelling or exceptions to spelling generalizations.

3. Pronounce each word orally and ask the student to write it spontaneously to your dictation. Place each word in a brief sentence so it has meaning for the student and possible homonyms are controlled. Repeat the stimulus word after reading the sentence.

4. As soon as the list of spelling words has been written, ask the student to check his or her own production as you reread the stimulus words. Allow the student to make any spontaneous corrections by writing the word a second time immediately beside the first attempt. Offer no assistance during this self-correction.

5. Check the student's written production immediately. Ask him or her to spell orally any words misspelled in writing. Write the oral spelling beside the attempted spelling on the paper.

6. Print any stimulus words not spelled correctly, either in writing or orally, on 3″ x 5″ index cards. Print three distractor cards for each word, providing a minimal contrast by varying only a single letter or at the most two letters from the correct spelling of the stimulus word.

7. Spread out the four cards for each stimulus word in random fashion. Read the stimulus word aloud and ask the student to point to the correct spelling on one of the four cards.

8. If alphabetizing skills are to be assessed, the distractor cards prepared for the previous step can be presented to examine the student's ability to arrange four cards on the basis of second, third, or fourth letters in the word.

Figure 8-6   Errors for Consideration in Constructing the ISI

Vowels

1. Silent vowels
2. Vowels represented by different symbols—eight, ai, ay
3. Reversals—"ie" for "ei"
4. Different sounds of same letter combinations—"ow," "oo"
    Bread   Wheat
5. Different spellings with same vowel sounds—
    Chief   Feast   Feeling
6. Diphthongs such as oi, oy, ow, ai, and ay

Consonants

1. Silent consonants
2. Doubling of consonants in some words and not in others
3. Sounds represented by different symbols—
    f, gh, ph; "celect" for "select"
4. Reversals—"garde" for "grade"

Careless

1. Poor handwriting
2. Omit letters and syllables
3. Addition of letters and syllables
4. Double wrong letter—speel for spell
5. Slips or accidental
    a. Errors from copying ending of word above
    b. Errors from including syllable from word to follow
    c. Errors from continuing dominant element of preceding word—"th Theeth" for "the teeth"

Miscellaneous

1. Trying an unknown word—unchecked guess
2. Poor pronunciation and enunciation on the part of the pupil *and* teacher
3. Spelling as it sounds
4. Meaning not understood—two, too, to
5. Poor auditory perception
6. Poor visual perception
7. Read mistakes due to wrong knowledge
8. Suffixes and prefixes (more trouble than root words)
9. Variations in word endings—le, el, al
10. Lack of ability to associate letters with sounds—aspel for weigh   elnust for running   eanut for receive

As mentioned earlier, the ISI should be constructed in anticipation of the types of errors a child will make. Figure 8-6 is a list of errors that should be considered in constructing an informal spelling assessment. This is an example of the type of checklist that can be developed by having a knowledge and understanding of the expected error patterns discussed in earlier sections of this chapter.

Preventing Spelling Problems

With spelling, as in perhaps most all achievement areas, many problems could be prevented through better instruction. Helping the child understand some simple rules or suggestions may go a long way in preventing spelling problems. Figure 8-7 illustrates ways in which the child can be assisted in making a structural and phonic analysis as well as other ways in which spelling failure can be prevented.

Figure 8-7   Phonic and Structural Analysis (From *Elementary English,* 1965)

Phonic Analysis
1. What other words can I write that sound like this word?
2. What other words can I write that begin like this word? End like this word?
3. What silent letters are contained in the word?
4. Which syllable is accented?
5. Do the vowels have long or short sounds?
6. Can I pronounce the word correctly?
7. If the consonants c, g, or s appear in the word, do they have a hard or a soft sound?
8. Does the word contain a sound that might be spelled in more than one way (e.g., phone; near)?

Structural Analysis
1. Is this a root word for formation of other words? If so, write the new words.
2. Is there a root word in the new word?
3. What is the prefix, if any, in this word? Can other prefixes be added?
4. What is the suffix, if any, in this word? Can other suffixes be added?
5. Can this word be made plural?
6. Are there any small words in this word?
7. Is this a compound word?

Figure 8-7   Phonic and Structural Analysis (From *Elementary English,* 1965) (*Continued*)

Structural Analysis

8. Is a new word formed by spelling this word backwards?
9. Can I arrange these words alphabetically?
10. Can I write this word correctly several times?
11. Does this word begin with a small or with a capital letter?
12. How does this word look in configuration?
13. Does the word contain any double letters?
14. Is this word a contraction?
15. Can I write the syllables for this word?

Meaning

1. What is the dictionary definition for the word? Does the word have more than one meaning?
2. What are some good synonyms for the word?
3. What are some good antonyms for the word?
4. Does the word have a homonym?
5. Is this an action word (verb)?
6. Is this a telling word (noun)?
7. Is this a describing word (adjective)?
8. Can this word be used in more than one of the ways stated above in 5, 6, or 7?
9. Can I find a picture to illustrate the word?
10. Can I find pictures to illustrate the plural of the word?
11. Which of the words appear in current events articles I have recently read or am now reading?
12. Which words appear in my other texts, reference books, and story books I am now studying?
13. If this word can be dramatized, can I do so?
14. Can I illustrate the word through art?

Usage

1. What good article can I write for the class or school newspaper using this word and others on the list?
2. Am I spelling this word correctly in my other school work?
3. Do I understand the word and synonyms, antonyms, and homonyms well enough to use them in my speech and writing?
4. What story, poem, announcement, report, letter, or instruction can I write using this word and others on the list?
5. Keep a spelling notebook in which examples of the usage of words —stories, sentences, poems, clippings from current events material, etc.—are kept.
6. Can I make a crossword puzzle using this word and others on the list?

Further, the teacher should be equipped to answer the following questions that will be helpful in assisting the child in having a successful spelling experience.

1. What are the aims of the spelling program? The answer to this should at least include the child becoming more proficient in spelling, as well as having a good feeling about the spelling task.

2. Does the child have the necessary spelling skills to complete the spelling task successfully? The answer to this should involve the teacher analyzing the child's visual and auditory acuity, fine motor abilities, as well as visual and auditory perception of words, letters, and sounds.

3. Does the child understand words in terms of the component parts, phonemes and graphemes representing the distinct sounds, and can the child enunciate and pronounce those sounds appropriately?

4. As the child gets older, an understanding of prefixes, suffixes, and compound words must also be determined. Is the child's understanding at an appropriate level?

5. How should spelling be taught to the child? The answer to this should at least involve a multisensory approach, where the child hears, sees, and spells the word. There should be constant feedback on the correctness and incorrectness of a word, with an emphasis on self-correction through application of the spelling rules. The child should be encouraged to apply spelling rules.

6. Should words be taught phonically or through other methods? As indicated earlier, a good number (over 85%) of all words in the English language lend themselves to the use of the spelling rules, which can therefore be used in learning how to spell a majority of the words. However, because there are a number (approximately 15%) that do not lend themselves in any way to those rules, phonic or structural, other methods such as rote memorization will have to be employed in teaching the child to spell the words.

7. In constructing an informal assessment of spelling, what word list can be used? The answer to this question is best found by an analysis of the instructional program being used. If the program is composed of a standardized word list, this can then be used in identifying words for spelling instruction. Also, all the major publishers of reading and spelling materials provide a word list that is usually broken down into age- or grade-level increments. A teacher wishing to assess third grade spelling ability using an informal assessment approach could select words from one of these scope sequence charts. Further, a number of word lists, such as the Dolch, Ayers, Thorndike, and Fitzgerald, are available for determining which words are commonly used in the English language. These word lists are also broken down into age and grade level increments.

In summary, any preventive program should be based upon success. The child must experience success in the instructional program. Success in many cases should be based upon the performance capabilities of the child. The performance capabilities can be determined only after a thorough application of the assessment procedures mentioned throughout this chapter. Guessing at what the child is capable of doing may not be a very productive means of helping the child to become a better speller.

Can You Answer These Questions?

1. What are the important skills required of the child to complete a spelling task successfully?
2. What skills must the teacher possess to assess the spelling behavior of children?
3. Can you identify and define the components of a spelling assessment?
4. What are spelling demons?
5. Can you name two rules for using long vowels and two rules for short vowels?
6. What are some formal spelling measures?
5. Rules for long vowels would include:
    a. a long vowel sound is given when the vowel is followed by a consonant and a final "e" such as in "bike";
    b. a long vowel sound is given at the end of a short word with an open syllable, such as "so."
    Rules for short vowels would include:
    a. a short vowel sound is given when only a single vowel is found in the beginning or medial position of a word: "bed," "bid," "egg";
    b. the short vowel sound is also given if the vowel is found before a consonant group such as "supper," "battle," and "apple."
6. Formal spelling test measures would include those that result in a norm-referenced or standardized spelling score. These would include the Wide-Range Achievement Test (Jastak, and Jastak, 1966) and the Peabody Individual Achievement Test (Dunn and Markwardt, 1970). Specifically designed tests of spelling would include the Webster Diagnostic Spelling

Test (1978) and the Test of Written Spelling (Larson and Hammill, 1976).

References

Anderson, P. S. *Language Skills in Elementary Education.* New York: Macmillan, 1964.

Dunn, L. M., and Markwardt, F. C. *Peabody individual achievement test.* Circle Pines, Minn.: American Guidance Service, 1970.

Hanna, P. R., J. S. Hanna, R. E. Hodge, and E. H. Rudorf. *Phoneme-Grapheme Correspondences as Cues to Spelling Improvement.* OE-32008. Washington, D.C.: Department of Health, Education and Welfare, 1966.

Hanna, P. R., R. Hodges, and J. S. Hanna. *Spelling: Structure and Strategies.* Boston: Houghton Mifflin, 1971.

Hildreth, G. *Teaching Spelling: A Guide to Basic Principles and Practices.* New York: Holt, Rinehart and Winston, 1955.

Horn, T. *Spelling Instruction—A Curriculum-Wide Approach.* Austin, Texas: University of Texas, 1954.

Hunt, B., A. Hadsell, J. Hannum, and H. W. Johnson. The Elements of Spelling Ability. *Elementary School Journal,* 1963, 63, 342–349.

Jastak, J. F., and S. R. Jastak. *Wide Range Achievement Test.* Wilmington, Delaware: Guidance Associates, 1965.

Larsen, S. C., and D. D. Hammill. *Test of Written Spelling.* Austin, Texas: Empiric Press, 1976.

Moran, M. R. "The teachers role in referral for testing and interpretation of reports." *Focus on Exceptional Children,* 1976, 8 1–15.

Ruddell, R. B. *Reading Language Instruction: Innovative Practices.* Englewood Cliffs, New Jersey: Prentice-Hall, 1974.

Webster Diagnostic Spelling Test. St. Louis, Missouri: Webster Division, McGraw-Hill, 1978.

chapter

Language Assessment

Objectives

At the conclusion of this chapter, the reader should be able to:

1. define and discuss the components of oral language assessment to include phonology, morphology, syntax, semantics, and vocabulary;
2. define and discuss the components of written language assessment to include grammar, punctuation, capitalization, and handwriting;
3. specify formal and informal assessment devices and techniques for use in conducting oral or written language assessment;
4. outline behaviors in oral and written language expected of children within specified grade levels;
5. outline procedures to be followed in conducting a language assessment.

Introduction

Language can be simply defined as a system of verbal and written symbols that are uniquely used by human beings in communicating information, thoughts, ideas, and feelings. This language system is the basis from which all knowledge is generated, defined, transmitted, and measured. Without an adequate language base or a language experience that involves the ability to speak or utilize that symbolic system, the child will experience difficulty in almost every aspect of the school world. Oral and written language systems are the foundation of our present educational systems and, as such, should be more thoroughly understood by all those involved in the educational process.

Understanding Oral Language

Major components of the oral language system include phonology, morphology, syntax, semantics, and vocabulary. *Phonology* is the study of sounds and the composite use of those sounds in producing words and sentences. The study of sounds and their meaning begins with an awareness of *phonemes* which are the specific sounds from which individual words can be constructed. A phoneme is the minimal sound unit for achieving meaning (Ruddell, 1974). By themselves, phonemes may not have meaning; however, in combination with other phonemes they produce words with meanings.

It is suggested from the research that the child of 4 to 5 years of age should have mastered a majority of the phonemes used in the English language (Ervin-Tripp and Miller, 1963; Ruddell, 1974). The individual production of phonemes is at the heart of normal language development. Inability to perceive and produce phonemes will impair not only the acquisition but the use of functional language for adequately communicating. Phonemes are considered, in part, to be vowels and consonants, as well as corresponding roughly to the letters of the alphabet (Brown, 1965).

Syntax refers to how words are arranged to produce meaning with that meaning being transmitted in the form of phrases or sentences. Syntax, or word order, has changed considerably over time. What was once considered proper syntax in old English would not be considered proper today. What is proper today will perhaps not be considered proper in the future. An important concept in understanding syntax is that words must be ordered in phrases or sentences to be meaningful.

Semantics refers simply to the meaning of words, phrases, and sentences. Word meanings have a great deal of variability owing to the attitudes, beliefs, and events within the multiplicity of cultures comprising America. This variability should be considered when evaluating a child's semantic performance in relationship to the educational task. The meaning of a word used by a child from one cultural background when compared to the meaning of the same word of a child from a different cultural heritage may not even be related. For example, Dexter (1978) identifies the word *ramp* as an illustration of differences in cultural understanding. Ramp, as used by a particular cultural group in eastern America, has more of a meaning related to the virtues of a wild vegetable, whereas the expected or most common meaning of the word may be that of a road structure. The meanings or semantics of words, phrases, and sentences is continually changing and is drastically variable within not only the American culture but other cultures as well. Meanings of words are not consistent across cultures or even among individuals. Due to this variability, the teacher will be wise to become informed of the word patterns and meanings characteristic of the school environment in which that teacher is placed.

Morphology is a study of the units of language called *morphemes*. A morpheme is the smallest meaningful unit of language which represents something in the real world or in the mind of speaker or listener. Morphemes can be characterized as free or bound. A free morpheme is a word that communicates meaning independently of any other morpheme—for example, "boy." A bound morpheme must be combined with a free morpheme to produce a meaningful unit of language. For example, combining "s" with boy produces the plural morpheme "boys" (Ruddell, 1974).

Vocabulary can be defined as those words that are understood and produced either in written form or orally. Vocabulary is most commonly thought of in terms of a speaking or hearing vocabulary; but it is also characterized by an individual's ability to read or write words with understanding and meaning.

Assessing Oral Language

The assessment of a child's oral language capabilities is dependent upon the teacher having an understanding of a number of critical variables and how these variables relate to the child. The variables include the child's maturational level, physical capabilities, intelligence, emotional capabilities, and environmental background. Each of these provides a basis from which the teacher can determine an expected level of oral language performance.

Maturation is most important, especially in the younger developmental years when the mechanisms for producing speech sounds are being formulated. Knowing the maturational level of the child will give an indication as to the types of sounds the teacher can expect the child to produce. Figure 9-1 provides an illustration of the maturational levels of oral language development that would be expected of children completing a normal growth and development cycle.

Physical capabilities, even though closely related to maturation, in this instance refer to the mechanisms used to receive (eyes and ears) oral language as well as to express (vocal cords, tongue, and the like) verbal communication. Being aware of these mechanisms is important in assessing the child's oral language ability. The child's physical capabilities for communicating orally must be determined. The physical mechanisms that are involved in producing or receiving oral language must be intact or distortions in oral language may occur. For example, a child with inadequate hearing or who has lost a larnyx as a result of injury or disease will have a more obvious difficulty in producing or utilizing oral language. Some physical incapabilities may not be as evident as the examples presented above; however, behaviors expressed by the child, such as inappropriate articulation, enunciation, or evidence of hearing impairment should be clues to the teacher to refer the child to an agency (speech therapist, audiologist, or physician) for an in-depth assessment of the impairment.

Another area, not as obvious as the lack or nonexistence of a physical mechanism, deals with the *neurological processes* that could affect that child's understanding, use, and production of oral language. A common neurological disorder is identified as

Figure 9-1 Language Development in Children

Approximate Age	Language
0–4 Months	Crying differential begins Front vowels k, l, g
4 Months	Cooing and chuckling One syllable sounds
6–12 Months	Babbling—playing with sounds 1. Reflexive sounds (crying) 2. Repeats self (babbling) 3. Repeats others (echolalia)
12–18 Months	A few first words (which are mostly nouns) "mama," "dada" Follows simple commands Responds to "no"
18–21 Months	Vocabulary 20–200 words Points to named objects Comprehends simple questions 2-word phrases
24–27 Months	300–400 words 2–3 word phrases
30–33 Months	Fastest increase in vocabulary (300–1000 words) 3–4 word sentences
36–40 Months	Vocabulary of more than 1500 words Well-formed sentences

childhood aphasia and is characterized by the limited use of speech or an inability to respond to oral language. In a word, the child's expressive or speaking capabilities and receptive or listening capabilities seem to be impaired for reasons other than physical impairment. This inability to respond is associated with dysfunction or damage in the neurological system. The behaviors that usually characterize this disorder include unevenness in the development of the child's language pattern. The child does not appear to develop language at a rate consistent with what would be expected within normal language development (Eisenson and Ogilvie, 1971). The child's overall academic performance is very erratic and uneven. Again, behaviors such as these should be clues to the teacher for requesting additional assistance in diagnosing and remediating the child's oral language difficulties.

Emotional factors may also affect the child's acquisition and functional use of oral language. The child unable to interact comfortably with other individuals on a social or emotional dimension will have a difficult time in developing a sound oral communication system. Children with severe emotional problems, such as autism or schizophrenia, manifest impairment in their oral language system. Patterns of behavior indicative of emotional problems include language that depicts the child as overly obsessive, overly impulsive, overly disordered in what language is used, or, in some cases, language that is perseverative to the point of being nonproductive.

To many professionals in the field, the child's ability to use language is a measure of the child's intellectual capabilities. For example, Macarthy (1960) has indicated that intellectually gifted children have unusually accelerated language development patterns. On the other end of the intellectual continuum, however, the severely retarded individual has a limited vocabulary and very few good language skills.

Environment is another variable in the acquisition and utilization of oral language that must be considered when planning or assessing a child's oral language capabilities. Environment plays a big role in the child's oral language development. This is especially so when making an analysis of the child's semantic and syntactical use of words. An understanding of the child's environmental background is most important in understanding the child's oral language performance; a measurement of performance must be based upon an analysis of the environment. As Ruddell (1974) points out, right or wrong language patterns will be difficult to ascertain in terms of meaningful communication in today's diverse cultural and ethnic world. No language or dialect should be considered better or worse than any other. An assessment of a child's oral language must be based upon an understanding of the dialect or cultural expectations that have been a part of that child's oral language development.

An understanding of the receptive and expressive components of the oral language system is vital to the assessment of the child's oral language capabilities. In making any assessment of oral language, a distinction between these components should be made to further pinpoint the area of greatest difficulty for the child. However, making the distinction between receptive or expressive abilities falls within the same controversial issue as that posed in Chapter 11 on modalities assessment. That is, in attempting to distinguish between receptive or expressive abilities, it is very difficult to ascertain which area may be affecting which area. For example, in a child having difficulty with speaking, is the difficulty a result of an inability to articulate language concepts or the child's inability to receive appropriate information that will later be verbally expressed? It is most difficult to determine or assess if the child's problem rests within receptive or expressive capabilities. The assessment process in this area should continually attempt to sort out this dilemma as it may be most helpful in developing the educational program for the child.

Formal Oral Language Assessment

A number of formal assessment devices can be used in determining the child's oral language capability as well as to assist the teacher in deciding if the child is having difficulty with receptive or expressive language. From the formal devices presented below information can be generated that should be of value to the teacher in determining the child's oral language capability. Some of the tests, by their structure and content, can be construed as being either expressive or receptive. However, no attempt will be made to classify the tests as such and the reader is requested to make a thorough analysis of the test content to determine the most functional use of the results in developing an oral language program for the child. Each of the tests below not only provides a formal assessment of the child's oral language capability, but can be a very good indication of the child's ability for completing school-related tasks involving the language components of phonemes, morphemes, semantics, syntax, and vocabulary. The discussion that follows will mention test results in light of these oral language components.

The Goldman-Fristoe Test of Articulation (Goldman and Fristoe, 1969). This test systematically assesses the articulatory skills of children. It was constructed to be used with distractable or mentally retarded children but can be used with all children to assess articulatory behavior. The test is composed of three subtests: sounds and sentence, sounds and words, and stimulability. The *sounds and words* subtest items include having the child respond to familiar pictures by naming and answering questions concerning each picture. The pictures and questions are used to have the child elicit consonant sounds found in the English language. In the *sounds and sentence* subtest, sound production is assessed by having the child listen to a story that is illustrated with pictures and then having the child recount the story using the pictures as an aid to recalling the story content. Through the child's production of sounds a chronological analysis of the child's understanding and use of sounds can be made. The third subtest, *stimulability*, attempts to measure the child's correct use of phonemes.

The test requires approximately 15 to 20 minutes to administer and score and is suitable for preschool children up to the upper elementary or junior high grades. The test was normed on children ages three to eight years. This assessment device can be appropriately used to determine a child's ability to use phonemes and to assess skills in the area of phonology.

The Templin-Darley Test of Articulation (Templin and Darley, 1960). This test is sometimes considered the standard in the field of articulation testing. It is sometimes described as a *phoneme inventory* comprised of 141 items grouped into 13 phoneme categories. The items assess the child's ability to produce vowels, diphthongs, single consonants, and consonant blends. The test can be administered to children with oral language skills beginning at about the third year of age and up. The test results can be compared to normative tables to give an indication of the child's articulation skills relative to age or grade level expectations. The Templin-Darley provides very specific information that can be used in not only assessing the phoneme skills of the child but the direction to be taken in developing an educational program related to those skills.

Carrow Elicited Language Inventory (Carrow, 1974). This test is a measure of the child's use of *grammar*. The child listens to a number of (fifty-two) sentences and phrases that are read by the teacher. The child is then asked to imitate what has been read. The child's imitations are taped and an analysis is made of the correctness of the imitation. Grammatical usage is then determined through the analysis of the child's imitation. The grammatical forms assessed in this device include the child's use of pronouns, prepositions, conjunctions, articles, adverbs, adjectives, verbs, declaratives, interrogatives, and imperatives. This test also provides a number of specific pieces of information that will assist the teacher in planning instructional strategies to correct a child's grammatical problems.

Northwestern Syntax Screening Test (Lee, 1969). This is an individually administered test designed to screen a child's grammatical usage. The test screens the grammatical structures of negatives, affirmatives, interrogatives, imperatives, and subject-verb agreement. The test is composed of two parts. The first part includes having the child listen to a pair of sentences accompanied by a picture with four distinct drawings, one of which correctly depicts the sentence content the child has just heard. The picture theoretically illustrates the syntactical organization of the sentence. The second part of the screening test is composed of 20 pairs of items that assess the child's ability to produce the grammatical forms. The child listens to a pair of sentences illustrated with a drawing depicting the sentence content. The child is then asked to imitate the sentence. In this way, an analysis of the child's verbal skills in grammar and syntax can be determined.

Information from this screening device is readily applicable to planning and developing instructional strategies to correct a child's syntax or grammatical deficiencies. Even though there are norms available for this screening test, the reliability and validity data are somewhat sketchy. When making normative comparisons, this information should be taken into consideration.

The Developmental Sentence Analysis (Lee, 1974). This test is a comprehensive and relatively thorough analysis of the child's syntactical ability. It is used for assessing a child's use of *grammatical rules*. This assessment is made through an analysis of the child's spontaneous speech that is elicited through a conversation with the examiner. A number of phrases are collected from the child's conversation and then analyzed in terms of grammatical correctness utilizing a procedure to determine the child's use of nouns, subjects, pronouns, plurals, affirmatives, negatives, and other grammatical instructions. Again, this test can provide the teacher with very specific information concerning the child's syntactical abilities and the ability to use and apply grammatical rules. The reliability and validity data are somewhat limited, therefore the application of test results should be done on an individual basis to assess individual skill acquisition and not be used as a comparative measure of how the child is doing in relationship to other children.

The Peabody Picture Vocabulary Test (PPVT) (Dunn, 1965). As the title implies, this test is an attempt to measure the child's *vocabulary* and *understanding of words*. A child is presented with a stimulus word in conjunction with a picture containing four distinct drawings. The child listens to the word and then identifies the picture that best describes that word. The test has been designed to be administered to persons from 2 to 18 years of age. This test has been used as a measure of intelligence and, in fact, was designed to assess an individual's verbal intelligence. From the normative tables available in the administration manual, an individual's raw score can be generated into an *Intelligent Quotient (IQ)* equivalent; however, an IQ score reported from the PPVT may be a misrepresentation of the individual's overall intelligence since in reality it reflects only one aspect of intellectual capacity, that of vocabulary usage or understanding.

The reliability data for this test are of two types. On the alternate form comparison of this test correlation coefficients ranged from .67 to .85, while correlation results from a test-retest procedure ranged from approximately .50 to .90. Validity involved both an analysis of content as well as correlating results of the test with IQs and MAs generated from the Stanford-Binet and Wechsler Scales. These concurrent validity data range from .30 to .92. This test, if used in its most appropriate mode, would provide the teacher with a very good idea of the child's vocabulary usage and understanding. The test is easily administered and therefore could be used as a good screening device for assessing the child's vocabulary.

The Utah Test of Language Development (Meacham, Jex, and Jones, 1967). This test has the expressed intent of assessing expressive and receptive verbal language skills in children. The test involves having the child complete a number of tasks related to sequencing, repeating sentences, digits, copying designs, and naming pictures. Although the test was constructed for use primarily with brain-injured children, it can be used to assess the language skills of any child experiencing difficulty with the processes of language. Perhaps the best use of this test would be through an analysis of the test items and performance of the child in relationship to being able to complete or not to complete those items. From this information the overall picture of the child's language development can be determined and instructional strategies identified. The reliability and validity data available for this test are somewhat vague and it is questionable whether the results could be generalized beyond the limited sample that was used to norm the test. The sample consists primarily of subjects ranging in age from 1 to 14 years who represented a normal population of white children. However, the test content, as mentioned above, can be useful in identifying a child's language difficulties as related to a child's performance of the tasks comprising this test which can be a valuable tool in program planning.

Test of Language Development (Newcomer and Hammill, 1977). This test is a comprehensive measure of the child's language ability. It is comprised of seven subtests designed to measure semantics and syntax skills. The subtests and what they measure include:

1. picture vocabulary, the ability to associate meaning with words;
2. oral vocabulary, the ability to define words;
3. grammatical understanding, the use of grammatical rules;
4. sentence imitation, the ability to reproduce correctly a sentence;
5. grammatical completion, the ability to comprehend and utilize syntax;
6. phonological, understanding of sounds;
7. word articulation, word arrangement.

This test can be a valuable tool to the classroom teacher in that it provides a comprehensive analysis of language development. Specific test items from each of the subtests and supplementary tests can provide very specific information as to the child's language difficulties and can be used for clues as to what the instructional strategy should be in correcting those identified deficiencies.

Illinois Test of Psycho-linguistic Abilities (Kirk et al., 1968). This test is an individually administered device for use with children between the ages of two years four months and ten years three months. It was designed to assess the child's verbal and nonverbal communication skills. The test is composed of 12 subtests, ten primary and two supplementary. These tests can be divided into three areas of communication assessment including, understanding, processing, and producing communication. A grouping of the 12 tests into these three areas follows:

1. Understanding communications
   a. Auditory reception. This subtest measures the child's vocabulary by having the child respond either yes or no to questions presented. For example, "Do hatchets chop?" "Do airplanes fly?"
   b. Visual reception. The child first views a single visual stimulus—for example, a picture of a boy running. The stimulus card is then removed and another visual stimulus is presented with four pictures, one of which corresponds to the previously viewed stimulus. In this example, on the stimulus card depicting the four pictures can be found a picture of a girl running, with no other picture of the four depicting a child running.
2. Processing communications
   a. Auditory association. This test is designed to measure the child's ability to complete verbal analogies. For example, if "grass is green, sugar is _____." The child must complete the analogy correctly. In this case, sugar is "white."
   b. Visual association. This is a measure of the child's ability to complete visual analogies. For example, the child is shown a stimulus of a pistol and holster and is instructed that these two pictures are related. Simultaneously with the picture of the pistol and holster the child is presented with a group of five pictures, with one picture arranged in the middle of four surrounding pictures. One of the four surrounding pictures depicts a relationship with the center picture that corresponds to the same relationship as the pistol and holster. In this case, the child is shown a picture of an envelope that would corre-

spond to the holster. The surrounding pictures include only one that would correspond to the same function that the pistol has, which in this example is a letter. The letter is inserted into the envelope much as the pistol is inserted into the holster.

c. Auditory closure. This supplementary test assesses the child's ability to complete words with missing syllables or letters. For example, the child is presented with the auditory stimulus of "__anta __aus." From this the child is to close the words into "Santa Claus."

d. Visual closure. This is a measure of the child's ability, when given a partial visual stimulus, to complete and make a whole item.

e. Grammatic closure. This test measures the child's ability to supply or to use grammatical forms correctly.

f. Auditory sequential memory. This test assesses the child's ability to reproduce a sequence of digits that has been presented auditorily.

g. Visual sequential memory. This is a test of the child's ability to produce a sequence of meaningless visual stimuli.

3. Producing Communication

a. Verbal expression. This test requires the child to describe a series of objects. The child's description is then written down and analyzed in terms of content. This task can also be used to determine the quality of the child's verbal expression in terms of grammatical understanding and usage.

b. Manual expression. This subtest is designed to measure the child's understanding of the use of specific objects. The child is provided with a visual stimulus of an object and then is asked to demonstrate how the object would be used. The child's response is observed and analyzed according to specifically identified behaviors necessary to complete this particular task.

The ITPA is used to determine a child's overall communication skills, both verbal and nonverbal. This requires the teacher to know and understand the content of the test and specific test items that relate directly to the classroom performance behaviors expected in the class. The normative data available on this test, including those data reported for reliability and validity, are somewhat inadequate. Validity data are lacking while the reliability data are at best questionable. The results from this test should be used in the assessment of a child's individual language abilities as measured by each of the subtests presented and that individual assessment should be based upon an interpretation of performance in relationship to test items. To use the normative data for comparative purposes, one child to another, would be questionable. However, the author feels that a great deal of good information can be generated from the test in attempting to assess the child's language capabilities as well as the direction that should be taken in remediating or planning instructional strategies to correct those language deficiencies.

Informal Assessment of Oral Language

At the heart of *informal assessment* of oral language can be found a very complete and thorough understanding of the oral language tasks that should be completed. A teacher wishing to assess the child's oral language ability must be able to determine what those abilities are and should be for the particular child that is to be assessed. If the tasks are understood, a more definite answer as to what language disorders the child is having can be determined. The elements in an informal assessment involve an understanding of the components of each of the oral language tasks and the expected level of development for a particular age or developmental level on the part of the learner. On the one hand, age or expectancy of performance must be determined and then each of the oral language components and the tasks comprising each component determined. Figure 9-2 illustrates this initial step in conducting an informal assessment. The illustration displays an age or expectancy level of six to seven years of age while the components of the oral language under consideration have been identified, in this case phonology, vocabulary, and syntax and each of the subcomponents of interest to the teacher is then identified. Under phonology is found vowels and consonants. Vocabulary acts as its own subcomponent. Syntax is broken down into nouns, pronouns, and verbs. Figure 9-2 is not inclusive of ev-

Figure 9-2 Grade Level Oral Language Expectations. (Most of the oral language components identified in this figure are well founded by the first grade).

Grade Level Expectancy	Phonemes		Vocabulary	Syntax		
	Vowels	Consonants		Nouns	Pronouns	Verbs
First	The child has mastered most of the consonants and vowel sounds and is now in a position to be taught their usage in the overall structure of language.		Over 2,500 words with good usage.	Most all parts of speech are correctly used (nouns, pronouns, verbs) and the child is now in a position to be taught formally how these concepts are used in the language.		
Second	Teaching the Sounds: *Vowels* Short a, e, i, o, u Long a, e, i, o, u	*Consonants* r, s, t, d, b, d, f, g, h, k, l, m, n	Speaking vocabulary is over 4,000 words. Fluent usage of the language.			
Third	Teaching the following words and consonants: *Vowels* Long i sound in fly.	*Consonants* j, y, qu, ck	Use of words increasing in size and complexity.	Correct or cultural usage of nouns, pronouns and verbs with sophistication developing with continual practice.		

erything that may be assessed in terms of oral language but it is an indication of what might be of concern to the teacher.

The teacher, in order to construct an informal assessment, must know the component parts of oral language. These include at least an understanding of phonemes, syntax, semantics, morphemes, and vocabulary and then an idea of the subcomponents of each of these. For example, phonemes might include vowels, consonants, digraphs, and blends. The next item of concern in constructing the informal assessment would be an understanding of the age level or sequence of development in which these items should or do occur. After the expectancy level and individual tasks have been identified, it becomes a matter of determining how best to assess the actual performance level of the child for each of these tasks. Should it be in the form of a checklist? That is, a checklist of expected behaviors that is completed through analyzing a sample of the child's oral language? The sample can be taken with a tape recorder or in an individual session with the child. Figure 9-3 provides a sample checklist of vowels and consonants expected of children. Through an analysis of the child's actual oral language behavior, it can be determined what deficiencies the child has.

Informal assessment is under the control of the classroom teacher and can therefore be constructed on the basis of the interests and concerns of the teacher in meeting instructional responsibilities. The development of an informal device can be tailor-made to meet those concerns and specifically directed to the teacher's instructional program needs.

Written Language Assessment

The components of written language to be considered in the following section include grammar, punctuation, and handwriting. Each of these components will be defined and the assessment technique, both formal and informal, discussed. *Grammar* is the manner in which order and structure are given to language to facilitate meaningful communication. Essentially, grammar is composed of the concepts discussed under morphology and syntax. There has been controversy over the value of teaching grammar in that instruction of traditional grammatical rules appears to have little value in teaching children to write or express themselves

Figure 9-3 Checklist of Initial Usage of Phonemes

Vowels	Adequate Usage	Needs Instruction
Long		
ā	——	——
ē	——	——
ī	——	——
ō	——	——
ū	——	——
Short		
ă	——	——
ĕ	——	——
ĭ	——	——
ŏ	——	——
ŭ	——	——
Consonants and Blends		
l	——	——
r	——	——
t	——	——
dr	——	——
bl	——	——
v	——	——
s	——	——
z	——	——
tr	——	——
sw	——	——
sp	——	——

more efficiently, especially if that instruction has been given prior to the sixth year of school. Grammar consists of having an understanding of the usage of nouns, verbs, adjectives, adverbs, conjunctions, prepositions, singular and plural forms, relationships between subjects and verbs, and parts of verbs. Even though it may be questionable to teach formal concepts of grammar to children prior to the sixth or seventh grade, it is vitally important for the teacher to have a grasp of these grammatical concepts in order to make a sound assessment of the child's ability to use those concepts and to assist the child in correcting deficiencies at as early an age as possible.

Punctuation and *capitalization* provide a means in which the organization and structure of language can be made. Through the use of punctuation, written communication finds meaning and can be given direction. The use of periods, commas, apostrophes, colons, exclamation points, question marks, all can be used to assist in the communication of an idea as well as to imply the meaning and intent behind that idea. Capitalization also assists in structuring where thoughts begin and demonstrating or highlighting words of importance. In a word, punctuation and capitalization provide *structure* to written communication.

Handwriting is the structuring, spacing, and legibility of written expression of one's thoughts and ideas. If an individual's thoughts and ideas are well conceived but are poorly recorded with handwriting, those thoughts and ideas may become misunderstood or misinterpreted. Handwriting is one method the individual has for communicating thoughts and ideas. Good handwriting is necessary in the communication of those ideas in making them understood by being easily read. Ruddell (1974) identifies the major goals of handwriting to be (1) to present ideas in a form that can be read by others or by one's self at a later time; (2) to develop fluency in producing legible written forms so as to exhibit thoughts; and (3) to develop speed and legibility in writing, be it for personal or public purposes (p. 256).

Assessing Written Language

A beginning step in the assessment of written language is a determination of the expected levels of performance. For *grammar*, it is necessary that the child have a good verbal or speaking vocabulary and be able to respond appropriately to spoken language. These are prerequisite skills to making an analysis of the child's use of grammar. The child must next be able to:

1. express thoughts in their written form. These are complete thoughts and ideas that are written down by the child and then read and interpreted by someone else. This level of performance usually occurs at approximately the age of 6 or 7.

2. conceive and write more sophisticated ideas as maturation continues.

3. recognize and distinguish between nouns and verbs at about the seventh to eighth year of development.

4. easily grasp the components of a sentence in terms of subject and verb by the ninth and tenth age level of development. At this age the child can begin to formulate and analyze written work to determine if it communicates complete and whole thoughts.

5. have a more sophisticated use of verbs, pronouns, adjectives, adverbs, conjunctions, and prepositions at about age 12. Even though the child may not name each of the items, the child at this age begins to demonstrate functional application and use of these concepts.

The development of *punctuation skills* usually begins with the recognition of the period early in the child's primary grade experience. The question mark is also understood at this time. The use of commas seems to be best understood after about the third grade, while colons, apostrophes, and quotation marks soon follow. What are the expected levels of understanding for each of these punctuation concepts?

1. For the period, the concepts to be learned
   a. are used at the end of a sentence for complete thought;
   b. can be used after an abbreviation, such as a title of a person's position (Dr.), or in the initials of proper names (C. F. Jones).

2. The question mark has two usual functions, one at the end of a direct question and two, at the end of a direct question within a sentence. For example, "Are you going?" the teacher asked.

3. Commas are a more difficult concept to learn in determining what is the accepted level of usage. Anderson (1964) points out that in some books there are still hundreds of rules for comma usage. He delineates 11 which are summarized below. Commas are used:
   a. to separate parts of the date and day of the year—September 25, 1980.
   b. to separate a city from a state—San Antonio, Texas,
   c. after a salutation in a letter—Dear Mom,
   d. after the close of a letter—Yours truly,
   e. to set off short, direct quotations—"Let's go," requested the children.
   f. after clauses in an introduction

    g. between parts of a compound sentence joined by a short conjunction—JoAnne assisted Jilleen, and Erin was helped by Danielle.

    h. before and after appositives—The department chairman, Dr. Gale, talked to the graduate students.

    i. before and after parenthetical expressions

    j. before and after a nonrestrictive clause

    k. of course, to separate words in a series.

4. An apostrophe is usually used to show possession (Paul's book), to show contractions (wouldn't for would not), to illustrate plurals for figures and letters (all the a's and all number 2's).

5. The use of the colon is primarily to set apart a long series of items (Mary has a number of jobs including: secretary, teacher, cub scout leader, and president of the PTA). The colon is used to separate hours from minutes (4:30 p.m.), after the greeting in a business letter, and to denote examples.

6. Quotation marks are used to indicate the direct quote and should enclose that quote entirely, including its punctuation. Quotation marks are also used to set apart the title of a story or article.

7. The expected usage of *capitalization* can be summarized as follows. Capitals are used at the beginning of a sentence, for proper names, for months, holidays, streets, states, schools, the first and last words of a title of a story or book and certain parts of speech of the title, the first word in the greeting and closing of a letter, and references to deity.

Handwriting is dependent upon good fine motor and eye-hand coordination. The child must be maturationally capable of completing the handwriting taks. This involves the following.

1. Understanding the physical readiness of the child and the age at which the child is maturationally ready to hold and grasp a pencil and has developed eye-hand coordination skills necessary for completing this task.

2. The next stage of handwriting begins at approximately the sixth year of development when the child usually begins to form manuscript letters.

3. A transition period follows which occurs at approximately the seventh and eighth years of age or second and third grade in which the child begins to transfer from manuscript to cursive writing.
4. At the succeeding levels of development, the child is continually in a state of refining handwriting behavior.

Handwriting, to be effective and productive for the child, should begin early and should be based upon the child's interests and maturational capabilities. Successful handwriting will depend upon the child learning the correct position and movements of arm, hand, and eyes. The child must then learn how the letters are formed and how numbers are constructed. Once this is understood, practice to improve is encouraged. It has been indicated that without proper motivation and interest, the child's handwriting appears to deteriorate over time. Therefore the writing task should be one in which constant motivation is provided to improve and produce good, legible written expressions.

Formal Written Language Assessment

The following standardized tests have components specifically designed for assessing grammar, punctuation, and capitalization. The California Achievement Test (CAT) (Tiegs and Clark, 1970) is a norm-referenced general achievement test that is group administered. The test is comprised of many subtests, of which the language mechanics subtest of usage and structure is designed to assess the child's use of grammar, punctuation, and capitalization skills. The test is designed for use in grades 3 through 12. The reliability data for the overall test are quite good. However, the language usage and structure subtest has reliability coefficients ranging from .69 to .83, making it less a measure of normative comparisons and more an analysis of individual skill deficiencies for use in individual program planning. The validity data for this test are vague, and the reader is encouraged to consult the technical bulletin for determining the relative validity of this particular achievement test. As with all norm-referenced devices, the items comprising the test, especially those related to language usage and structure as well as capitalization and punctuation, should be helpful tools to the teacher in deciding the relative efficiency a child has in utilizing these written language components.

The Stanford Achievement Test (SAT) Madden, Gardner, Rudman, Carlson, and Merwin, 1973) is also a group administered, norm-referenced test designed to assess a child's overall academic achievement. However, several of the subtests comprising the Stanford Achievement Test assess the child's understanding of punctuation, capitalization, and grammatical structure. The test can be administered to children between grade levels three through nine. The *word study skills* subtest provides information as to use of consonant blends, digraphs, and vowels. The *language arts* subtest provides information relative to punctuation, capitalization, and grammatical usage. An extensive amount of reliability and validity information is available for this particular test. Overall, the reliability correlation coefficients were found within the .90 range. The validity is again a matter of interpretation and the reader is invited to review both the reliability and validity data available on this test. It must be indicated that most all achievement tests depend upon an analysis of content for determining validity. Therefore, the test items themselves must be scrutinized by the individual user to determine if the information will be valid for making decisions relative to instructional programs.

The Metropolitan Achievement Test (MAT) (Durost, Bixler, Wrightstone, Prescott, and Barlow, 1971) is a norm-referenced, group-administered achievement test that can be used to assess the child's understanding of grammar, punctuation, and capitalization. The test has been designed for use in grades three through nine. The subtest used for language assessment is *language*, which attempts to determine the child's understanding of the rules of punctuation, capitalization, and grammar. Reliability data provided for this test fall within the .90 range, while the validity data again will have to be individually judged by the user. The reader is invited to attend to the technical manuals that can be obtained describing the validity and reliability data for this test.

The Iowa Test of Basic Skills (Hieronymus and Linquist, 1971, 1974) assesses the child's overall achievement in a number of academic areas. It is designed for use with children grades 3 through 8. The *language* subtest from the Iowa Test of Basic Skills is designed specifically to assess the child's use and understanding of capitalization, punctuation, and grammar. The reliability and validity data are comparable to those of other achievement tests previously discussed and the reader is referred to the technical part of the manual (1974) for a more in-depth discussion of these data.

All of the tests presented above can provide the teacher with some very definite and distinct information concerning the child's written language abilities as they relate to punctuation, capitalization, and grammatical usage. It is important in utilizing any of these test data to become familiar with the test items used to assess these written language components. Also, it is suggested that the normative data provided be used only as an indication of strengths and weaknesses in relationship to other children within the same environmental setting as the child being assessed. That is, the test data should be used to complete an *intra-individual* analysis of skill level attainment as opposed to comparing the child with national norms. The teacher should find use of these data in this way to be more functional for program planning.

Informal Assessment Techniques

Informal assessment of the written language components of *punctuation, capitalization,* and *grammar* can be best accomplished by taking the information from expected levels of performance and developing a checklist of the child's acquisition or nonacquisition of those behaviors. Further, if the expected level of achievement is understood, the child can then be assessed as to the relative level of proficiency for each of those written language components. The teacher, in conducting an informal assessment, must be well aware of what grammatical concepts and rules are to be learned and used by the child. This applies equally to the area of punctuation and capitalization.

Figures 9-4 and 9-5 are examples of checklists that have been constructed from the expected levels of achievement in the areas of grammar, punctuation, and capitalization. The teacher should be able to use these as a guide in more specifically delineating the tasks within each of the areas to accommodate his/her needs in assessing and planning instructional programs for written language.

Informal assessment of *handwriting* can be made on the basis of

Figure 9-4 Checklist of Grammar Usage in Written Language

Grade Level Expectancy	Grammar Component	Adequate Usage	Needs Instruction
Sixth	Can the child correctly use verbs?	——	——
	Can the child correctly use pronouns?	——	——
	Can the child correctly use singular and plural nouns?	——	——
	Can the child recognize pronouns?	——	——
	Can the child recognize adjectives?	——	——
	Can the child correctly use adjectives?	——	——
	Can the child correctly use conjunctions?	——	——
	Can the child correctly use prepositions?	——	——
Fifth	Can the child use a simple subject?	——	——
	Can the child use a compound subject?	——	——
	Can the child use a complete subject?	——	——
	Can the child use a simple predicate?	——	——
	Can the child use a compound predicate?	——	——
	Can the child use a complete predicate?	——	——
	Can the child use common and proper nouns?	——	——
	Can the child use singular and plural nouns?	——	——
	Can the child use nouns as subjects?	——	——
	Does the child recognize verbs and nouns?	——	——
Fourth	Does the child recognize nouns?	——	——
	Does the child recognize verbs?	——	——
	Does the child recognize adjectives?	——	——
Third	Does the child recognize nouns?	——	——

***Figure* 9-5**   Checklist of Punctuation and Capitalization

Punctuation	Yes	No
Use of the Period		
In using the period, does the child place it:		
1. At the end of a sentence?	____	____
2. After an abbreviation in titles of persons and things?	____	____
3. After initials in proper names?	____	____
Use of the Comma		
In using the comma, does the child place it:		
1. To separate the words in the series?	____	____
2. To separate the parts of the date and the day of the year?	____	____
3. To set off the name of a city from a state?	____	____
4. After a salutation in a letter?	____	____
5. Before and after appositives?	____	____
6. Between parts of a compound sentence joined by a short conjunction?	____	____
7. After close of a letter?	____	____
8. To set off short direct quotations?	____	____
9. Before and after parenthetical expressions?	____	____
10. Before and after a nonrestrictive clause?	____	____
Capitalization		
Does the child capitalize:		
1. The beginning of a sentence?	____	____
2. Names of months and holidays?	____	____
3. Names of people, pets and initials of people?	____	____
4. First word and important words of a title?	____	____
5. References to deity?	____	____
6. Names of particular streets and schools?	____	____
7. Names of countries, cities, rivers and mountains?	____	____
8. First word in greeting and closing of a letter?	____	____

the child's quality as well as speed in the handwriting task. Good handwriting is based upon the child's having reached the necessary *maturational level* to accommodate the handwriting task. This includes being able to grasp, hold, and manipulate the writing in-

Figure 9-6 Analysis of Handwriting

		OK	Pretty Good	Need More Practice
Slant	Do all letters lean the same way?			
Spacing	Are the spaces between letters and words even?			
Size	Are all small letters small; all tall letters evenly tall?			
Alignment	Do all letters touch the line?			
Loops	Are l, f, h, g, y, k, b well formed?			
Stems	Are down strokes really straight?			
Closings	Are a, d, g, o, p, s closed?			
Roundness	Are m, n, h, u, v, w, y rounded?			
Retraces	Are t, i, d, m, n retraced?			
Endings	Are they without fancy swinging strokes?			
Capitals	Are they well formed and legible?			

strument; to visually discriminate letter forms and words; and to coordinate eye-hand movements. Readiness skills to be considered are:

1. Can the child sit in a writing position?
2. Can the child draw shapes to include triangles, circles, and squares?
3. Can the child print from the left to the right side on the page?

Figure 9-7   Analysis of Cursive Handwriting

Position	**Alignment**
____Incorrect	____Off the line in places
Size	____Uneven in height
____Too large	
____Too small	
____Varying in size	

Line

____Too heavy
____Too light
____Varying
____Kinky (looks slow)

Slant

____Too slanting
____Too nearly vertical
____Irregular

Form

____Angular letters	____Capital letters weak
____Places illegible	____Small letters need strengthening
____Ending strokes poorly made	____Poor figures
____Poor loop letters	

Spacing

____Too scattered (wide)	____Poorly arranged on page
____Crowded	____Margins uneven
____Irregular	

4. Can the child grasp the writing instrument in a three-finger hold near the tip of his pencil?
5. Can the child copy a simple word from the chalkboard correctly?
6. Can the child copy a word correctly when that word is printed on the same piece of paper which he is to copy?

These items are of fundamental consideration in assessing the child's handwriting capabilities.

Once these capabilities have been determined, the next step is to analyze the child's handwriting to determine areas of deficiency. *Legibility* can be determined by looking at the slant and size of letters, word and letter spacing, alignment of letters and words, and the child's posture to include arm and finger movements. Body position and arm and finger movements relate directly to most of the deficiencies in handwriting. For example, too much slant may be due to the child writing with the arm too near the body or the fingers too stiff. The child that is writing too light may be holding the writing instrument too straight or too obliquely or at too much of an angle. Spacing too heavily may be due to the fingers too tightly grasping the writing instrument.

The proper formation, slant, spacing, and size of letters can be readily determined through a number of different commercially made devices, such as those scales produced by Zaner and Bloser (1975). Figures 9-6 and 9-7 are checklists for assisting the teacher in analyzing the child's handwriting abilities as they relate to manuscript and cursive writing.

As was mentioned earlier, good handwriting skills are necessary for expressing thoughts and ideas through the written form. If the handwriting is illegible, the thought that has been illegibly written may be misconstrued or misinterpreted. Therefore, it is important to assist children in developing good handwriting skills.

Summary

This chapter has focused on both oral and written language assessment techniques to determine a child's relative skill level in both of these areas. The information provided should be of assistance to the classroom teacher in determining the skills needed and at what levels of expectancy they should occur in functionally and appropriately completing oral and written language tasks. Both the formal and informal information can be used in the development of instructional strategies to include the identification of specific goals and objectives for the individual child. The assessment techniques discussed, if followed and if understood by the teacher, readily lend themselves to the identification of instructional strategies. For example, in determining or assisting the child's functional understanding of punctuation, an analysis of how well the child has punctuated a sentence should be illustrative to the teacher of, not only the deficiency, but what the instructional goal or objective should be. It is suggested that the teacher become thoroughly aware of the content of both the formal assessment devices, as well as the expected levels of behavior for each of these two levels of language development.

Can You Answer These Questions?

1. What are the components of oral language assessment?
2. What are the components of written language assessment?
3. Can you list three formal tests for use in an oral language assessment?
4. Can you list three formal tests for use in a written language assessment?
5. What are rules governing the use of commas?
6. What are two usual functions of the question mark?
7. What are the readiness skills for handwriting?
8. Can you define phonemes and graphemes?

References

Anderson, P. S. *Language Skills in Elementary Education.* New York: Macmillan, 1964.

Brown, R. W. *Social Psychology.* New York: Free Press, 1965.

Carrow, E. *Carrow Elicited Language Inventory.* Austin, Texas: Learning Concepts, 1974.

Dexter, B. "Classroom Forum." *Focus on Exceptional Children,* 1978, 10, 11–12.

Dunn, L. *Peabody Picture Vocabulary Test.* Circle Pines, Minnesota: American Guidance Service, 1965.

Durost, W., H. Bixler, J. Wrightstone, G. Prescott, and I. Barlow. *Metropolitan Achievement Tests.* New York: Harcourt Brace Jovanovich, 1970.

Eisenson, J., and M. Ogilvie. *Speech Correction in the Schools.* New York: Macmillan, 1971.

Ervin-Tripp, S., and W. Miller. *Language Development.* Sixty-second Yearbook NSSE. Chicago: University of Chicago Press, 1963.

Goldman, R., and M. Fristoe. *Goldman-Fristoe Test of Articulation.* Circle Pines, Minnesota: American Guidance Service, 1969.

Hieronymus, A. N., and E. F. Lindquist. *Iowa Tests of Basic Skills: The Teachers Guide for the Levels Edition.* Boston: Houghton Mifflin, 1971.

Hieronymus, A. M., and E. F. Lindquist. *Iowa Tests of Basic Skills: Manual for Administrators, Supervisors, and Counselors.* Boston: Houghton Mifflin, 1974.

Kirk, S., J. McCarthy, and W. Kirk. *Illinois Test of Psycholinguistic Abilities.* Urbana, Illinois: University of Illinois Press, 1968.

Lee, L. *Developmental Sentence Analysis.* Evanston, Illinois: Northwestern University Press, 1974.

Lee, L. *Northwestern Syntax Screening Test.* Evanston, Illinois: Northwestern University Press, 1969.

Madden, R., E. R. Gardner, H. C. Rudman, B. Karlsen, and J. C. Merwin. *Stanford Achievement Test.* New York: Harcourt Brace Jovanovich, 1973.

McCarthy, D. *Language Development.* Monograph of Social Research and Child Development, 1960, 25, No. 77, 5–14.

Meacham, M., J. L. Jex, and J. D. Jones. *Utah Test of Language Development.* Salt Lake City, Utah: Communication Research Associates, 1967.

Newcomer, P. L., and D. D. Hammill. *The Test of Language Development.* Austin, Texas: Empiric Press, 1977.

Ruddell, R. B. *Reading Language Instruction: Innovative Practices.* Englewood Cliffs, New Jersey: Prentice-Hall, 1974.

Templin, M. C., and F. L. Darley. *The Templin-Darley Test of Articulation.* Iowa City: Bureau of Educational Research and Service, University of Iowa, 1960.

Tiegs, E. W., and W. W. Clarke. *California Achievement Test.* Monterey, California: CTB/McGraw-Hill, 1970.

Zaner-Bloser Creative Growth with Handwriting. Columbus, Ohio: Zaner-Bloser, 1975.

chapter

10

Assessing Social/ Emotional Development

Objectives

At the conclusion of this chapter, the reader should be able to:

1. present a rationale for conducting an assessment of social/emotional development;
2. define the role of social/emotional development in the child's academic performance;
3. identify formal and informal diagnostic measures that can be used to assess social/emotional development;
4. interpret the results of these measures and specify their uses in educational planning.

Rationale

A child's level of success in school is not only dependent on how well the appropriate academic responses are learned. Achievement is also influenced by adequate development of social and emotional skills. Social/emotional development plays a vital part in the child's ability to interact successfully with teachers, peers, the environment, and the academic program. Lack of development in any of these areas presents a barrier to learning.

A good educational program must attempt to provide a complete therapeutic environment. This is especially true of a program for children who experience learning problems. The goal of the program should be to provide an environment that is educationally and psychologically supportive to the child. Confidence, self-acceptance, self control, persistence, initiative, and successful relationships with peers and authority figures are important factors in successful school experience. Questions that a teacher should constantly seek to answer are: "How does the child feel?" "Are the child's needs being satisfied?" "What is the child's emotional status?" Lerner (1976) states that a child's emotional well-being and favorable attitude toward school-related tasks are essential prerequisites to effective learning.

The Role of the Teacher

Social/emotional assessment is often more difficult than assessment of academic performance for the following reasons.

1. It is not always possible to establish absolute criteria to differentiate between normal and abnormal behavior.
2. Teacher training in the social/emotional area is more highly varied than in the academic areas.
3. Emotional problems are often manifested as inappropriate classroom behavior. The teacher is forced to deal with a symptom instead of a cause. Referral for further assessment on the basis of the *symptom* is occasionally interpreted as a lack of ability on the part of the teacher to maintain effective discipline. Therefore teachers may be hesitant to make a referral for further assessment.

The teacher's role in this process consists of determining whether a problem exists and, if so, how severe it is. Many resources are available to the teacher who is confronted with a child suspected of having a problem in this area. The school principal, nurse, guidance counselor, and psychologist can provide assistance. The teacher should become familiar with those people in the community who are available to assist in generating information concerning a child's social/emotional well-being. It is necessary that a teacher be able to conduct a cursory assessment of a child's abilities and performance in this area and to determine whether the problem is one that should be referred to these resource people.

Discrepancy Analysis

Comparing the child's behavior to the behavioral norm for his age group can establish the existence of a discrepancy. The severity of the discrepancy can be determined by the age group difference. For example, a junior high boy experiencing highly irrational fears has a more severe problem than a primary grade boy displaying the same behavior.

Both an intra- and inter-individual comparison require the teacher to possess a knowledge of what social/emotional behaviors can be expected of a typical child in a particular group. The normal developmental sequence of social and emotional skills for preschool to senior high school children is well illustrated by Biehler (1974). A summary of typical social and emotional behaviors identified by Biehler is found in Figure 10-1.

In an intra-individual comparison, it is important to notice the frequency of occurrence of behaviors that are not acceptable. It is of less value to say, "Johnny has temper tantrums" than "Johnny had three tantrums in six days." Of even greater value is to specifically describe the behavior Johnny exhibited during the tantrums. On an intra-individual basis, it is important to remember that behaviors that might interfere with one child's learning process may actually be promoting another child's learning experience. For example, tapping a pencil while reading may totally distract one child but set a reading rhythm for another.

Figure 10-1 A Developmental View of Typical Social/Emotional Behavior (Adapted from Biehler's *Psychology Applied to Teaching* [1974])

Age Group	Social	Emotional
Preschool and Kindergarten Ages 3 to 6 years	1) Has one or two best friends but these may change rapidly. Quite flexible socially—willing to play with most classmates. Favorite friends tend to be of same sex but may develop heterosexual friendships. 2) Small, not too highly organized play groups; hence they change rapidly. 3) Frequent quarrels—but of short duration and quickly forgotten. 4) Enjoys dramatic play, often based on TV shows or own experiences. 5) Beginning awareness of sex roles.	1) Expresses emotions freely and openly. Frequent anger outbursts especially when tired or hungry. 2) May have many fears including some highly irrational ones—due to vivid imagination and many new and strange experiences. 3) Often jealous of classmates—competing for teacher's affection and approval.
Primary Grades Ages 6–9 years	1) More selective in their choice of friends. May select a more or less permanent best friend and often a semipermanent "enemy." 2) Likes organized games in small groups but may be overly rule-conscious. 3) Still frequent quarrels. Now uses words, more than physical aggression—but boys may still indulge in wrestling, punching, shoving. 4) Noticeable competition and boasting. 5) Boys and girls begin to show different interests, both in play and schoolwork.	1) Becoming alert to the feelings of others—can lead them to hurt others deeply by attacking a sensitive spot without realizing how devastating his attack is. 2) Sensitive to criticism and ridicule. May have difficulty adjusting to failure. Needs frequent praise and recognition. 3) Eager to please the teacher. Likes to help, enjoys responsibility, wants to do well in schoolwork.

Elementary Grades Ages 9–12 years	1) Peer group becomes powerful—replaces adults as major source of behavior standards and recognition of achievement. "Gang age." 2) Interests of boys and girls even more divergent. Battle of the sexes in the exchange of insults and competition in schoolwork and games. 3) Team games become more popular. Strong class spirit. 4) Crushes and hero worship common (of teacher as well as movie stars).	1) Conflict between group code and adult rules may cause difficulty, even juvenile delinquency. 2) No longer such "sticklers" for rules—can take into account extenuating circumstances and see rules as suggested courses of action, rather than absolute dictums.
Junior High Grades Ages 12–15 years	1) Peer group is source of general rules of behavior. Conflict between peer code and adult code. 2) Real need to conform. Cliques common. 3) Concerned about what others think about them. Friendships and quarrels are more intense. 4) Girls are more advanced socially and may date older boys. The younger boys may try to cover up immaturity and lack of confidence by teasing and being critical of girls.	1) Likely to be moody, temperamental, unpredictable—due to role confusion and sexual maturation. 2) May behave boisterously to conceal lack of self-confidence. 3) Anger outbursts are common—could be due to psychological tension, biological imbalance, and fatigue (from lack of sleep or proper diet or by over-exertion). 4) Often intolerant and opinionated. Needs to think that there are absolute answers and that he knows them.
Senior High Grades Ages 15–18 years	1) Peer group dominates. Adult and peer codes conflict. Extreme pressures to conform (fads). 2) Preoccupation with opposite sex. Dating and marriage a dominating concern. 3) Girls still more socially mature and have smaller number of close girlfriends. Boys have a wider circle of more casual male friends but cannot completely trust his friends.	1) "The adolescent revolt"—no clearcut way to make transition from youth to adult. Must demonstrate maturity by defying adult authority. 2) May be in frequent conflict with parents due to increasing independence. 3) Moody and preoccupied.

Task and Behavior Analyses

It is important to note that in relation to social/emotional assessment, the reference point of the task itself is a behavior that the child does or does not perform. A specific description of behavior, rather than a categorizing label, is an important aspect of social/emotional assessment.

Formal Assessment Procedures

In order to determine the child's social/emotional level and establish appropriate remedial activities, a teacher should become familiar with the formal and informal techniques available. There are a number of formal devices for assessing social/emotional development. Many of these require trained examiners and therefore should be administered and interpreted by school psychologists, guidance counselors, or psychiatrists. Such tests are often of the projective type—for example, the Thematic Apperception Test (Morgan and Murray, 1935), the Minnesota Multiphasic Personality Inventory (Hathaway and McKinley, 1943), and the Bender Gestalt Visual Motor Test (Bender, 1938).

However, there are many formal devices that can be administered and interpreted by the classroom teacher. The following fit this category and can be used readily by the teacher in generating information concerning a child's social/emotional well-being. The teacher should keep in mind that these devices are merely *indicators* of a child's social/emotional well-being and, as with all tests, *should not* be used to *label* or *classify* a child. Instead, test results should be used only to generate information that will guide the teacher in developing an appropriate education program.

The Vineland Social Maturity Scale (Doll, 1953). This scale offers a profile of social growth in the areas of self-help skills, self-direction, communication, locomotion, and socialization. Based on observations of a child's performance of everyday tasks, the referrant (parent, teacher, or counselor) checks off items arranged according to age norms.

One major value in using this scale is the use of parents to generate information about the child. It helps to provide insight and awareness into the child's growth and development. This scale provides a definite outline of detailed performances showing the child's progressive capacity for self care and for participating in those activities which lead toward ultimate independence as an adult.

This scale is somewhat out of date and, as such, should be cautiously used. However, the Vineland can generate a great deal of good information about the child that will give direction to the teacher for program planning.

The Preschool Attainment Record (PAR) (Doll, 1967). This record is an extension of the Vineland Social Maturity Scale, directed to the first seven years of life. Its eight categories (ambulation, manipulation, rapport, communication, responsibility, information, ideation, and creativity) are designed to measure physical and intellectual development, as well as social development. Each item is norm-referenced for the average age at which a child can perform it; thus, the PAR provides a quick assessment of a child's general strengths and weaknesses.

Problem Behavior Identification Checklist (PBIC) (Walker, 1976). Because the PBIC is an easily administered formal device for classroom use, it will be presented in some detail. The checklist is used to identify children with behavior problems who should be referred for further psychological evaluation and treatment. Based on the teacher's responses to a list of 50 classroom problem behaviors, a profile analysis chart can be drawn up, by sex, in the areas of:

1. acting out;
2. withdrawal;
3. distractability;
4. disturbed peer relations;
5. immaturity.

Minimum recommended observation period before scoring a child's typical behavior on the checklist is two months. A visual examination of the profile chart can point out particular areas of social or emotional disturbance. *T* scores above 60 are a significant indication of disturbance. Boys with total scores of 22 or over and girls with total scores of 12 or over should be referred for further psychological evaluation and treatment.

In developing an appropriate intervention program for an individual student, the teacher can examine:

1. overall areas of disturbance from the profile. A student scoring high in Scale 1 (acting out) would require a different intervention strategy than a child scoring high in Scale 2 (withdrawal).
2. specific trouble spots, by looking at each circled problem behavior. For example, a contingency contracting approach could be selected for a child with item 27 (temper tantrums) or item 39 circled (physical aggression). A circled item 40 (hypercritical of himself) could possibly be overcome by a program emphasizing small skill sequences and providing much opportunity for success and positive reinforcement for appropriate behavior.

Informal Assessment Techniques

There are a multiplicity of informal assessment techniques that can be used by the classroom teacher to assess the child's social/emotional ability. The techniques range as far and as wide as the teacher's own creative abilities. There are, however, some techniques that are more easily applied than others. These include classroom observation, informal checklists, sociograms, and sentence completion.

Perhaps the most valuable assessment technique that a teacher can use is *classroom observation*. It is within the classroom that behaviors signaling social or emotional problems would be manifest. An observant teacher can uncover indicators of social or emotional problems with the assistance of *behavior rating scales, checklists,* or *peer-rating techniques.* As mentioned in previous chapters, one characteristic of scales and checklists is that the behavior listed on the scale defines the task. The behavior in relation to the task is evaluated by noting the individual's performance on that task.

The completion of checklists and behavior rating scales requires the classroom teacher or independent observer (preferably both) to focus on the behavior of the child in question to determine the extent of the child's social or emotional problem. When observing a child's behavior, a teacher should keep in mind the following procedures.

1. A child should be closely observed for a minimum of at least one week. This allows the teacher to determine not only the extent of the behavior but also events or activities that precede the behavior and the consequences that follow which may be reinforcing that behavior.

2. The teacher should note the characteristics of the response as well as its frequency. To accomplish this, the behavior must be clearly defined in "countable" or "measurable" terms. That is, a behavior described as "distractable" has little meaning, whereas the behavior described as "being off task everytime an auditory stimulus is presented" can be counted and measured. Once this has been accomplished, its frequency of occurrence can be more readily noted. For example, if the task is adequate control of emotions, inappropriate behavior in relation to the task may consist of the following description. In one day, within a 30-minute interval, John performed the following behaviors:

   a. hit Susan once;
   b. yelled four times;
   c. threw his pencil at someone twice;
   d. kicked his desk over twice.

   This is a more accurate assessment than "John has a bad temper."

3. Once the checklist is completed, the teacher must analyze the severity of the problem; this last step is as critical as the previous two. Many times a teacher feels a problem exists when in reality it does not.

Checklists and Behavior Rating Scales. Figures 10-2 and 10-3 are examples of teacher observation checklists for both screening for children with social/emotional problems as well as determining the extent or severity of those problems.

Teacher should observe each child closely for a minimum period of at least one week. According to his/her interpretation of what can be considered maladaptive for that age group of children, and upon a marked demonstration of the behavior over a period of time, the teacher can score the checklist items according to the frequency of occurrence:

—Characteristic response
—Frequently
—Average
—Seldom
—Never

Figure 10-2 Teacher-made Checklist of Potential Social/Emotional Problems

Name _____	Key:
Age (CA) _____	0 Behavior not present to
Date of Record _____	4 Behavior is excessive

Variability of Behavior in the Classroom	0	1	2	3	4
1. Personal reactions					
a. tantrum					
b. crying					
c. pouting					
d. using profane language					
e. destructive					
f. explosive					
g. hitting, fighting					
2. Poor adjustment to environment					
3. Poor adjustment to change in routine					
4. Response to authority figures					
a. disobedient					
b. difficulty accepting criticism					
c. resentful					
d. defiant					
e. stubborn					
f. has little regard for rules, etc.					
5. Behaviors related to class assignments					
a. appears to be bored					
b. does not finish work					
c. constant need for teacher's attention					

Figure 10-3 Checklist of Social/Emotional Behaviors (Modified from Wallace and Kauffman [1975])

Teacher Observation—Informal Assessment

	Characteristic response	Frequently	Average	Seldom	Never
I. Indications of Low Self-Concept					
a. Speaks disparagingly of self					
b. Is unwilling to attempt new or difficult tasks					
c. Is fearful of new situations					
d. Is excessively shy and withdrawn					
e. Lacks self-reliance—often says, "I can't"					
f. Shows excessive concern over acceptance by others					
g. Is usually unhappy or depressed; seldom smiles; cries or frowns often					
h. Demonstrates inability to make everyday decisions					
i. Demonstrates inability to accept errors or correct mistakes					
j. Shows extreme negative reaction to minor failures					
k. Has slovenly, unkempt appearance					
l. Is unable to evaluate his behavior realistically; brags or denigrates his accomplishments					
II. Disturbed Relations with Peers					
a. Has no close friends or "chums" in peer group					
b. Is avoided by children in games or activities					
c. Hits, bites, kicks, or otherwise physically assaults peers					
d. Is incessantly teasing or teased by others					
e. Seeks company of much older or younger children					
f. Withdraws from group activities					
III. Inappropriate Relationship to Teachers, Parents, and Other Authority Figures					
a. Refuses reasonable requests					
b. Defies direct commands					
c. Disobeys classroom rules					

Figure 10-3 Checklist of Social-Emotional Behaviors (*Continued*)

Teacher Observation—Informal Assessment

	Characteristic response	Frequently	Average	Seldom	Never
III. Inappropriate Relationship to Teachers, Parents, and Other Authority Figures (*Continued*)					
d. Encourages peers to disrupt the class or defy adults					
e. Strikes, bites, kicks, or otherwise attempts to injure other children or adults					
f. Runs away from school or home or leaves the classroom without permission					
g. Steals					
h. Lies					
i. Manipulates adults to his advantage					
j. Is overprotected; seldom allowed to enter new age-appropriate situations alone, or allowed to take reasonable risks					
k. Is overindulged; "spoiled" by being given noncontingent or excessive rewards					
IV. Other Signs of Social-Emotional Problems					
a. Exhibits inappropriate behavior for a given context (e.g., laughs when someone is hurt, interprets figures of speech literally)					
b. Is overly suspicious or jealous of others					
c. Complains of physical symptoms, pains, or fears in mildly stressful situations; complains of every little hurt					
d. Is in constant motion; compulsively manipulates objects; moves about the room excessively					
e. Engages in repetitive, stereotyped motor behavior; has tics, bites nails, sucks thumb, rocks, etc.					
f. Talks incessantly; frequently talks out without permission or interrupts conversations					
g. Explains inappropriate behavior by rationalization or intellectualization					
h. Does not seem to learn from experience; behavior does not improve with usual disciplinary methods					

Teacher Observation—Informal Assessment

	Characteristic response	Frequently	Average	Seldom	Never
IV. Other Signs of Social-Emotional Problems *(Continued)*					
i. Is retained in grade or excluded from school					
j. Fails to learn when there is no evidence of intellectual, sensory or health problems					
k. Makes meaningless or "animal" noises					
l. Acts impulsively and shows poor judgment; does not consider or understand consequences of his behavior					
m. Is easily distracted; cannot concentrate or attend for more than a few minutes					
n. Has not mastered bowel or bladder control					
o. Shows extreme interest in monsters, war, fighting or gruesome events					
p. Is overcome frequently by drowsiness or sleep					
q. Places inedible objects in mouth or shows appetite for inedible objects					
r. Has violent outbursts of temper					
s. Lacks curiosity					
t. Daydreams; sits with a vacant expression, doing nothing productive					
V. Language Indicators					
a. Does not speak					
b. Speaks only when spoken to					
c. Speaks with inappropriate pitch—too high-pitched or low-pitched for age and sex					
d. Speaks with inappropriate volume—too loud or too soft					
e. Speaks with marked dysfluency; stutters, clutters or otherwise interrupts the flow of speech					
VI. Disordered Temporal Relationships					
a. Is chronically late					
b. Refuses to talk about the past					
c. Cannot shift readily from one activity to the next					

Once the checklist is completed, the teacher can judge whether the child is demonstrating a severe problem within a given area or social/emotional maladjustment in general. The checklist can thus be used to pinpoint areas of behavior that need immediate attention.

Sociogram. An example of an effective peer rating technique is the sociogram. This device is used to reveal the child's social position within the class. Biehler (1974) has presented an effective model (Figure 10-4) for using the sociogram.

Each child was asked to write down the names of the most liked classmates—the most fun to be with, the nicest to sit next to. The selected choices were plotted on the diagram with the "stars" in the center and the "isolates" outside the circle. After having identified the isolates, the teacher can determine whether the child desires to be a loner or desires interaction with other children. In the former situation, attempts to promote social interaction could lead to other types of social/emotional problems. In the latter situation, the child may desire interaction but lack the necessary skills. The teacher may help by pairing the child with another classmate, who is chosen by the child, for various classroom activities.

Figure 10-4   Sociogram (From Biehler [1974]).

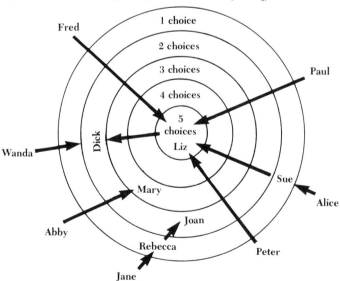

This device can be used to identify those children whose social, motor, or academic skills need additional attention to assist them in better fitting into the mainstream of the class. It also aids in adjustment of the program according to the identified social and emotional needs of the child.

Sentence Completion. Sentence completion is a device that is at the control and manipulation of the classroom teacher. A number of different kinds of information can be generated informally by asking the child to respond to the sentence stem of the sentence completion device. A child's attitude toward family, friends, school, and self can be revealed through the child's response on the sentence completion.

Many commercial sentence completion devices are available, and many teachers construct their own. The sentence completion test presented in Figure 10-5 is used as an example of a teacher-made sentence completion device. This device has two good features for generating information. These are as follows.

1. It is designed to assess specific areas of interest; in this case these are perception of family, self in relation to family, social and school environment, self-concept (needs and personal evaluation), and general mental health.
2. It has criteria for scoring responses. Positive and negative responses can be assigned a definite value by a teacher. For example, 50 percent or more (four responses) negative responses may be indicative of a problem area. This provides for a much more thorough analysis.

More Specific Assessments

Once the teacher has assessed, through classroom observation and formal tests, that a child is experiencing problems in the social/emotional area, several interpretations can be made according to the specific problems observed in the child. The first step is an accurate definition of the child's inappropriate responses. Figure 10-6 presents examples of adequate and inadequate descriptions of behavior.

As the chart indicates, the clearly defined behaviors of the first assessment more readily lead to clearly defined, implementable program strategies. Program strategies are based on the type of assessment results obtained. As an example, classroom observa-

Figure 10-5 Example of a Teacher-made Sentence Completion Test (Adapted from the Southeastern Education Service Center, Carbon County Schools, Carbon, Utah).

| Areas | Affect Impact | | | Comments |
	+ Positive	0 Neutral	− Negative	
Family				
Self-Needs				
Peer Relations				
School				
Self-Appraisal				

SOUTHEASTERN EDUCATION SERVICE CENTER
SENTENCE COMPLETION TEST

Name _____ Sex _____ Birthdate _____ Age _____
School _____ Grade _____ Date _____

F S P S S -

1. My father _____

2. I wish _____

3. Most boys _____

4. For me, reading _____

5. What I like best about me _____

6. Having a brother or a sister _____

7. I'd really be happy if _____

8. I don't like people who _____

9. My teachers think I _____

10. My body _____

11. When mother and dad are together, they _____

_____

12. I need _____

13. The other kids think _____

14. Math _____

15. The thing I can do best _____

16. At home I get _____

17. What I want more than anything _____

18. To the other kids, I_____

19. My grades in school _____

20. I am the _____

21. I sure wish my father _____

22. When I am older_____

23. Girls _____

24. At school I am _____

25. I should_____

26. My mother thinks I_____

27. The thing that makes girls different from boys

_____

28. When I play with the kids, they_____

29. When the teacher _____

30. The worst thing about me _____

31. My family treats me _____

32. A kiss_____

33. I wish the kids _____

34. School should_____

35. What I would change about me is _____

36. In my home _____

37. Someday I will_____

38. A friend should _____

39. The best thing about school_____

40. I can't _____

Totals

Figure 10-6   Adequate and Inadequate Descriptions of Behavior (From Hammill and Bartel [1975])

	Description of Behavior	Specific Intervention
Adequate assessment	(1) Withdrawal from class participation	(1) Initial use of role playing and/or puppetry
	(2) Fighting during reading	(2) Proper sequencing of reading materials plus reinforcing incompatible responses
Inadequate assessment	(1) Emotionally disturbed	(1) Therapeutic milieu
	(2) Socially maladjusted	(2) Counseling
	(3) Behavior disordered	(3) Psychoeducational therapy

tion, including use of a behavior checklist, indicated that Mary was experiencing some emotional problems to an extent that exceeded the average of her classmates.

Because of those observations, the Walker Problem Identification Checklist was selected for further analysis of the severity of Mary's social or emotional problems. Her scores are shown in Figure 10-7.

Remember any T scores over 60 indicate a significant problem area; both withdrawal and disturbed peer relations are areas of concern for Mary. Such a disturbance in her social and emotional relationships could very easily be affecting her successful interaction with the academic curriculum as well as with class members. Also, if her raw scores are totaled, a score of 22 is obtained. As one score over 12 for a girl suggests further psychological evaluation and treatment, Mary should probably be referred to the school psychologist for further testing and counseling.

The results obtained above can also provide direction in classroom program planning by the teacher. In addition to such basic procedures as carefully sequencing academic curriculum and providing numerous opportunities to achieve success and positive reinforcement, there are several classroom activities that are especially geared to helping the child develop appropriate

Figure 10-7   Mary's Walker Problem Identification Checklist Scores

	Scale 1 Acting Out	Scale 2 Withdrawal	Scale 3 Distract- ability	Scale 4 Disturbed Peer Relations	Scale 5 Immaturity
Raw Score	3	11	1	7	0
T Score	57	81	48	111	47

social/emotional responses. Because Mary's main areas of disturbance are withdrawal and disturbed peer relations, the teacher may want to consider one of the following intervention strategies.

"Sharing" or "Show and Tell" Periods. Short time blocks are devoted to the class members sharing important events in their lives. These periods would provide an opportunity for Mary to receive much positive reinforcement for attempts to communicate and would help her develop a more positive self-concept.

Magic Circle. In a series of daily, twenty-minute sharing sessions the class members are gathered together in *Magic Circle* (Bessell and Palomares, 1971) groups of approximately ten and respond to questions such as "What did you do that someone liked? What did you do that someone disliked?" These questions are designed to explore both positive and negative feelings, thoughts, and actions. Pictures and physical activities are presented to stimulate these responses.

The aim of the Magic Circle program is to develop greater self-confidence, self-awareness, and an understanding of social interaction (Biehler, 1974). By means of such a program, Mary can learn to share feelings and to listen to and observe others. She will also be provided with numerous activities to interact with her peers in a positive, controlled environment.

Role Playing, Creative Play, Stories, Discussion. These activities can be used to help Mary anticipate consequences of social acts, as well as provide opportunities to experience peer interactions. Puppetry, play therapy, and modeling are also effective techniques to draw out a child and encourage more appropriate peer relationships.

Commercial Kits—DUSO (Developing Understanding of Self and Others) **and TAD** (Toward Affective Development) **(Dinkmeyer, 1970).** Such kits provide numerous activities and materials to stimulate affective and psychological development. Self-image, peer relationships, accepting responsibility, and setting realistic expectations are just a few of the topic areas covered by such kits.

Behavior Modification. Consequences are carefully arranged to increase or decrease the occurrence of a given behavior. In the area of education, contingency and behavior management are widely used techniques. For example, under a contingency approach, Mary would contract to remain at a task for a given period of time in exchange for several minutes of free time or a preferred activity. Using a behavior management approach, Mary would be reinforced positively whenever she performed a desired behavior (staying on task or interacting with peers without fighting or hitting). Behavior modification is a widely used remediation technique to develop more appropriate social and emotional responses in children through arrangement of the environment to better accommodate appropriate behavior.

Work Record Cards (Hewett, 1968). This strategy encourages self-competition and self-directed behavior. Appropriate educational tasks are selected, based on the student's individual needs. For example, remaining in seat, starting assignment, completing assignment, and remaining on task would be behaviors to consider if Mary's score in "distractibility" had been high. A reward meaningful to the individual student is identified. For example, at the beginning of each day, Mary is given a new work card (see sample card in Figure 10-8) and a check for appropriate behaviors (one check each for starting an assignment and for remaining on task). At the end of the day or week, Mary can exchange her completed cards for rewards she has previously selected.

The above activities are a sample of the intervention strategies teachers can implement once the assessment techniques have demonstrated social or emotional problems in a particular student. Because social or emotional problems can effectively impede Mary's academic progress as well as her emotional well-being, it is essential that those problems be identified and remediated.

Figure 10-8   Sample of a Work Record Card

Work Record Card				
Name: Mary Date : Monday, March 11 Tasks: Staying in seat, on task, completion of assignments without hesitation				

Summary

The teacher must be aware of potential behavior problems that can be manifest by children. This allows for not only more efficient program planning, but for better communication with other professionals (psychologist, social worker, and the like) who may be requested to assist in developing the most appropriate programs for the child. The following list of behaviors and their descriptors are presented as a means of acquainting teachers with possible remediating techniques that could be used for specific types of problems. An awareness of these techniques may prove helpful when the teacher is planning the child's educational program.

1. Hyperactive—shorten the length of tasks, cut seat work papers into sections for greater variety and varying degrees of difficulty.

2. Talkativeness—allow the child to gain some catharsis through talking in order to reduce the tension which builds up.

3. Flightiness—patience, understanding, and acceptance of the child will help develop stability.

4. Annoying, teasing—this is an attention-getter and comes from feelings of inadequacy—patience and praise for appropriate behavior is needed. Many of these behaviors can be ignored.

5. Impulsivity—patient and persistent reminders that the child is one of many and must stop to think before acting (to be done in a positive manner).

6. Excessive reaction—use the positive approach, accept the child as is, set limits on behavior and be sure they are understood; consistently maintain the limits.

7. Anxiety—provide a structured environment, a routine environment, and success experiences; avoid failure experiences, design tasks within the ability of the child, and provide guidance only when necessary to avoid failure.

8. Insecurity—constant reminders the child is doing well, prod and encourage when necessary, insist upon accuracy and completion of tasks, always give recognition and praise when deserved.

9. Excitability—provide a minimal amount of stimuli, low noise level, low movement level about the child, gradually introduce more normal levels of stimuli.

10. Day dreaming—the child withdraws to provide self-protection, therefore, he doesn't try things; simplify tasks by giving them one at a time, in proper sequence, to be done that way, and compound directions and tasks gradually.

11. Irritability—noises seem louder, movements more rapid and numerous, lights seem brighter; reduce external stimuli in his environment, find ways to conserve his energy, the child may need a shortened school day.

12. Distractability—reduce auditory and visual stimuli, teach others to understand, keep noise at a minimum, avoid exciting, noisy, running games, avoid flashy jewelry and bright clothes.

13. Short attention span—minimize distractions, design goals to match ability, even to the point of giving one problem at a time, or three spelling words instead of ten, patiently prod and remind, avoid placing the child in a position that requires over-trying to accomplish a task, offer help and encouragement to avoid failure.

14. Retention—do not give a long series of instructions or items, get the child emotionally involved in the learning situation at hand, present information that is meaningful and be sure it's understood, present concepts in many and varied situations.

15. Perseveration—the child is unable to change from activity to activity, so involve the child emotionally in the learning task, avoid rote learning, present practice sessions in various forms, avoid drills.

Moving from Assessment to Program Planning. After the assessment has been completed and the teacher has a pretty good

Figure 10-9   Problem Behavior Data Collection Chart

Problem Behavior Data Collection

Day	Frequency of Behavior	Antecedents of Behavior	Consequences of Behavior
1			
2			
3			
4			
5			

idea of what the child's problem is, the next step that should be taken is to pinpoint the direction the instructional strategy should take. The following steps are provided as an example of what the teacher could do to determine that direction.

I. Profile the strengths and weaknesses.
   a. Analyze the observation information.
      1. If a child often makes derogatory remarks about him/herself, plan something where the child can experience success to improve his or her self-image.
      2. If the student is particularly proud of something, make plans for the student to share it.
   b. Select a target behavior and collect data. (Figure 10-9 shows an example chart.)
      1. Be specific about the behavior. Mary is distractible is not a very specific behavior. Mary never completes assigned tasks within a specified time period is more specific, is measurable, and also indicates the direction the remediation strategy should take.
      2. Be sure the behavior is measurable.
      3. Chosen behavior should imply the desired direction of change.
      4. List the behaviors in order of urgency.

     5. Be sure the behavior is really undesirable.

     6. Be sure the expectations for change are realistic.

II. Analyze the baseline data to determine where to start and set goals.

    a. Tally the baseline data collected. See Figure 10-10 for example of tally chart.

    b. From this tally a teacher determines that fighting occurs most often during reading periods. Therefore, collect the data during the reading period and translate the tallies into a frequency graph (Figure 10-11).

III. Questions to ask to specify the direction of the instructional program.

    a. What seems to motivate the student?

    b. What seems to distract the student?

    c. Where is the failure level?

    d. What outside pressures are apparent?

    e. Does the child need instruction with others or solitude in which to learn?

    f. Is structure needed or does an aura of freedom need to prevail?

    g. Does the child see or understand the problem?

    h. What parts of the school environment can be removed or controlled to facilitate reduction of the problem?

Can You Answer These Questions?

1. Why should a teacher be concerned about assessing the social/emotional well-being of a child?

2. What are the expected social behaviors of children three to six years of age?

3. What are the expected emotional behaviors of adolescents twelve to fifteen years of age?

4. What are three formal devices that teachers can use in their classrooms to assess children's social/emotional behaviors?

5. What are some informal techniques a teacher can use to assess a child's social/emotional behaviors?

Figure 10-10   Sample Tally Chart

Day and Time (20 minutes)	Number of Fights
1 Monday, reading	11111
2 Tuesday, art	1
3 Wednesday, arithmetic	11
4 Thursday, reading	1111
5 Friday, reading	11111

Figure 10-11   Frequency Graph of Behavior Tallies

BEHAVIOR TALLIES

Reading Days	Number of Fights
1. Monday	1111
2. Tuesday	111111
3. Wednesday	111
4. Thursday	11111
5. Friday	111111

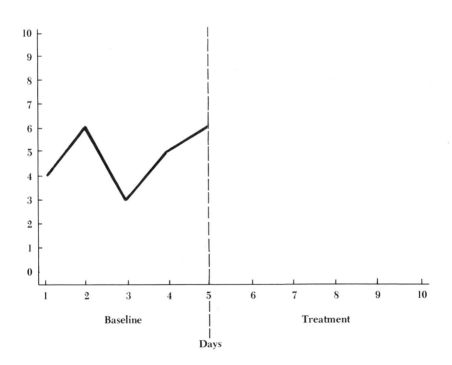

6. Can you list two behaviors descriptive of adequate assessment of a child's social/emotional behavior?
7. Can you identify a strategy or strategies for helping a child overcome inhibition and shyness as manifest by a lack of self-confidence and self-directed behavior?

References

Bessell, H., and U. Palomares. *Methods in Human Development: Theory Manual*. San Diego: Human Development Training Institute, 1971.

Bender, L. *The Visual-Motor Gestalt Test for Children*. New York: American Orthopsychiatric Association, 1938.

Biehler, R. F. *Psychology Applied to Teaching* (2nd ed.). Boston: Houghton Mifflin Company, 1974.

Dinkmeyer, D. D. *Developing Understanding of Self and Others*. Circle Pines, Minnesota: American Guidance Service, 1970.

Doll, E. A. *Vineland Social Maturity Scale*. Minneapolis: Educational Test Bureau, 1953.

Doll, E. A. *Preschool Attainment Record*. Circle Pines, Minnesota: American Guidance Service, 1967.

Hammill, D. D., and N. Barter (eds.). *Teaching Children with Learning and Behavior Problems*. Boston: Allyn and Bacon, 1975.

Hathaway, S. R., and J. C. McKinley. *The Minnesota Multiphasic Personality Inventory* (rev. ed.). Minneapolis: University of Minnesota Press, 1943.

Hewett, F. *The Emotionally Disturbed Child in the Classroom*. Boston: Allyn and Bacon, 1968.

Lerner, J. *Children with Learning Disabilities* (2nd ed.). Boston: Houghton Mifflin, 1976.

Morgan, C. D., and H. A. Murray. "The Thematic Apperception Test." *Arch Neurol. Psychiatry*, 1935, 34, 289–306.

Thorpe, L. P., W. W. Clark, and E. E. Tiegs. *California Test of Personality*. Los Angeles: California Test Bureau, 1953.

Walker, H. M. *Problem Behavior Identification Checklist* (rev. ed.). Los Angeles: Western Psychological Services, 1976.

Wallace, G., and J. M. Kauffman. *Teaching Children with Learning Problems* (2nd ed.). Columbus, Ohio: Charles E. Merrill, 1978.

chapter

11

Modality Assessment

Objectives

The reader at the conclusion of this chapter should be able to:

1. present a rationale for conducting a modality assessment;
2. discuss the research relative to the value of modality assessment in the educational process;
3. identify and define the modalities and their components;
4. specify formal and informal devices for use in the assessment of modalities.

Introduction

Simply defined modalities refer to the pathways of learning (Wallace and Larsen, 1978). Throughout this chapter, three modalities, or pathways of learning, will be discussed; the visual modality, the auditory modality, and the motor modality. The research conducted in this area appears rather controversial and has established neither a definitive role nor the degree of significance modalities play in the educational process. It appears obvious, however, that without modalities a person would have a difficult time learning anything.

Modality assessment is usually broken down into two parts, the assessment of *acuity* and the assessment of *perception*. Acuity relates primarily to determining if the mechanisms for providing a pathway to learning exist. That is, is the child able to see appropriately? Does the child possess all the necessary parts of the hearing mechanism to allow sufficient auditory stimuli to be heard? Are the child's motor capabilities adequate enough to allow for performance in those areas involving motor skills?

The other part of modality assessment deals with perception. It is within this area that most of the controversy lies. It appears that the assessment of modality perceptual disorders involves the determination of a child's ability to discriminate visual and auditory stimuli, to store and recall that stimuli, and then to integrate the stimuli into other areas of learning. Motor perception involves the determination of how well the child senses through touch (tactile) information for use in acquiring skills and muscle movement (kinesthetic) that allows for moving efficiently and productively. The purpose of this chapter is to review the modalities in terms of definition as well as the instruments and techniques used to assess both the child's modality acuity and perception. Also a review of the literature relative to developing an understanding of modalities in the educational process will be presented. The determination as to the relative efficacy of assessing the modalities and the ultimate use of that information in program planning will be left to the reader. The author would like to indicate that the research, even though controversial, is also very limited. The area of modality assessment is in its infant stages of investigation and will be for some time before more definitive techniques will be developed for assisting the teacher in generating useful, worthwhile information for planning instructional programs.

What appears obvious is that learning takes place through the modalities and that educators and experimenters should attempt to continue investigating the most efficient ways to learn and to determine how the modalities affect learning efficiency.

One of the first areas which should perhaps be thoroughly investigated is the difference in semantics used to describe the process of perception. This appears to be at the root of the controversy surrounding modality assessment. If there were agreement on what perception is, then a more definitive research effort could be directed toward the identification of the part perception plays in learning. Very few educators or educational psychologists would argue against the concept that perception is an integral part of learning. Few, however, can agree as to what the perceptual basis for learning actually is. Several researchers and educators also contend that without an adequate perceptual base, children will fail in school.

One issue that appears throughout the literature concerns the neglect of the perceptual disorder assessment, utilizing specially developed training programs designed to correct an identified perceptual problem and improve a child's overall achievement in academic areas. That is, when a child is identified as having a modality perceptual deficiency which is then corrected through a modality perceptual training program, it appears that the training does not have much of an effect on increasing the child's overall academic performance. As Wallace and Larson (1978) point out, the modality assessment and training may detract from teaching directly to the child's observed academic deficiency. (For a more thorough discussion of the history and background of the area of modality assessment and application in the educational setting, the reader is referred to Hallahan and Cruickshank, 1973, who quite thoroughly trace the study of perceptual motor problems in exceptional children and outline the work of major contributors in the area of perceptual motor disorders.)

As a conclusion to this introductory section, the author would like to quote from Wallace and Larson (1978): "At best perceptual assessment should be considered experimental with little empirical support for its usefulness in school. Consequently, we do not recommend the use of these techniques except for research (p. 180)." To this the author would like to add that if decisions relative to a child's instructional program are to be made based upon the assessment information taken from a modality assessment instrument, the teacher must then determine through a thorough analysis of that instrument's content the relative value of the information generated in constructing an instructional program. Moran (1976) provides one other dimension for developing a rationale for study in this area. She states:

> Although testing of psychological process dimensions is discouraged by the research literature, one has only to observe school testing situations or inspect record folders to determine that such testing is being done and that education decisions are being made on the basis of such test results. Indeed some state mandates for special education services have been written in such a way that testing of psychological correlates such as visual and auditory discrimination, memory sequencing and other school constructs must be reported for funding purposes (p. 3).

Under these conditions, then, the teacher must at least be aware of what perceptual motor tests are available and what these tests purport to tell the teacher relative to a child's modality development.

What the Research Says

Reger, Schroeder, and Uschold (1968) identified auditory, visual, and motor modalities as being important to the learning process. However, the role played by the modalities as well as the relationship of modalities to the learning process has not been well established. Even though modality preference can be determined (Wolpert, 1971), preference alone may not be indicative of the manner in which the child actually processes information, nor does it determine how efficiently the child may learn information. The modality preference appears simply to be one indication of the many ways in which the child acquires and therefore learns information. The question as to whether a specific preference produces more efficient learning is one that has received a great deal of interest in the literature. Sabatino and Streissgurth (1972) found that visual learners performed higher on specified tasks than did auditory learners. Cooper (1971) found similar results in his comparison of modalities between good and poor readers.

Another question of interest in the literature is that issue dealing with teaching to the child's identified modality preference. Studies by Bateman (1967), Harris (1965), and Bruininks (1977) attempted specific modality preference teaching and found no significant relationship to a child's performance as a consequence of specifying and then teaching toward the child's identified modality preference. Spache (1976) refers to specific studies utilizing the Learning Methods Test (Mills, 1970) and concludes that "fitting method to children's modality as determined by tests or the Mills Procedure . . . works logically in some instances and is apparently fruitless in equally as many" (p. 70).

A third question that has received a great deal of emphasis in the literature is the relationship of modality preference to ability. Cooper (1971) reports infrequent modality preferences in brighter children. Arnold's (1968) study reports no relationship between teaching to a child's identified modality preference and the child learning new words. In this study disabled readers were used as subjects. Subjects being taught through their modality preference, when compared to those not being taught in this manner, showed no difference in the number of new words learned.

The application of information concerning a child's modality preference and school achievement has been investigated quite extensively. Hammill and Larsen (1974) reviewed approximately 33 studies in which the relationship between measures of academic achievement, in most cases reading, and measures of auditory discrimination, memory, and auditory visual integration were correlated. The overall findings of this review seemed to indicate that little predicted value can be made from the use of modality assessment devices. That is to say, diagnostic information about a child with a perceptual difficulty, as measured by a perceptual test, can not necessarily be used as a predictor of the child's success in school. An equal percentage of those students who perform poorly on perception tests were distributed equally in adequately or inadequately completing academic tasks.

Although the significance of the role of modality assessment has not been established, Moran (1976) and Wallace and Larsen (1978) have identified wide use in schools and in planning individual education programs as the reason for including the study of modality assessment in the training program of teachers. Spache (1976) states that "inconclusiveness about determining modality and results from modality teaching should not discourage further investigation in this area. And in fact this is an area which warrants even more continuous and thorough investigation." Learning can be viewed as a multisensory act involving the modalities and their component parts. It becomes our part as educators and researchers to determine the value and usage of modalities in the overall learning system. Effective use of information about an individual's ability to perceive and conceptualize must continue to be an area of investigation.

Definition of the Modality

The modalities to be discussed in this chapter include visual, auditory, and motor with the motor area being composed of kinesthetic and tactile processes. Components of the modalities include sensation, perception, memory, and conceptualization. The *visual modality* is defined in terms of sensation and perception. The mechanisms involved in *visual sensation* include the eye composed of the cornea, pupil, and retina. The retina, at the rear portion of the eyeball, receives light and activates the optic nerve which carries the visual stimulus to the brain for further processing. *Visual perception* has been defined in a number of different ways but is essentially the manner in which the visual stimuli is processed resulting in interpretation of what the perceived stimuli is or means to the individual. Visual perception is usually thought of in terms of the following dimensions:

1. *Visual discrimination*, which is the ability to identify differences and similarities in the stimuli. In terms of academic tasks this may be the ability to differentiate between letters, numbers, words, or graphic forms.
2. *Figure ground*, which is the ability to select a figure from a background of confusing or irrelevant stimuli. A related academic task

would involve having the child focus on one word, letter, or number on a page, keeping it distinct and apart from all other letters, words, and numbers on that page.

3. *Visual memory*, which is the ability to recall the sequence of visually presented stimuli. A related academic task may be recalling the sequence of numbers placed on the blackboard after they have been erased.
4. *Visual closure* is the ability to complete from a partial visual stimulus a complete figure. If, for example, a child is presented with  or 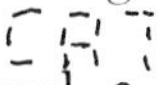, the child is able to complete the figure into a whole word C A T.
5. *Visual motor integration* stimuli is the utilization of perceived visual stimuli in making more efficient body movements or in more efficiently moving within the environment through adequately processing the visual stimuli.

The *auditory modality* and the acuity mechanisms involved in *auditory sensation* include the outer, middle, and inner ear plus the auditory nerve which transmits auditory stimuli to the brain for processing. As with the mechanisms in visual sensing, a breakdown with any of these mechanisms will impair the child's ability to receive, and therefore process, auditory stimuli. *Auditory perception* is also vaguely defined in the literature, but appears to be composed of the following parts.

1. *Auditory discrimination*, or the ability of the child to distinguish between sounds. In an academic task, this may include being able to discriminate the phonics sounds of specific letters, digraphs, or blends.
2. *Sound ground* is much like visual figure ground in which the individual selects out an auditory stimulus from a background of conflicting or competing auditory stimuli. In terms of school-related tasks, sound ground may include having the child focus on the teacher's verbal directions while the other students in the class are creating a great deal of competing or conflicting noise.
3. *Auditory memory*, which is an ability to recall the sequence of stimuli presented auditorily. An academic task related to this is having a child follow a teacher's auditory direction, "Mary, go to the office and pick up a ream of white art paper and 40 pencils for today's art assignment."
4. *Auditory blending* involves blending distinct sounds into whole words.

The *motor modality* is composed of the tactile or touch sense and the kinesthetic, or movement, sense. Leading theorists in this area (Kephart, 1960, and Barsch, 1966) indicate that adequate motor development is essential to the development of an efficient learning system. This concept is supported by others in this field (Bruininks, 1977; Cratty, 1970, 1975) who support the notion that the motor areas of posture, coordination, awareness laterally, and ambulation are fundamental to learning.

Modality Assessment Techniques

Children differ widely in the methods by which they learn. Spache (1976) correlates this to other traits by stating that children are no more homogeneous in their learning modalities than they are in any other of a number of traits. In order to help the child use his own learning system more efficiently and efficaciously, assessment of this area can be of value to the classroom teacher. Some children are able to learn, for example, the steps in solving a math problem by watching the teacher perform the operations on the chalkboard. Others require only hearing the procedure explained in a programmed listening center or lecture approach, while other children require manipulative objects to assist them in understanding the math process fully. A teacher having a combination of these approaches available will be able to provide a more beneficial learning environment for a majority of students. Modality assessment is not suggested in order to establish the answer to a child's learning problem, but rather as one additional technique in which information can be generated that will assist the teacher in identifying strategies and methodologies for instructing the child. Further, the information generated from a modality assessment must be used in light of the controversial issues presented earlier.

Visual Assessment. Visual acuity is one of the first areas to be assessed. The classroom teacher is usually in a position only to screen the child's visual acuity to determine if the child's field of vision is restricted in any way. A child manifesting problems through the screening process should be referred to an appropriate diagnostician, such as an ophthalmologist or optometrist, for further investigation. A Snellen eye chart, the Keystone Visual

Survey Telebinocular (revised 1974), or the Spache Binocular Reading Test (Spache, 1961) can be used to screen a child's visual acuity. Children having problems on any of these devices should be referred immediately for a more in-depth diagnosis with that diagnosis not only checking acuity but fusion, muscle imbalance, and depth perception. Informal assessment of a child's visual acuity can be made through observation of a child's behavior. An overabundance of eye-blinking or rubbing of the eyes may be an indication that the child is having difficulty in focusing on the visual stimuli presented. Frequent trips to the chalkboard to complete a copying assignment may also indicate an acuity problem.

Formal assessment of visual perception can be made with a number of tests. These include the Marian Frostig Test of Visual Perception (DTVP) (Frostig, LeFever, and Whittlesey (1966). This test is composed of five areas of visual perception: (1) eye-motor coordination, (2) figure ground, (3) form constancy, (4) position in space, and (5) spatial relationships. This test is designed for use with individuals or small groups between the ages of four and eight. Raw scores from this test can be computed into a perceptual quotient or perceptual age. The perceptual age equivalent is used to determine if a child is having a problem in any of the five subtest areas. That is, a child that does not receive the maximum perceptual age for any of the subtests up to that child's age level is said to have difficulty in that area. The DTVP manual indicates that scaled scores below eight should be considered as a weakness in any area they occur and should be of concern for instructional program planning. The reliability data for this test, using test-retest and split half reliability procedures, reveal a wide range of correlation coefficients between each of the subtests utilizing both methods. The test-retest data ranged from .42 to .80 while the split half coefficients ranged from .68 to .89 (the reader is referred to the DVTP administration manual for a more definitive answer to the questions he may have concerning reliability). The validity of the test was conducted through a correlation of test scores and teacher ratings of children's classroom adjustment, motor coordination, and intellectual functioning. The correlation coefficients conducted were at about the .50 level, indicating a slight correlation between the scores from the test and teacher ratings. However, the amount and type of validity data available for this test would certainly indicate that further investigation is warranted. The recommended use of the DTVP is as a screening device for preschool and primary aged children. It could also be used to screen older children suspected of having visual perceptual difficulties. The important use of the test is to relate its findings with related school tasks. In this way an identified weakness may be better understood and remediation developed to assist the child in overcoming school related problems.

The Developmental Test of Visual Motor Integration (VMI) (Beery and Buktenica, 1967) is designed to assess visual motor functioning of the child. It can be used as a group or individual test. It, too, should be considered as a screening device. The test has been designed for use with children ages 2 through 15 and is easily administered by the classroom teacher. The test is composed of a booklet in which the child is asked to reproduce 24 geometric designs that are sequenced in increasing difficulty. The test attempts to localize the child's visual motor integration problem and the level at which that development occurs. Raw score data are converted into a developmental age equivalent illustrative of the developmental level at which the child is performing visual motor integration tasks adequately. The reliability data for this test are rather extensive and the reader is referred to Beery, Keith, and Butentica (1967) for information relative to both reliability and validity data as well as the standardization procedures used in constructing this test. The reliability data indicate correlation coefficients ranging from .80 to .85 from a test-retest procedure. The validity data available are somewhat vague even though correlation coefficients between VMI scores and those of the Frostig DTVP were .80. Other validity indicators do not give a clear picture as to the overall validity of this test.

Like the VMI, the Bender Visual Motor Gestalt Test (Bender, 1938) is a test designed to assess the child's ability to motorically reproduce visual stimuli. The test was designed for use with children and adults and non-brain-injured individuals. This test is currently used quite extensively by clinical psychologists for differentiating between brain-injured and non-brain-injured individuals. The test is composed of nine geometric figures which the person taking the test is asked to copy one at a time. One scoring system used to interpret the results was developed by Koppitz

(1963) and is the most commonly used system in scoring the test performance of children. Koppitz (1975) has published a compilation of the research completed on the Bender, to which the reader is referred for more specific information relative to the utility of this test. Reliability and validity data from the Koppitz (1975) system are somewhat questionable. The reliability coefficients range from .50 to .90 with a mean of approximately .70. Validity for this test suffers from the same perils as other like tests in that the semantics involved in defining perception, in this case visual motor perception, are very inadequate, which result in any number of interpretations, therefore leading to the potential misinterpretation and misuse of test results. The test should not be used to predict a child's academic performance (Koppitz, 1975), but can be used as a screening device of visual motor functions by the classroom teacher. To make any other conclusions such as to the child's intellectual, social, or brain-injured status would require the professional opinion and experience of a trained psychologist or psychometrist.

Memory for Designs Test (Graham and Kendall, 1968) is a test designed to measure the visual perception ability of children. The child is presented with 15 designs that are sequenced in terms of difficulty. The child is presented the design and asked to reproduce it from memory. The test, designed for use with persons eight years of age and older, has the expressed intent of assessing those persons who are suspected of being brain-injured. The raw scores result in a determination of suspected brain damage as well as the developmental level of visual memory performance. The reliability data appear quite good in that the split half reliability coefficients were reported to be .92. These, however, were computed on the performance of only 140 subjects. Validity data seem to support the contention that the test will discriminate between brain-injured and non-brain-injured persons. It must be pointed out, however, that the test assesses skill in copying designs from memory and that it is not clearly indicated in the literature that this skill is necessarily a measure of brain injury. The value of this test to the classroom teacher rests in assessing a child's memory for copying visual stimuli, as well as in determining the expectancy level of what a child can functionally copy from a visual copying exercise in the classroom. Determination of brain injury should be left to the professional opinion of those trained in that area.

The tests reported above are representative of those found reported in an exceptional child's cumulative folder. There are several other tests that can be used to assess the visual perception abilities of children, and can be administered by the classroom teacher. These include the Slosson Drawing Coordination Test (Slosson, 1967), plus the subtests from the Metropolitan Readiness Test on Matching and Copying (Hildreth, Griffith, and Magauvran, 1969); the Visual Attention to Letters subtest from the *Detroit Test of Learning Aptitude* (Baker and Leland, 1935) and the Visual Sequential Memory and the Visual Closure subtests from the *Illinois Test of Psycholinguistic Abilities* (Kirk, Macarthy, and Kirk, 1968).

Informal assessment of visual perception can be made by the classroom teacher by understanding a few of the characteristics associated with visual perception problems. These include:

1. The child may completely fail or be very clumsy in performing simple motor tasks at home or at school. The tasks of cutting, pasting, drawing, writing, sports, and games will be much more difficult for him than for the child's schoolmates.
2. The child appears to be inattentive and disorganized; attention tends to jump to any stimulus that moves, no matter how irrelevant it may be.
3. The child appears to be careless in completing assigned school work due to the mobility required to find the place on a page or to find the word in a dictionary; the child may skip sections of assigned work.
4. Academically, a child with poorly developed shape and size constancy will recognize a number or letter in one particular form or context, but will be quite unable to recognize it when presented in a different manner. The following two checklists (Figures 11-1 and 11-2) provide an informal means of assessing a child's potential visual perception problems. A check in any *Yes* column may be a *clue* to the child's inability to perform visual tasks and would warrant closer observation and investigation.

Auditory assessment.   In determining the child's auditory acuity an audiometer should be used in conjunction with the services of a well-trained audiologist. Informal assessment of audi-

Figure 11-1   Informal Checklist of Symptoms Indicative of Potential Visual Perception Difficulties

	Yes	No
1. Does the child complain about headaches, dizziness or nausea associated with use of the eyes?	____	____
2. Does the child complain about an inability to work accurately at blackboard or with books?	____	____
3. Does the child complain about hurting, itching, or "tiredness" of the eyes?	____	____
4. Does the child complain about blurred or double vision?	____	____
5. Does the child shut or cover one eye?	____	____
6. Does the child tilt or thrust head forward?	____	____
7. Does the child rub eyes frequently?	____	____
8. Does the child scowl, squint, frown, or give other facial contortions when reading or doing close work?	____	____
9. Does the child blink more than usual?	____	____
10. Does the child appear to be irritable, restless, or nervous when called upon to use the eyes for close work?	____	____
11. Does the child have temper tantrums, fatigue, or listlessness after doing close work?	____	____
12. Does the child stumble or trip frequently?	____	____
13. Does the child have poor eye-hand coordination?	____	____
14. Does the child hold a book too near or too far away?	____	____
15. Does the child write with face too close to paper?	____	____

tory acuity would include identifying the child who (1) is always asking to have things repeated, (2) is asking to be moved closer to the origin of the sound, or (3) doesn't respond to others' verbal commands unless visual or physical contact is made. The teacher noting any of these behaviors should possibly have the child recommended for screening and diagnosis by the audiologist.

Formal assessment of perception includes the application and use of the following devices. The Wepman Auditory Discrimination Test (Wepman, 1958) is an easily administered test requiring the child to identify similarities and differences in word pairs. Performance on this test gives an indication of the child's ability

Figure 11-2   A Checklist for Use in Screening for Children's Potential Visual Perception Problems

	Yes	No
1. Does the child appear to lack prerequisite skills of visual-motor perception, such as ability to identify sizes, shapes, colors, and differences or similarities in letters?	____	____
2. Does the child have difficulty classifying or categorizing objects or pictures?	____	____
3. Does the child appear to observe objects within the visual field?	____	____
4. Does the child attach meaning to visual symbols, such as signs and gestures?	____	____
5. Does the child care for picture books, and is able to identify pictures of objects rapidly?	____	____
6. Does the child fail to use context clues from pictures or book illustrations in reading?	____	____
7. Does the child find absurdities in pictures?	____	____
8. Does the child have difficulty in grasping content of a story from a series of pictures?	____	____
9. Does the child have difficulty in putting series of pictures in proper or logical sequence?	____	____
10. Does the child require frequent verbal instruction in completing what is required?	____	____
11. Does the child respond better to spoken words than to visual aids?	____	____
12. Does the child fail to understand what is read?	____	____

to discriminate between sounds of letters and words. It must be emphasized that it is important to establish if the child can distinguish between the concepts of same and different before administering or making judgments about the results of the test. Too often children have been identified as having auditory discrimination problems on the basis of this test when, after interviews with the children, it was found that they could not adequately distinguish between same and different. Because there is little reliability and validity data available for this test, its usability will have to be determined by the individual user. The selection of this test as a diagnostic indicator of auditory discrimination should be done in relationship to the type of auditory discrimination tasks to be learned in the classroom by the child.

The Goldman, Fristoe, Woodcock Test of Auditory Discrimination (Goldman, Fristoe, and Woodcock, 1971) was designed to determine the child's discrimination of speech sounds utilizing a quiet and noisy background. The test can be administered to children from three years of age and into adulthood. The results from this test give an indication of the amount of intensity of auditory stimuli that a child can handle under quiet and noisy conditions. To use the test results most effectively, the teacher should become familiar with the test content. Once familiar, the test results will have greater meaning for selection and development of instructional strategies involving auditory stimuli. The reliability data from this test are quite good for both of the noisy and quiet subtests, with the reliability coefficients ranging from .81 to .87. Little validity data are provided with the apparent validity of the test being primarily based upon the opinion of the authors. Teacher use of this test, again, should be based upon a thorough understanding of what the test is measuring; then teacher utilization of the generated information in developing appropriate instructional strategies should reflect the amount and intensity of auditory stimuli that a child has been able to handle adequately as measured by the test results.

Goldman, Fristoe, and Woodcock also have another test of auditory skills, the Goldman, Fristoe, Woodcock Auditory Skills Test Battery (1976) which provides a more comprehensive assessment of auditory assessment skills. This test assesses skills in the area of auditory attention, auditory discrimination, auditory memory, and sound-symbol associations. The test was designed for use with individuals 3 years and older. This test follows somewhat the same pattern as the GFW Auditory Discrimination Test, the results of which should also be used in conjunction with a careful analysis and thorough understanding of what each of the subtests is attempting to measure. Other formal assessment devices that could be of value to the classroom teacher in assessing auditory perception include the Auditory Sequential Memory and the Sound Blending subtests from the Illinois Test of Psycholinguistic Abilities (Kirk, Macarthy, and Kirk, 1968). From the *Wechsler*

Scales (see Chapter 4 on cognitive assessment), the Digit Span subtest score could be of some value in assessing a child's auditory memory. The Roswell-Chall Auditory Blending Test (Roswell and Chall, 1963) is another relatively good test of auditory skills for use by teachers.

Informal assessment of auditory perception problems is facilitated as the teacher becomes familiar with the following concepts and the behaviors that characterize each. Simply asking if the child manifests any of the behaviors will greatly aid in determining if an auditory perception deficit exists.

1. *Signal-ground* (analytic closure). Children with signal-ground problems find it difficult to distinguish the signal from the ground. In other words, they may have difficulty attending to the message because of the presence of competing noises. They may also have difficulty identifying a sound in its word context.

2. *Auditory closure.* Auditory closure difficulty is a percept retrieval problem. Children with poor auditory perceptual retrieval have difficulty in supplying the missing auditory parts.

3. *Auditory constancy.* Teachers are aware that some children have particular difficulty in recognizing a vowel sound or other speech sound or letter from one day to the next. This is part of the process of learning to read in which many children must have considerable practice. Also, some children may have very little skill at recognizing rhyming patterns so they fail to appreciate such sound families as "and" which form the basis of a series of words such as band, land, hand, sand.

4. *Sound discrimination.* Difficulty in distinguishing between sounds that closely resemble one another may account for some of the speech production problems in which children substitute an "f" for a "th," such as in "fumb" for "thumb." Not being able to make these fine discriminations may also interfere with the child's learning to read and spell. Speech sounds are relatively refined, requiring fine discrimination. Most children may be expected to have some speech sound discrimination difficulty in the beginning stages of their auditory perceptual development. Some children, however, may have marked sound discrimination problems to the extent that they cannot distinguish easily among more gross sounds, such as the sounds of various animals or other environmental sounds.

5. *General auditory memory.* A child who has difficulty remembering a sound in several different words but no trouble remembering it in a particular word has a constancy problem rather than a general memory problem. The child, on the other hand, who cannot remember the sound from day to day regardless of its con-

text may be said to have a memory difficulty in perceptual recognition of a sound. Memory problems may be those of immediate memory or remote memory. Some children have facility for immediate memory—that is, they are able to repeat what has just been told them rather accurately, whereas on the following day they may have forgotten what they were told.

6. *Auditory attention.* Attention and memory are closely related. An inability to hold in auditory memory of something that has just been said by someone else may result in the person's loss of attention to the thing that has just been said or to the person who said it. Conversely, if a person does not give sufficient attention to the details of something that was said, that person's memory of the spoken message or auditory stimulus may be very short. Children who are extremely distractible may not be able to give sufficient attention to perceive a stimulus accurately in the first place and, thus, exhibit poor memory for auditory stimuli to which they have been exposed.

7. *Sequential auditory memory.* Immediate and remote memory differential is of considerable significance in tasks involving a sequence of auditory percepts. When there is severe sequential memory difficulty, children may not be able to recall appropriate word order to constitute acceptable syntax in a sentence. They may, as they read words, have difficulty holding the memory of sounds of letters in their auditory processing system long enough to recognize the word and to be able to read it. Or they may not be able to hold in their auditory memory long enough, instructions they have been given in order to carry out more than one commission.

Observation on the part of the teacher of the following behaviors would also be indications that the child may have auditory perception problems: The child (1) continually fails to follow verbal directions; (2) is constantly asking for repetitions; (3) is unable to concentrate on a task due to the extraneous auditory stimuli in the classroom; (4) manifests confusion of letters or words; (5) is unable to blend sounds in a phonic exercise; and (6) has pronunciation problems in speech patterns. Any or all of these may be indicative of a child's auditory perception difficulties.

Motor assessment. Two formal motor assessment devices will be discussed in this section, along with selected informal techniques. The Purdue Perceptual-Motor Survey (PPMS) (Roach and Kephart, 1966) was developed to determine the qualitative perceptual motor abilities of children in the early grades. The survey is intended for use in observing the motor behavior of children within a structured environment. The manual provides very specific directions, including photographs, for administering the survey items. Scoring is accomplished through the use of a rating scale which specifically identifies behaviors the child should be able to perform relative to each of the eleven subtests that compose the entire survey. The subtests of the survey assess a child's (1) balance and postural flexibility; (2) jumping; (3) identification of body parts; (4) imitation of movement; (5) movement through an obstacle course; (6) ability to perform angels in the snow; (7) perceptual motor matching; (8) rhythmic writing; (9) ocular control; and (10) form perception. Each of the subtests is composed of specific tasks including walking a balance beam, jumping on each foot, and activities through which the ability to use both sides of the body can be assessed. These individual tasks allow for easy analysis of a child's performance and can assist the teacher in better determining a child's gross and fine motor capabilities. From the assessment more exact instructional strategies can be identified that would benefit the child in better performing those particular tasks. The reliability data available on this test show that the correlation coefficients taken from a test retest as being .95. The validity information is somewhat less definitive and is of a content nature.

The usability of this test is found more in the informal information that can be generated than in attempting to identify normative levels of behavior. As mentioned above, the individual subtests are composed of distinct items of specific behavior. Those specific behaviors can be identified by the teacher that best fit the overall educational program the child is functioning within. Behaviors identified as being deficient from the survey can then be specifically programmed for remediation. This allows the teacher far greater control between the overall educational program of the child and those parts of that program that require the child performing tasks similar to those assessed by this survey. Data are not available to support the use of this survey in making comparisons with a normative population for classification or placement purposes. This survey, in the author's opinion, is a very effective informal device for assessing children's motor abilities.

The Bruininks-Oseretzky Test of Motor Proficiency (Bruininks, 1977) is designed for use with children between the ages of 4 and 18 years. It is to be individually administered and is designed to assess both the fine and gross motor capabilities of the child. It is composed of eight subtests including: (1) running speed and agility; (2) balance; (3) bilateral coordination; (4) strength; (5) upper-limb coordination; (6) visual-motor control; (7) response speed; and (8) upper-limb speed and dexterity. Results of the test scores can be interpreted in terms of age equivalence or percentile rankings. The test provides an estimate of the child's general motor ability and can be used much like the Purdue Perceptual Motor Survey as a checklist of motor behaviors expected of a child at a particular age or developmental level. The reliability data on this test are of a retest nature with a correlation coefficient for the subtests approximately at the .80 level. Educational uses of the data from this test should not include the determination of a child's relative motor development age but as an indication of those motor areas in which the teacher ascertains the skill development needs of the child. From this information appropriate instructional strategies can be identified and planned to assist the child in increasing motor performance in any particular area.

Figure 11-3   Informal Motor Assessment

	Yes	No
1. Can the child get up quickly on command from a prone position, kneeling position, sitting position?	____	____
2. Can the child catch a large ball two out of four tries from six feet?	____	____
3. Can the child hold a pencil and write name legibly?	____	____
4. Can the child maintain balance while walking a straight line, forward and back?	____	____
5. Can the child stand on one foot for five seconds, ten seconds?	____	____
6. Can the child close eyes and touch nose with both hands?	____	____
7. Can the child draw a straight line between two points six inches apart?	____	____
8. Can the child turn right or left on command?	____	____
9. Can the child hop on both feet, right foot, left foot?	____	____
10. Can the child imitate the body movements of others?	____	____
11. Can the child throw a ball, throw for distance, and throw for accuracy?	____	____

Other formal motor tests include the Perceptual and Motor Development (Cratty, 1970), as well as parts of the Denver Developmental Screening Test (Frankenburg and Dobbs, 1967).

Informal motor assessment can be accomplished through the use of a number of different procedures, one of which is illustrated in Figure 11-3, a rating scale of motor tasks. Teacher observation provides a very worthwhile means of determining the motor abilities of the child. The teacher can construct a number of procedures to determine if the child is able to identify and locate body parts as well as to perform gross and fine motor tasks such as catching and throwing a ball or using scissors to cut a specified object from a sheet of paper. An obstacle course such as that suggested in the PPMS is an excellent device for assessing a child's general motor abilities to include left-right orientation, identification of body parts, balance, and flexibility in movement.

The observation of a child in terms of body control—clumsiness and uncoordinated movements are indications of potential motor difficulties—may warrant remediation especially if it is determined that the child's overall performance in school, either academic or emotional, can be improved through improving the motor areas. For example, putting the child through a remediation program to develop better coordinated body movements to directly improve the child's performance in a sports area may increase better peer relationships as well as self-image. These, in turn, may positively affect the child's overall academic performance. The development of fine motor control may assist the child in increasing his performance involving handwriting tasks as well as the willingness to perform those types of tasks. The important concepts involved in motor assessment are the identification of the motor skills required within the overall instructional program. Once they are identified, a child's ability to perform those tasks can be more readily determined either utilizing formal or informal methods. After the child's ability has been assessed, the instructional strategies can be more exactly identified and planned.

Summary of Modality Assessment

The assessment as well as remediation of modalities, especially in the area of perception, appears to be somewhat controversial and in need of further investigation. However, several authorities seem to feel modality information should continue to be included in the child's instructional program; and there is substantial information to indicate that this information will continue to be requested and required of children attending public school classes serving exceptional children. Both of these reasons provide the emphasis behind the rationale for teachers becoming familiar with the concepts and techniques involved in the assessment of modalities. That is, teachers should become familiar with formal and informal procedures that can be used or are used to assess modalities. For instructional program planning from a modalities frame of reference, the teacher must be equipped with information relative to what requirements the instructional program has for involving each of the modalities mentioned in this chapter. The identification of this information can then be used to more appropriately select and utilize formal and informal assessment techniques to determine a child's visual, auditory, or motor deficiency. Even though little conclusive research evidence is available concerning this area, every possible element that can affect school performance should be taken into consideration. The information generated from the modality assessment may have important implications for both program planning and classroom teaching. That information may provide or suggest a direction of possible adjustment within the methodology or strategy being used to teach the child. Further, the information generated from this type of assessment may give light as to what other types of diagnostic information are needed to understand the child better.

Another implication of the results taken from a modality assessment would be an attempt to establish the causes of behavior within the child instead of reacting to the child's behavior directly. That is, the child manifesting behavior problems in the classroom when viewed from a modality reference may be found to have difficulties with auditory acuity. As such, the child's external behaviors imply something totally different to a teacher not having that information concerning the child's auditory acuity. With the information the teacher can not only make more accurate decisions relative to instructional program planning; he can also make an appropriate referral for further diagnosis. Modality assessment is one of many areas that comprise the total assessment process. It is of more value in some situations than others and should be used cautiously, especially when consideration is made of the controversial research presented earlier in this chapter. Children who experience learning problems, however, can benefit from this area of assessment if the results are correctly applied and interpreted within the total learning environment of the child.

Can You Answer These Questions?

1. Can you define modalities?
2. What is visual figure ground?
3. What is visual motor integration?
4. Can you differentiate between acuity and perception?
5. What are three formal tests of visual perception?
6. What are three formal tests of auditory perception?
7. What are some of the controversial issues pertaining to the assessment of modalities?
8. What would be included in an informal assessment of motor function?

References

Arnold, R. D.   "Four Methods of Teaching Word Recognition to Disabled Readers." *Elementary School Journal*, 68, 1968, 269–74.

Baker, H. J., and B. Leland. *Detroit Test of Learning Aptitude.* Indianapolis: Bobbs-Merrill, 1935.

Barsch, R. H.   "Teacher Needs—Motor Training." In W. M. Cruickshank (ed.), *The Teacher of Brain-injured Children.* Syracuse: Syracuse University Press, 1966.

Bateman, Barbara.   "The Efficacy of an Auditory and a Visual Method of First Grade Reading Instruction with Auditory and Visual Learns." *Curriculum Bulletin* (School of Education, University of Oregon), 23, 1967, 6–14.

Beery, Keith, and N. Buktenica. *Developmental Test of Visual-Motor Integration.* Chicago: Fallett Publishing Co., 1967.

Bender, L. *A Visual Motor Gestalt Test and Its Clinical Use.* New York: American Ortho-psychiatric Association Monograph, No. 3, 1938.

Bruininks, R. H. *Bruininks-Oseretzky Test of Motor Proficiency.* Circle Pines, Minnesota: American Guidance Service, 1977.

Cooper, J. David. "A Study of the Learning Modalities of Good and Poor First Grade Readers." In Nila B. Smith (ed.), *Reading Methods and Teacher Improvement.* Newark, Delaware: International Reading Association, 1971, 87–97.

Cratty, B. J. *Perceptual and Motor Development in Infants and Children.* New York: Macmillan, 1970.

Cratty, B. J. *Remedial Motor Activity for Children.* Philadelphia: Lea and Febiger, 1975.

Frankenburg, W. K., J. B. Dobbs, and A. W. Fasdal. *Denver Developmental Screening Test.* Denver: Ladoca Propet and Publishing Foundation, 1970.

Frostig, M., W. Lefever, and J. Whittlesey. *Frostig Developmental Test of Visual Perception.* Palo Alto, California: Consulting Psychologists Press, 1966.

Goldman, R., M. Fristoe, and R. Woodcock. *Goldman-Fristoe-Woodcock Test of Auditory Discrimination.* Circle Pines, Minnesota: American Guidance Service, 1970.

Goldman, R., M. Fristoe, and R. Woodcock. *The Goldman-Fristoe-Woodcock Auditory Skills Test Battery.* Circle Pines, Minnesota: American Guidance Service, 1976.

Graham, F. K., and B. S. Kendall. "Memory for Designs Test." *Perceptual and Motor Skills,* 1960, 11, 147–190.

Hallahan, D. P., and W. M. Cruickshank. *Psychoeducational Foundations of Learning Disabilities.* New York: Prentice-Hall, 1973.

Hammill, D. D., and S. C. Larsen. "The Effectiveness of Psycholinguistic Training." *Exceptional Children,* 1974, 41, 5–15.

Harris, Albert J. "Individualizing First Grade Reading According to Specific Learning Aptitudes." *Research Report*, Office of Research and Evaluation, Division of Teacher Education of the City University of New York, 1965.

Hildreth, G. H., M. Griffiths, and M. E. McGauvran. *The Metropolitan Readiness Test*. New York: Harcourt Brace Jovanovich, 1969.

Kephart, N. C. *The Slow Learner in the Classroom*. Columbus, Ohio: Charles E. Merrill, 1960.

Keystone Visual Survey Tests, Davenport, Iowa: Keystone View Division, Must Development Co.

Kirk, S., J. McCarthy, and W. Kirk. *Illinois Test of Psycholinguistic Abilities*. Urbana, Illinois: University of Illinois Press, 1968.

Koppitz, E. M. *The Bender-Gestalt Test for Young Children*. New York: Grune and Stratton, 1964.

Koppitz, E. M. *The Bender-Gestalt Test for Young Children*. Vol. II: *Research and Application, 1963–1973*. New York: Grune and Stratton, 1975.

Mills, R. E. *Learning Methods Test Kit, Revised*. Fort Lauderdale: The Mills Educational Center, 1970.

Moran, M. R. "The Teachers Role in Referral for Testing and Interpretation of Reports." *Focus on Exceptional Children*, 1976, 8, 1–15.

Reger, R., W. Schroeder, and K. Uschold. *Special Education: Children with Learning Problems*. New York: Oxford University Press, 1968.

Roach, E. G., and N. C. Kephart. *The Purdue Perceptual-Motor Survey*. Columbus, Ohio: Charles E. Merrill, 1966.

Roswell, F., and J. Chall. *Roswell-Chall Auditory Blending Test*. New York: The Essay Press, 1963.

Sabatino, D. A., and W. O. Streissgurth. "Word Form Configuration Training of Visual Perceptual Strengths with Learning Disabled Children." *Journal of Learning Disabilities*, 5 (August–September 1972), 435–41.

Slosson, R. I. *Slosson Drawing Coordination Test.* East Aurora, New York: Slosson Educational Publications, 1967.

Spache, G. D. *Spache Binocular Reading Test.* Davenport, Iowa: Keystone View Division, Mast Development Company, 1961.

Spache, G. D. *Diagnosing and Correcting Reading Disabilities.* Boston: Allyn and Bacon, 1976.

Wallace, G., and S. C. Larsen. *Educational Assessment of Learning Problems: Testing for Teaching.* Boston: Allyn and Bacon, 1978.

Wepman, J. M. *The Auditory Discrimination Test.* Chicago: Language Research Associates, 1973.

Wolpert, E. M. "Modality and Reading: A Perspective," *Reading Teacher,* 24 (April 1971), 640–43.

chapter

12

Mathematics Assessment

Objectives

At the conclusion of this chapter, the reader should be able to:

1. identify formal and informal procedures for conducting a math assessment;
2. outline the sequence of math behaviors expected at specified grade levels;
3. conduct a math assessment to identify a child's math deficiencies.

Introduction

The academic area of math is perhaps the most neglected of all the academic areas. This is especially evident when the number of assessment devices and commercially prepared instructional programs are used as a measuring stick. Wallace and Larsen (1978) have pointed out that there is very little professional literature dealing with the remediation and assessment of math problems for children with learning difficulties and that few assessment devices and remedial materials are available in the same magnitude as found in other academic areas. This apparent lack of diagnostic measures as well as remediation techniques may be due in part to the more clearly and specifically defined skills that one must possess to complete different levels of the math task.

The commercially prepared remediation materials as well as the diagnostic tests in the area of math assessment are usually designed to identify a performer's specific strengths and weaknesses in skill development. As indicated by Salvia and Ysseldyke (1978), mathematical operations depend on successful skill level performance of specific operations or related operations—that is, multiplication is dependent somewhat upon addition. They conclude that it is, therefore, easier to sequence skill development in math than in other academic areas.

Children having difficulty in math do so for a number of different reasons. The reasons relate either to their deficiencies with specific skills or may be related to factors beyond skill level deficiencies. Spencer and Smith (1969) note that arithmetic skills are so complex in their interrelationships that children may have difficulty in achievement for a number of reasons. They identify three basic questions which the classroom teacher must be concerned with when determining what the reasons are behind a child's failure in math:

1. What deficiencies in number readiness skills prevent the child from achieving in arithmetic?
2. What are the difficulties in computational skills, time and money concepts that seem to be interfering with progress in arithmetic performance?
3. What specific skill difficulties prevent achievement in problem solving?

The success of any mathematics program depends on how closely it relates to the needs and interests of the child benefitting or participating in the program. The teacher must know what the needs and interests of the child are in conjunction with a very solid idea as to the child's readiness, computational skills and problem-solving skill levels. Assessment of both a formal and informal nature should be geared to the identification of this information.

Children's Math Problems

Following are a number of specific arithmetic areas in which children appear to have problems. These include readiness, computational and problem-solving skills. A brief discussion of types of problems encountered by children in each area will be presented.

Arithmetic Readiness Skills. Prior to performing adequately on basic computational skills a child should exhibit competency with a number of the skills basic to understanding other arithmetic or math processes. The child should be able to: (1) discriminate among different sizes, shapes and quantities; (2) demonstrate an understanding of one-to-one relationships; (3) count numbers; (4) order numbers by name; and (5) arrange numbers into sets.

Computational Skills and Time and Money Concepts. A great portion of the arithmetic problems manifest by children are directly related to basic computational skills, including a demonstrated ability to add, subtract, multiply and divide at their most fundamental level. Having an understanding of place value as well as fractions is a step that many children have difficulty in demonstrating mastery and which may affect time and money concepts; however, taken separately, time and money concepts is an area where children have difficulty grasping and applying the concepts functionally. The ability to tell time and to identify monetary values is a deficient area in many children.

Problem-solving Skills. Some children with arithmetic difficulties are unable to operationalize number skills and story problems due to specific problem-solving deficiencies. Adeuate problem-solving skills in math are based upon the child's ability to: (1) understand the language of arithmetic; (2) reason and interpret information from reading a story problem; and (3) conceptualize the appropriate operation for solving that problem.

Teacher Skills. Wallace and Kauffman (1978) indicate that learning problems in general may be due to inadequate or inappropriate teaching. Since math deficiencies seem more directly related to skill acquisition, it is paramount on the part of the teacher to possess the necessary teaching skills needed for teaching children appropriate math operations. As Wallace and Larsen (1978) point out, remedial arithmetic teaching methods may not be included in many teacher training programs and inservice programs for teachers in remedial arithmetic techniques are almost nonexistent. This, of course, all results in teachers not being adequately trained to deal with children's math problems appropriately. Other problems underlying the students' successful performance in the math area may be related to the emphasis placed on it in schools (Otto, McMenemy, and Smith, 1973). Math is not emphasized as much because it is not perceived as being as important as other academic areas, especially reading.

Conducting a Math Assessment

The most common reasons for conducting an assessment in the area of math are usually found among the following.

1. Grouping. Grouping is to assist the classroom teacher in determining how best to place children according to skill level. This is usually done under the guise of more efficient use of the teacher's time.

2. Achievement level placement. The assessment is conducted to identify the best or most appropriate math program that the child should be placed within.

3. Planning a curriculum. Even though related to grouping and placement, the assessment information is a guide that allows a teacher to identify, select and plan the lessons to be given to the child.

4. The ultimate reason for conducting any assessment including math is to determine the child's specific areas of skill, strength, or weakness, and more particularly to generate such information that will more clearly delineate the reasons behind the child's difficulty. For example, identifying the child as unable to compute two-digit addition with sums not to exceed 50 is a more specific

level of information than to merely indicate that the child is performing math at a first grade level of proficiency.

Discrepancy Analysis. In conducting the math assessment the teacher must determine the expectancy level that is desired for each individual child. Expectancy levels can best be extracted from a number of different, related sources, such as a scope and sequence chart from a standardized math program, or a skill level chart outlining the sequence of behavior that is necessary in performing progressively more difficult math skills taken from the local education agency or state education agency's list of expected math behaviors of children attending that agency's schools. Figure 12-1 is a skill sequence chart depicting the math skills expected at different grade levels (Utah State Board of Education, 1976). It is merely an example of the type of scope and sequence chart that can be obtained or should be available from the local or state education agency.

The usual manner in which a scope and sequence skill chart is prepared is either in terms of grade level, as found in Figure 12-1, or in terms of age expectancy levels. In either case, the skills depict the sequence of difficulty in determining the expectancy level of the child. The teacher merely needs to survey the list and focus on that particular skill sequence that is most appropriate to the child. Having this information will assist in guiding the programmer or teacher in selecting diagnostic as well as remedial program strategies.

A next step in math assessment is to determine the actual performance level of the child and then to pinpoint as specifically as possible the type of problem the child is manifesting. This can be accomplished through either the application of formal diagnostic tests or informal assessment measures. Comparing the actual performance to the expected performance level allows the teacher to determine the severity of problems as well as to locate the most appropriate starting place for developing instruction. Figure 12-2 is an illustration of Eloise's expected and actual math performance. As can be seen, Eloise is in the sixth grade, and it has been determined by her placement that her math performance is *expected* to be at that level. Her actual *tested* math performance was found to be at approximately the second-grade level of development in the basic computational areas.

Figure 12-1   Math Skills Sequence by Grade Levels

Grade Level	Operation	Expected Behaviors
Pre-academic (K–1)	Geometry/ Measurement	Identifies largest, smallest, from three objects.
		Distinguishes between two geometric shapes.
		Recalls events of yesterday.
		Matches like geometric forms.
		Predicts events using *tonight*.
		Identifies the missing object from a set of three.
		Identifies *middle* size.
		Arranges three objects by size: big to little, little to big.
		Selects a specific shape from a set: square, circle, triangle.
		Identifies *birthday* as a recurring event.
		Recalls events of *last night*.
		Associates clocks and calendars with telling time.
		Compares sizes of two sets using *more* and *less*.
		Identifies the missing object from a set of four.
		Identifies shapes: circle, square, triangle, rectangle.
		Indicates comparison of size: tall, short, long.
		Indicates comparison of volume: full, empty, more, less.
		Identifies shapes of familiar objects.
		Associates clock with school routine.
		Associates calendar with days, weeks, months.
		Reproduces sequence or patterns of geometric shapes.
		Reads number data from science activities.
		Identifies geometric objects by one characteristic: shape, size and color.

Grade Level	Operation	Expected Behaviors
Pre-academic (K–1)	Geometry/ Measurement	Indicates one-half of symmetrical shapes. Locates numbers (1–9) on primary ruler. Tells time with hours and half-hours.
	Numbers/ Numerals	Stacks a set of objects and places a set of objects in a row (linearity). Identifies three objects as *more than* two. Distinguishes between *one* and *many*. Identifies two *uses* of numerals. Distinguishes between *letters* and *numerals*. Counts by rote to 3, perhaps without understanding. Counts aloud three objects. Identifies one object and one more as *two*. Participates in games that involve counting. Participates in group recitation of poems and songs involving numbers. Indicates his age, address, and telephone number. Indicates comparison of quantities: some, all, many, same. Identifies larger and smaller sets. Arranges a set in order by size. Constructs a set with the same number of members as a given set (1–5). Identifies a set with *one more* member than a given set. Matches objects one-to-one. Counts by rote to 30. Counts backward from 10 to 1. Indicates the set with a given number of members from among sets of various sizes (1–9). Counts objects in order (1–9). Reads numerals (0–9). Constructs sets of 1–9 members using concrete objects.

Figure 12-1   Math Skills Sequence by Grade Levels (*Continued*)

Grade Level	Operation	Expected Behaviors
Pre-academic (K–1)	Geometry/ Measurement	Identifies numbers as *more than* or *less than*. Recognizes pictures of sets of 0–9 objects. Draws a set with 0–9 members. Identifies on the number line 1–9. Writes the numerals 1–9. Reads words: one to five. Constructs a number line (1–9).
1st	Geometry/ Measurement	Constructs geometric shapes on geo-board. Draws shapes from geo-board on dotted paper. Describes common objects in geometric terms. Constructs a monthly calendar. Names five basic geometric shapes. Draws an acceptable circle, square, rectangle and triangle. Recognizes time in quarter-hours. Observes, reads, and records data from science activities. Constructs a set of geometric forms by shape, by size, and by color. Groups geometric objects by two characteristics: red-round, small-square. Reads and records the temperature from a thermometer. Tells time to nearest five minutes.
	Numbers/ Numerals	Counts by rote with fives and tens to 100. Reads words: zero–nine. Reads and writes numerals through 19. Writes different names of numbers through 5. Reads ordinal numbers: first through tenth.

Grade Level	Operation	Expected Behaviors
1st	Numbers/ Numerals	Counts by rote with 2s through 20.
		Indicates values of coins: penny, nickel and dime.
		Counts from a small number through 100.
		Shows numbers through 99 as tens and ones by grouping concrete objects.
		Tells difference in sizes of two sets.
		Identifies the face value and place value up to 99.
		Uses < > to compare two numbers.
		Regroups numbers through 99 as tens plus ones.
		Reads and writes numerals through 99.
		Identifies on a number line 1–99.
		Writes number sentences to represent experiences.
		Uses number line to locate nearest 10 with numbers up to 90.
		Matches values of sets of coins up to $1.00.
	Basic Computations (add, subtract, multiply, divide)	Joins sets of 1 to 5 objects and records results using + and = signs.
		Writes addition facts to sums of 5 from memory.
		Separates sets of objects with 2–5 members and records results using − and = signs.
		Writes subtraction facts related to sums through 5 from memory.
		Uses placeholders (i. e. □) in all three positions in addition and subtraction sentences with answers through 5.
		Demonstrates commutative property with sums 2 through 5 (3 + 2 = 2 + 3).
		Joins and separates sets of objects with 2–10 members and records results.
		Uses number line for addition and subtraction through sums of 10.

Figure 12-1 Math Skills Sequence by Grade Levels (*Continued*)

Grade Level	Operation	Expected Behaviors
Pre-academic (K–1)	Basic Computations (add, subtract, multiply, divide)	Writes addition and subtraction facts with answers of 6 through 10 from memory.
		Uses place holders in all three positions in addition and subtraction sentences to answers through 10.
		Uses vertical addition with three addends to sums of 10.
		Solves word problems to sums of 10.
		Represents addition and subtraction facts with sums/differences from 11 to 18 using concrete materials.
		Demonstrates on a number line addition and subtraction facts with answers from 11 to 18.
		Completes a table of addition facts with sums of 11 to 18 using aids.
		Completes math sentences with a missing addend or sum with sums 11 to 18.
1st–2nd	Geometry/ Measurement	Arranges geometric objects by three characteristics: small, red, square.
		Recognizes inch, foot, yard.
		Reads and writes specific times such as 6:35.
		Identifies points on a coordinate plane.
		Uses arbitrary units to measure length, width, and height.
		Converts days to weeks and weeks to months using a calendar.
	Numbers/ Numerals	Compares two number names to determine *more than*, *less than* and *equal to* relationships.
		Rounds numbers less than 99 to nearest 10.
		Identifies half, third, and fourth of a set of concrete materials.
		Identifies halves, thirds, and fourths of a set of pictorial materials.

Grade Level	Operation	Expected Behaviors
1st–2nd	Numbers/ Numerals	Writes cardinal numbers as words. Renames two-digit addends by using expanded notation. Represents two-digit addition and subtraction on number line. Finds total value for each set of coins up to $1.00. Writes ordinal number words, first to tenth, from memory.
	Basic Computations	Writes addition and subtraction facts with sums/differences to 18 from memory. Uses 10's in regrouping addends in addition to sums of 18. Adds three addends, sums to 18. Employs associative property in adding two-digit numbers to one-digit numbers, sums to 18; i.e. 12 + 5 = (10 + 2) + 5 = 10 + (2 + 5). Adds and subtracts by 10's. Performs two-digit addition and subtraction with no regrouping. Performs two-digit addition and subtraction involving regrouping in the one's place. Writes number sentences to solve problems to sums of 18. Computes total value of a set of coins using penny, nickel, dime, quarter, half-dollar.
2nd–3rd	Geometry/ Measurement	Locates and places points on a coordinate plane. Measures to nearest inch.
	Numbers/ Numerals	Shows numbers through 999 as hundreds, tens, ones by grouping concrete objects. Reads and writes numerals through 999. Identifies and locates numbers through 999 on a number line.

Figure 12-1   Math Skills Sequence by Grade Levels (*Continued*)

Grade Level	Operation	Expected Behaviors
	Basic Computations	Renames numbers through 999 with expanded notation. Performs two-digit addition and subtraction with regrouping in ones and/or tens. Performs three-digit addition and subtraction involving regrouping in ones or tens.
3rd–4th	Geometry/ Measurement	Converts cups, pints, quarts, gallons, using physical materials. Converts inches, feet, and yards, using physical materials. Measures to ½ inch. Estimates the areas of irregular shapes drawn on graph paper. Converts cups to pints, pints to quarts, and quarts to gallons, using pitchers. Converts inches, feet and yards. Measures to ¼ inch. Represents specific times with numerals and with clock faces. Represents times that are earlier or later than that on a given clock face. Measures lengths of line segments correct to centimeters and ¼ inches. Converts liquid measures and linear measures.
	Numbers/ Numerals	Represents (A) multiplication with products of 25 or less and (B) related division facts using concrete objects. Represents multiplication and related division facts of 25 or less with arrays. Represents multiplication and related division facts of 25 or less on number lines. Writes fractional numerals: ⅓, ⅔, ¾. Uses decimal notation to record money.

Grade Level	Operation	Expected Behaviors
3rd–4th		Performs multiplication of two-digit numbers by one-digit numbers, using expanded notation.
		Reads, writes and represents numbers through 999,999.
		Reads and writes Roman numerals to XII.
		Identifies prime numbers: 2, 3, 5, 7.
	Basic Computations	Performs three-digit addition and subtraction involving regrouping in ones, tens, and hundreds.
		Solves word problems involving addition or subtraction.
		Performs column addition of five, three-digit numerals, with regrouping.
		Computes products to 25.
		Adds and subtracts money values to three digits.
		Performs multiplications through products of 81 and related divisions.
		Solves word problems involving multiplications to products of 81 and related divisions.
		Uses distributive property.
		Uses $<$ $>$ or $=$ to express relations between numbers to 999.
4th–5th	Geometry/ Measurement	Converts value of all U.S. coins.
		Converts pounds and ounces.
		Converts ones and dozens.
		Computes areas using coordinate paper.
	Numbers/ Numerals	Identifies fractional parts of units fifths to eighths.
		Locates fractional numbers on the number line.
		Identifies even or odd numbers.
		Reads and writes mixed numbers.
	Basic Computations	Divides two-digit numbers by one-digit numbers, using two-stage process.

Figure 12-1 Math Skills Sequence by Grade Levels (*Continued*)

Grade Level	Operation	Expected Behaviors
4th–5th		Adds and subtracts dollars and cents involving regrouping.
		Adds like fractions (halves through eighths) to sums of 1.
5th–6th	Geometry/ Measurement	Constructs bar graphs to record data.
		Identifies common objects as cubes and spheres.
		Converts scale distance on maps to real distances. (Scale: 1″ = 1 mile)
	Numbers/ Numerals	Identifies a number as a product of prime numbers.
		Recognizes the second factor of a product as the size of a set.
		Skip counts by 2s, 3s, 4s, 5s, 6s, and 8s to eight skips.
	Basic Computation	Adds and subtracts to 9,999,999 involving regrouping and carrying.
		Multiplies three-digit numbers by one-digit numbers through 9 × 999.
		Divides three-digit numbers by one-digit divisors through 9.

On a gross level the teacher has at least a beginning place from which to start instruction. The next step would be to review the skill sequence such as is found in Figure 12-1 to determine more specifically the basic math concepts that have been mastered by Eloise (approximately the second grade level) and then to select the next sequence of behavior to which the instructional program should be directed. In the case of Eloise a good beginning place for instructional programming would include the following behaviors selected from Figure 12-1. The teacher would ensure that Eloise could complete these basic computations before going on to higher skill development.

Math behaviors for Eloise:

1.   Represents addition and subtraction facts with sums/differences from 11 to 18 using concrete materials.

Figure 12-2 Discrepancy Analysis of Eloise's Math Performance

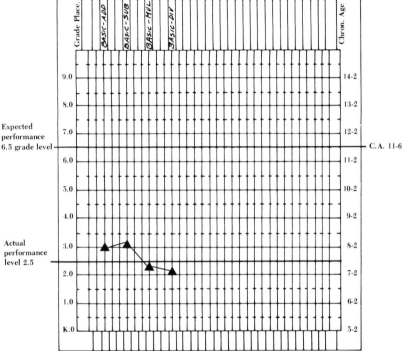

PROFILE CHART

Name __Eloise__ Date _____ Profiler _____
              Yr. Mo. Day
School _____ B.D. _____ Report to _____
              Yr. Mo. Day
Grade _____ Age: _____ Address _____
              Yr. Mo. Day

2. Demonstrates on a number line addition and subtraction facts with answers from 11 to 18.

3. Completes a table of addition facts with sums of 11 to 18 using aids.

4. Completes math sentences with a missing addend or sum with sums 11 to 18.

5. Writes addition and subtraction facts with sums/differences to 18 from memory.

6. Uses 10s in regrouping addends in addition to sums of 18.

7. Adds three addends, sums to 18.

8. Employs associative property in adding two-digit numbers to one-digit numbers, sums to 18; i.e. $12 + 5 = (10 + 2) + 5 = 10 + (2 + 5)$.

9. Adds and subtracts by 10s.
10. Performs two-digit addition and subtraction with no regrouping.
11. Performs two-digit addition and subtraction involving regrouping in the one's place.
12. Writes number sentences to solve problems to sums of 18.
13. Computes total value of a set of coins using penny, nickel, dime, quarter, half-dollar.
14. Performs two-digit addition and subtraction with regrouping in ones and/or tens.
15. Performs three-digit addition and subtraction involving regrouping in ones or tens.

Formal and informal math assessment measures will be reviewed in the following discussion. First a review of formal diagnostic tests will be presented beginning with instruments that are easily applied by the classroom teacher and then concluding with a discussion of informal techniques.

Key Math Diagnostic Arithmetic Test (Connolly, Nachtman, Pritchett, 1971). This test is an individually administered test designed for use with children from the ages of preschool through grade nine. The Key Math is composed of 14 subtests that are organized into three areas: content, operations, and applications. The *content* area is specific to assessing a child's basic knowledge of mathematics and the concepts underlying basic math operations. In the *operations* area, the child demonstrates an understanding of addition, subtraction, multiplication, and division through computation of specific problems. In the *applications* section, the child demonstrates an understanding of money, time, and measurement.

Four kinds of diagnostic data can be generated from the child's performance on this test. These include the child's total test performance, which can be transformed into a grade equivalent. The second type of interpretation is focused on the performance of the child in each of the three general areas of the test. That is, the child's performance across the three areas is thoroughly analyzed to determine potential areas of deficit, either in content, operations, or applications. A third area of interpretation relates to the child's performance on each of the 14 subtests which can be nicely illustrated on the profile sheet provided with the test materials. The profile is a graphic illustration of strengths and weaknesses. Certainly, an identified weakness on a subtest should be thoroughly scrutinized before decisions relative to program planning are made. The last area of interpretation, and perhaps the most unique feature of the Key Math Test, is the reference of each test item that is written in an objective statement of the math behavior expected for each item of the test. This allows the teacher to determine more objectively what the child's deficiency might be relative to the tasks the child was unable to perform: That is, once the teacher knows which task the child failed on any of the subtests, he or she can refer to the specific behaviors (located in the back of the administrator's manual) to obtain a more definitive description of the child's problem. Figure 12-3 gives a sample of the types of specific behaviors that depict the test items.

In terms of program planning the Key Math is a most useful device. It provides good information enabling the teacher to identify a child's specific skill deficiencies. With the information obtained from the specific objectives or specific behaviors sequence, the teacher can plan math programs. The test can be used both as a normed reference measure to establish actual grade level performance or as a criterion measure from which expected behaviors for completing specified math skills can be identified. It should be noted that the test has been designed for use by teachers who have had little if any diagnostic training. The test can be easily administered, scored, and interpreted by classroom teachers.

Stanford Diagnostic Mathematics Test (Beatty, Madden, Gardner, and Karlsen, 1976). This test is group administered and can be used as both a norm-referenced as well as criterion-referenced device. There are four levels of the test for administration to students in grade 2 through high school: Level 1 is designed for grade 1.5 through 4.5; Level 2, grades 3.5 to 6.5; Level 3, grades 5.5 to 8.5; and Level 4, grades 7.5 to high school. Each level is composed of three parts to assess number and numeration, computation, and application. In the *number and numeration* section the child's understanding of numbers, sets, and complex mathematics operations is assessed. The primary function of this component of the test is to determine the child's understanding of numbers and their properties. The *computation* sec-

Figure 12-3 A Sample of Behavioral Objectives Selected from the Key Math Diagnostic Arithmetic Test

Subtest	Item Number	Behavioral Objective
Fractions	B-1	Given an object and its half, identifies the half part
	B-2	Given a group of objects, identifies half the group
	B-3	Given a measuring cup with fractional markings, identifies the quantity contained
	B-4	Given a whole divided into unequal parts, indicates the fraction formed by one of these parts
	B-5	Given a fractional numeral, identifies it by name
	B-6	Given a whole divided into unequal parts, indicates the fraction formed by combining two of these parts
	B-7	Given a set of objects, identifies the fraction which represents a subset of the elements
	B-8	Given a group of objects, identifies the number of elements composing one-third
	B-9	Given a number, obtains a specific fractional part
	B-10	Given a group of objects, identifies the number of elements composing three-fourths
	B-11	Given an improper fraction, changes to a mixed number
Geometry and Symbols	C-1	Given a variety of geometric shapes, identifies the circle
	C-2	Given a disc shape, identifies which of two parts needs to be joined with another to make an identical disc figure
	C-3	Given a star shape, identifies which of three parts needs to be joined with another to make an identical star figure
	C-4	Given a variety of geometric shapes, identifies the square
	C-5	Given a variety of geometric shapes, identifies the tallest

Subtest	Item Number	Behavioral Objective
Geometry and Symbols	C-6	Given a variety of geometric shapes, identifies the triangle
	C-7	Given a disc shape, identifies which of four parts needs to be joined with another to make an identical disc figure
	C-8	Given a number sentence, identifies the symbol for addition
	C-9	Given a number sentence, identifies the symbol for subtraction
	C-10	Given a number sentence, identifies the symbol for equality
	C-11	Given an amount of money, identifies the dollar sign
	C-12	Given a number sentence, identifies the symbol for multiplication

tion of the test assesses a child's understanding of the primary math facts involving addition, subtraction, multiplication and division. In the *application* part of the test, the child's skill in applying basic math facts is assessed. During this part of the test the child is required to solve simple to complex story problems involving basic computation skills and measurement. The overall focus of the test is to assess the child's understanding of numbers as well as the child's skill in working with basic math concepts.

The test is criterion-referenced in terms of the "progress indicator." For each part of the test the child is determined to be competent or incompetent within each of the levels and subtests (number and numeration, computation, and application) on the basis of performance, the performance being valued through the *progress indicator*. Those children reaching the indicator level specified for a particular subtest item are considered competent and those not reaching that indicator level are referred for additional help or program assistance. The test is also norm-referenced in that it was standardized on a public school population within the United States, involving approximately 40 school districts and approximately 40,000 pupils. The reliability data from an alternate form procedure resulted in coefficients ranging from .64 to .94. The validity of this test was primarily established through an analysis of the test's content and should be evaluated by the user in much the same way. In other words, each subtest and test item should be reviewed to determine its usability in diagnosing and planning for a child's math problems.

General Math Achievement. A number of devices exist that can be used to screen a child's general math ability. These include the math subtest of the Peabody Individual Achievement Test (PIAT) and the math subtest from the Wide-Range Achievement Test (WRAT). Both of these tests provide a standardized norm-referenced score or an indication of actual performance level. Both tests are easily administered and scored by the teacher and can be used to generate information for use in determining the child's overall math performance level. Further, the test results will help the teacher specify the direction that more specific diagnosis should take. The PIAT (Dunn and Markwort, 1970) is an individually administered test. This test is composed of five academic achievement subtests, one of which is mathematics. The math subtest contains multiple choice items that are designed to assess a child's general math skills from pre-academic through the upper grades including some advanced concepts in trigonometry. The reliability data for this subtest, from a test-retest procedure, were found to be at about .75. The validity of the test was determined through an analysis of the content. The teacher must determine how useful the test can be through a thorough review of the test items, keeping in mind the use of this measure as a screening instrument.

The WRAT (Jastak and Jastak, 1965) is also an individually administered test composed of three subtests, one of which assesses skills in mathematics. Each subtest is composed of two levels, with level 1 being administered to children twelve years and under and level 2 being administered to those children over twelve years of age. The math subtest of the WRAT is designed to assess a child's understanding and application of basic math skills to include counting, reading numerals, and performing written computations involving the four major math processes. This test can be quickly administered and should be used only as a screening device. The reliability coefficients generated from a split half procedure were in the .90 and above range. There is very little validity data available on this test, but again by thoroughly analyzing the content a decision can be made relative to its validity for the individual user. Scores from this test certainly should be used with caution and should not be considered for making instructional program decisions but could nicely be used for identifying potential math problems.

The Stanford Achievement Test (Madden and Gardner, 1972) and the Metropolitan Achievement Tests (Durost, Bixler, Wrightstone, Prescott and Barlow, 1971) have subtest components in the area of mathematics and are designed for use with groups of children. The Stanford Achievement Test (SAT) mathematics subcomponents measure math concepts, math computation skills, and math application while the math subtests of the Metropolitan Achievement Test (MAT) assess math computation, math concepts, and mathematical problem solving skills. Reliability data for both the MAT and SAT were determined using split half procedures and result in coefficients that are found within the .85 to .90 range. As with all other achievement tests, validity was determined through an analysis of the content; therefore, the use of the math subtest data from either of these measures should be based on a careful analysis of the content items comprising the test. (Note: The validity data for the SAT were also of a concurrent nature with a current measure used being the Metropolitan Achievement Test. The Metropolitan Achievement Test validity data are not included in the materials accompanying the test but are available through a series of technical publications provided by the publishers of the test materials.) Other normative or standardized achievement tests that have mathematics subcomponents include the California Achievement Test (Tiegs and Clark, 1970) and Iowa Test of Basic Skills (Hieronymus and Lindquist, 1974). These are group administered tests.

The validity of any general achievement test or the value of any achievement test to the classroom teacher is found in the careful analysis of the individual test items to determine a child's math problems more specifically. The teacher would have to make a thorough analysis of each individual test item and then relate those items to the math program to be used or to the math concept to be taught within the classroom. If these two sets of information do not correspond, then the achievement test has relatively little value to the classroom teacher. If decisions are to be made relative to placing or planning for a child's specific math instructional program, only those tests and test items should be selected that will best aid the teacher in generating information for appropriate decision making relative to that program.

There are criterion-referenced devices available to assist the teacher in determining the achievement level of the student. Two of these will be discussed in this chapter. One, the Basic Skills Inventory for Math (BESI) (Adamson, Shrago, and Van Etten, 1972), is a criterion-referenced inventory of basic educational skills with a subcomponent in mathematics. The other device is the System Four in Utah (1977) criterion measure that has also a subcomponent that assesses a child's math sequence. In the BESI Math the child's readiness, as well as number related skills, is assessed. The math subtest from BESI illustrates a sequential, almost scope and sequence, of basic math skills. Figure 12-4 is a summary of the math skills found from the BESI.

The BESI can be administered to an individual or small group and can be administered in part or the entire inventory can be given. The results from this measure identify specific math skill strengths and weaknesses relative to each of the skills mentioned in Figure 12-4. System Four results in similar types of diagnostic information as the BESI. The math subtest from System Four assesses three primary areas: geometry and measurement, numbers and numerals, and operations and applications and is a sequence of skills from primary to secondary levels of difficulty with general math skills. As illustrated in Figure 12-1, this, too, is a test that can be used to determine a child's relative mastery of math and to pinpoint the level of proficiency that the child can demonstrate with selected math concepts. Both the BESI and System Four can be administered by classroom teachers and the results of the information can be more readily applied to program planning and development.

Informal Assessment and Math Abilities

Both the BESI and System Four or any like measures that are designed with a sequence of behavior can be easily adapted in

Figure 12-4   Basic Math Skills Assessed in the Basic
Educational Skills Inventory

Quantity
Naming
Matching Numbers
Counting Objects
Dot to Dot Number Sequences
Counting Orally
Writing Numbers
Number Sequencing—Before and After
Ordinal and Cardinal Concepts
Number Words

Addition Facts	Subtraction Fractions
Subtraction Facts	Multiplication of Fractions
Multiplication Facts	Division of Fractions
Addition Problems	Addition of Decimals
Subtraction Problems	Subtraction of Decimals
Multiplication Problems	Multiplication of Decimals
Division Problems	Division of Decimals
Fractional Parts	Decimal-Fraction-Percent
Reducing	Transformation
Fractions	Time
Adding Fractions	Money

making informal assessments of a child's math ability. Utilizing information from Figure 12-1, a checklist of math behavior can be developed for an area of development that is of concern to the classroom teacher. For example, the teacher is responsible for developing an understanding of numbers sequence. How those numbers can be constructed is found within the sequence chart. Utilizing this information, a checklist can then be made similar to the one found in Figure 12-5.

The teacher usually has several methods and procedures that can be followed in informally assessing a child's performance in math. One of the most beneficial is the *anecdotal record* which can be maintained very nicely on each child with relatively little expenditure of time on the part of the teacher. In effect, the teacher merely maintains a record of a child's behavior. The record can be in the form of completed work assignments in the class or can be written descriptions of the child's math behavior.

Figure 12-5   Informal Methods to Assess Basic Math Skills

Skill	Informal Diagnostic Activity
The Language of Math (All, more, take-away, less than, add, subtract, borrow, carry)	Using blocks, ask children questions which require them to respond with an expression characterizing a quantity or relation.
Classification	Have children group objects by size, shape, use, or color.
Correspondence (Relating elements in one group to elements in another group)	Have children match an object in one set to an object in another set. Use objects that are similar and then objects that are dissimilar.
Conservation (Number of units in a set remains the same regardless of changes in the arrangement.)	Using sticks or blocks arranged in a particular way, ask children to change arrangement and see if the original number of objects has been changed.
Reversibility (Units can be restored to their original position without changing their nature or relationship to other groups of objects.)	Using blocks, alter the positions of them, asking the pupils to place them in their original order. Question the children to see if they realize that it is possible to restore the blocks to their original arrangement without changing the characteristics of the blocks.
Ordering	Using objects of different sizes, ask children to order them according to length, from smallest to largest.

Maintenance of these types of records over a period of time can reveal many distinct areas of a child's math deficiencies and abilities.

It is recommended that the teacher develop a habit of maintaining some completed work copies from the child's normal or daily math assignments and make a periodic notation about the child's behavior. This record will not only assist in diagnosing but can also be used as an evaluation of how effective the math program has been with the child. The anecdotal record, especially in the form of teacher's notations of a child's behavior, may also reveal diagnostic information about other factors that may be influencing, indirectly or directly, the child's overall math performance. Over time, the recurring statement about a particular child's expressed dislike for the math task or fear of the math task may be valuable information for assessing the math program in which the child is placed or may be used to specify more exactly the direction the math program should take in altering the child's attitude.

Informal Arithmetic Inventory (IAI). This informal assessment procedure can provide the teacher with objective data concerning the achievement level as well as the areas of strengths and weaknesses of a child without using formal assessment devices. Its most valuable use is found in constructing a math program specific to the perceived needs of both the child and the teacher. A strong feature of the IAI is its flexibility in that the teacher has complete control of the content and development of the test. A properly constructed IAI will allow the teacher to determine information in the following areas:

1. an approximate level of the child's math achievement;
2. strengths and weaknesses of math skills;
3. math skill areas in need of further assessment.

The procedures involved in the development of an IAI include the *construction, administration,* and *interpretation* of results. Each of these procedures will be discussed below.

Construction. Constructing an IAI can best be accomplished through completion of each of the following steps:

1. Identify and secure math texts and/or workbooks in sequence from grade one through at least grade five or six.
2. Select up to 20 problems from the text with ten being selected from the first half of the book and ten from the middle to the end of the *first grade* copy. From successive grade levels select 10 to 20 examples of *new types* of problems avoiding duplication of lower grades as much as possible.
3. Write the selected problems onto master sheets, with a code for each in terms of the grade level the problem represents. For example, 245 code number may indicate that the problem is from the second (2) half of a fourth (4) grade textbook covering mul-

tiplication (5). One purpose of the code is to ensure the teacher is aware of the grade level difficulty of selected items but that the grade level indicator is not readily apparent to the child.

4. The sheets should be composed of items testing the same concept at the same grade level. For example, carrying, when adding two-digit numbers, should be the only concept found on the sheet given to the child. Having adding with three-digit numbers with no carrying involved may be confusing and upsetting to the child.

5. Construct a "key" answer sheet for each master sheet.

Administration. Prior to the administration, review as much of the work as is available on what the child has done in the past to determine the approximate level to begin the testing. If this is not available, observe the child and begin the test at a level easily accomplished by the child. The test is administered by having the student complete answers for the problems provided in writing. The test is not timed, but speed can be an added factor by specifying a time limit for the test or part of the test. The student should be told to illustrate all work (carrying, borrowing, etc.) on the answer sheet.

If the student cannot *write* the answers because of physical handicaps (cerebral palsy, for example), administer the test verbally; however, caution should be taken to avoid giving so much help as to invalidate the results. In this situation a multiple choice type of answer format may be used.

Interpretation. Each grade level master sheet should be scored to determine a percentage. A score of 90% or better should be considered an *independent level* of functioning. That is, the child should be able to successfully and independently complete problems from that level. Testing should continue until a level of 75%–90% accuracy is obtained. This would be considered the child's *instructional level* and should be the point at which instruction should begin. A score of less than 75% accuracy would indicate that the level of materials is too difficult and should be avoided in instructional planning.

Ideally in planning a program of math instruction the teacher would want to begin at a level that is successfully completed by the child. For this reason, it is suggested that beginning instruc-

tion should be at the independent level (90% or better). Performing at this level will afford the child much opportunity to be successful and to receive a great deal of positive reinforcement from
both the teacher and self.

The child could in all probability profit by assistance at the instructional level (75–90 percent), but the occasions for reinforcing
performance are obviously restricted. Beginning at the frustration
level (less than 75 percent) would well turn the child off to the
subject itself. The teacher should examine carefully the types of
mistakes made, particularly at the independent and instructional
levels, as these are the levels at which instruction will begin
before moving on to the next sequence of math skills.

The IAI can be of great value in identifying a child's specific
strengths and weaknesses. By testing beyond the independent
level, the teacher is provided with data on skills within one or
more of the four processes (addition, subtraction, multiplication,
and division). For example, a given child may score 60% at the
fifth-grade level. Such a score may result in the teacher assigning
a math level of 4–6 or 4–7, which in and of itself is not necessarily incorrect. However, upon closer observation, the teacher may
find that the child did not miss any addition problems even at the
fifth-grade level when carrying was involved, while the child's
performance was inconsistent in the other process areas. Certainly this could be considered a strength in relation to the other
procedures. Conversely, a child may conceivably demonstrate an
independent level at the sixth grade while repeatedly missing,
even at the fourth-grade level, subtraction problems which
require borrowing, illustrating a possible weakness.

Once a deficit has been identified or at least a process is questioned, the teacher may want to explore this area in more detail.
For example, in the case of the child who repeatedly missed subtraction problems requiring borrowing, the teacher would want to
construct a specific skills test in the area of subtraction. Such a
test should be developed in a sequential fashion starting with
simple one subtrahend and one minuend problems and gradually
increasing the degree of difficulty to assess higher levels of computation, (i.e., two-place minuend, one-place subtrahend with no
borrowing; two-place minuend, two-place subtrahend with no
borrowing; two-place minuend, one-place subtrahend with bor-

rowing, and so on). Such a test provides a means of isolating not only the deficit function (subtraction) but also the level it occurs on.

The number and type of problems on this form of in-depth test will vary, but several problems involving each of the skills to be assessed should be included to reduce the possibility of a careless error on one problem being interpreted as a skill deficiency. Actually, the greater number of problems involving each skill that the child has to compute increases the chances of isolating specific problem areas. By having each master sheet composed of only one type of problem at one particular level of difficulty with several test items will help to pinpoint more exactly a child's area of deficit.

Summary

To summarize the actual conducting of the math assessment, it is first of all important to identify the expectancy level of math performance for the child. This is accomplished by identifying the specific math behaviors to be performed. Math behaviors can be selected from a scope and sequence or skill sequence chart similar to the one presented in Figure 12-1. The next step is to ascertain the actual achievement level of the child. This can be accomplished through the application of a number of standardized criterion or informal methods of assessment. It is also important to observe the child in attempting to identify any other factors (that is, social-emotional, motor) that may be or could be influencing the child's overall performance. Once obtained, the actual performance and the expected performance are compared with the results being used to assist the teacher in determining the (1) level at which instruction should begin, (2) goals and objectives to be met by the instructional program, and (3) instructional program content.

Can You Answer These Questions?

1. What are four formal measures that can be used to identify a child's actual performance level?

2. How would you determine a child's expected level of performance in math?

3. What are three procedures in developing an IAI?

4. What are several math behaviors expected of children between the second and third grades in the area of understanding numerals and numbers?

5. The BESI could best be used for what assessment purposes?

6. What are the diagnostic strengths of the Key Math?

7. Can you specify two informal procedures for assessing math skills?

8. What tests would you use for screening math skills?

9. An IAI can be used to generate information in at least three areas. What are these areas?

10. What is the value of the Key Math profile?

References

Adamson, G., M. Shrago, and G. Van Etten. *Basic Educational Skills Inventory*. Olathe, Kansas: Select-Ed., 1972.

Beatty, L. S., R. Madden, E. F. Gardner, and J. Karlsen. *Stanford Diagnostic Mathematics Test*. New York: Harcourt Brace Jovanovich, 1976.

Connolly, A. J., W. Nachtman, and E. M. Pritchett. *Keymath Diagnostic Arithmetic Test*. Circle Pines, Minnesota: American Guidance Service, 1971.

Dunn, L. M., and F. C. Markwardt. *Peabody Individual Achievement Test*. Circle Pines, Minnesota: American Guidance Service, 1970.

Durst, W., H. Bixler, J. Wrightstone, G. Prescott, and I. Barlow. *Metropolitan Achievement Tests*. New York: Harcourt Brace and Jovanovich.

Hieronymous, C., and A. P. Lindquist. *Iowa Test of Basic Skills*. Boston: Houghton Mifflin, 1974.

Jastak, J. F., and S. R. Jastak. *Wide Range Achievement Test*. Wilmington, Delaware: Guidance Associates, 1965.

Madden, R., E. R. Gardner, H. C. Rudman, B. Karlsen, and J. C. Merwin. *Stanford Achievement Test.* New York: Harcourt Brace Jovanovich, 1973.

Otto, W., R. A. McMenemy, and R. J. Smith. *Corrective and Remedial Teaching* (2nd ed.). Boston: Houghton Mifflin, 1973.

Salvia, J., and J. E. Ysseldyke. *Assessment in Special and Remedial Education.* Boston: Houghton Mifflin, 1978.

Spencer, E. F., and R. M. Smith. "Arithmetic Skills." In R. M. Smith (ed.), *Teacher Diagnosis of Educational Difficulties.* Columbus, Ohio: Charles E. Merrill, 1978.

Systems Four in Utah, Salt Lake City, Utah: Utah State Department of Education, Special Education Division, 1977.

Tiegs, E. W., and W. W. Clark. *California Achievement Tests.* New York: CTB/McGraw-Hill, 1970.

Utah State Board of Education. *Systems Fore.* Salt Lake City, Utah: Utah State Board of Education, 1976.

Wallace, G., and S. C. Larsen. *Educational Assessment of Learning Problems: Testing for Teaching.* Boston: Allyn and Bacon, 1978.

3

Developing an Educational Program

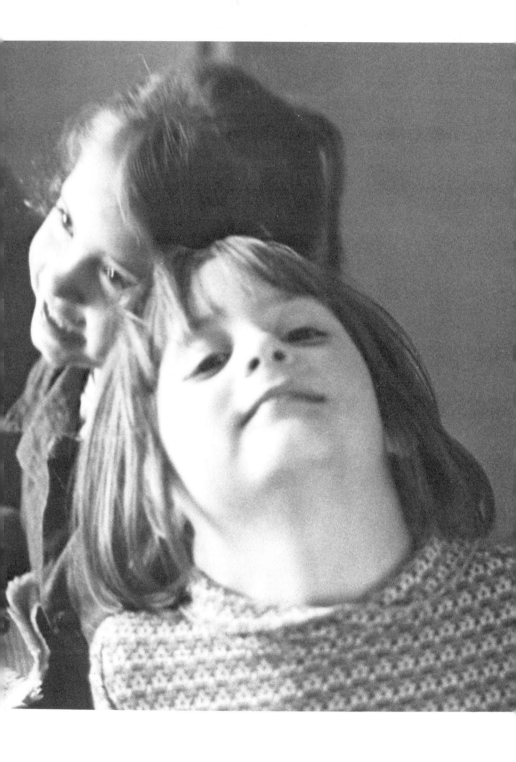

13

Organizing Assessment Information

Objectives

At the conclusion of this chapter, the reader should be able to:

1. organize assessment information for determining a child's relative strengths and weaknesses;
2. discuss the value of profiling assessment information;
3. profile assessment information;
4. specify procedures to be followed in answering these questions: What are the child's expected actual performance levels? What are the child's relative strengths and weaknesses? What are the potential underlying reasons for the child's performance discrepancies?

Introduction

The purpose of this chapter is to provide examples and exercises that will assist the teacher in the interpretation and organization of assessment information which has been completed or collected on a child. An attempt will be made to synthesize information from previous chapters into a system for organizing the assessment information for interpretation and use in developing instructional programs.

A teacher preparing a program for disabled children is usually confronted with the task of sorting out a myriad of diagnostic information. This information usually comes in the form of interpretation of formal or nonreferenced test data, criteria-referenced data, parents' and others' observations, samples of a child's work, case study reports, anecdotal records, and a number of other means. Following is a sample of the type of information that a teacher can expect to find within a child's cumulative folder:

Assessment Information

Name: Mark
C.A.:   9.5
Present Grade Placement: 4th
Assessment Information Available:

WISC-R	VS	78
	PS	100
	FS	92
SIT	IQ	95
DAP	MA 9-6	
WRAT	Spelling:	1.6
	Math:	3.8
	Reading:	2.3
PIAT	Math:	4.2
	Rdg Recog:	2.0
	Rdg Comp:	1.8
	Spelling:	3.1
	Gen Info:	4.4
Key Math	Total Raw Score:	119
	Grade Score:	3-9

Woodcock　Letter Id.　　4.3
　　　　　　Word Id.　　　1.9
　　　　　　Word Attack　2.2
　　　　　　Word Comp.　1.6
　　　　　　Passage Comp. 2.1
　　　　　　Total Reading　2.3
Wepman Auditory Discrimination
　　　　　x errors = 1
　　　　　6 errors = 2
Slosson Drawing Coordination Test
　　　　　5 errors　90%

Behavior Observations:
Mark has been referred for planning an educational program to assist him in improving his reading performance. His teacher reports as well that he has been observed to function well with his peers on the playground and in physical education classes. He communicates well with adults and peers and seems to be somewhat competent in his social interactions and relationships with people. The diagnostic data that are available on Mark have been collected over a period of time but essentially reflect a pretty accurate description of his present academic skill level. In the classroom he appears to be a little behind in most academic subjects, especially the area of reading. This deficit was so great that the teacher was concerned enough to have Mark referred to a special education teacher in an effort to improve reading performance and to stimulate growth in other academic areas.

Organizing the Information

Given this information, the teacher must decide what to do with it, what it means, how to determine the child's strengths and weaknesses, and what the primary focus of the instructional effort should be. Should it be in the social/emotional area, the academic area, the cognitive or physical/motoric area, or some combination of these? As can be readily ascertained, the teacher is confronted with a number of complex questions related to the interpretation and utilization of diagnostic information.

Following the assessment model proposed in Chapter 1, the

teacher can attempt to synthesize this assessment information into more meaningful and usable data by answering the following questions.

1. What are the expectations for this child? That is, what are the cognitive, behavioral, social, motoric, and academic expectations that the teacher should have for Mark?
2. What is the child's actual performance relative to these expectations? To answer this question, some data either from norm-referenced or criterion-referenced measures must be found to substantiate what Mark's actual performance is in relationship to his expected performance level. This question can also be answered through a review of anecdotal records, case histories, interviews with the teachers, and a review of Mark's school work.
3. What are the child's relative strengths and weaknesses and what doesn't seem to be a problem? In other words, it is important to sort out what the child is most capable of doing about which the teacher will not have to worry. Why waste precious instructional time attempting to have Mark do tasks that he can perform adequately? To answer this question requires a thorough understanding of the tasks to be performed and the behaviors expected to be manifest. Without this knowledge and understanding, a great deal of time can be wasted in nonproductive adventures. It should also be pointed out that the teacher's usual focus of attention is on the child's weaknesses. As Strang (1969) illustrates, it is not what the child can do, but what the child cannot do that concerns the teacher. It is just as important to identify those things that can be easily accomplished for use in strengthening or providing successful experiences for the child; in other words, one of the most important steps in sorting out the assessment information is identifying what the child is capable of doing.
4. What are the potential underlying causal factors related to the problem? That is, is there anything related to Mark's academic weaknesses that can be attributed to factors other than a lack of knowledge of what is to be learned? For example, is Mark unable to see or hear written or spoken language adequately to process it? Is he emotionally able to concentrate on reading or other academic tasks?

It must be noted from the information provided in the sample that not all the information to the questions can be found. However, through a systematic attempt at answering these fundamental questions, the teacher will generate a more composite picture of the child's abilities as well as uncover potential disabilities.

Further, by systematically answering these questions, specific areas can be identified where further assessment information is needed or would be helpful for making instructional program decisions.

Profiling

One of the first steps in sorting out the assessment information provided in the example above is to profile that information into graphic form. This allows for more easily viewing and analyzing that information. If the profile has been completed accurately, it will also provide a record of initial performance that can be used as an evaluative measure later on to illustrate what effect the instructional program has had on meeting specified goals and objectives. To do this, one has only to record the initial data and first-of-year test results on the profile sheet and consider it as baseline data and then to profile subsequent, mid-year or end-of-year, assessment data against these initial data (see Figure 13-1). A comparison of the two will allow the teacher to determine relative effects of instructional strategies.

Answer the Questions

What are the expectations for this child?

To answer this question, the teacher must look at Mark's age and grade placement, be familiar with that grade level's academic, social/emotional, and physical/motoric development and curriculum. Further, the teacher must consider all the information from all sources—parents, other teachers, and Mark's past performance and current test results—in making a decision concerning expectations for him.

Figure 13-2 illustrates the sources of information that should be surveyed in making a decision about a child's expected level of performance. No one source can provide a definitive answer to what that expected level should be. A child's *capabilities* must first be considered. These capabilities are determined through *observing* the child's performance in a number of school-related activities such as completion of assigned math and reading tasks, behavior on the playground, interaction with peers and classmates and other related activities. A review of the child's *history*

Figure 13-1 Using the Profile Chart as a Measure of Instructional Program Effectiveness

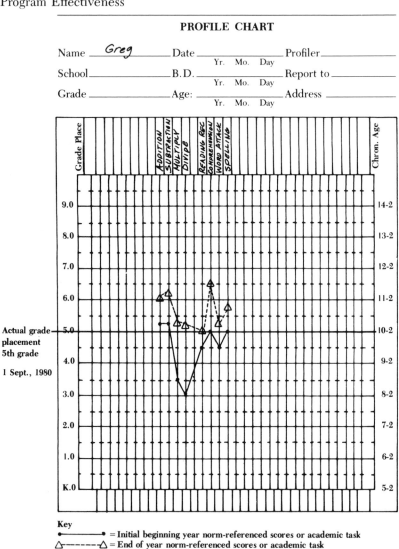

PROFILE CHART

Name _Greg_ Date _____ Profiler _____
　　　　　　　　　　Yr. Mo. Day

School _____ B.D. _____ Report to _____
　　　　　　　　　Yr. Mo. Day

Grade _____ Age: _____ Address _____
　　　　　　　　Yr. Mo. Day

Key
●————● = Initial beginning year norm-referenced scores or academic task
△------△ = End of year norm-referenced scores or academic task

will also reveal information about what to expect from the child. Parents and previous teachers plus examples of previously completed school work tasks are all valuable sources of information that must be considered. Performance on criterion and norm-referenced *tests* will also provide information about expected levels of performance.

Figure 13-2 General Model for Developing Educational Programs for Exceptional Children

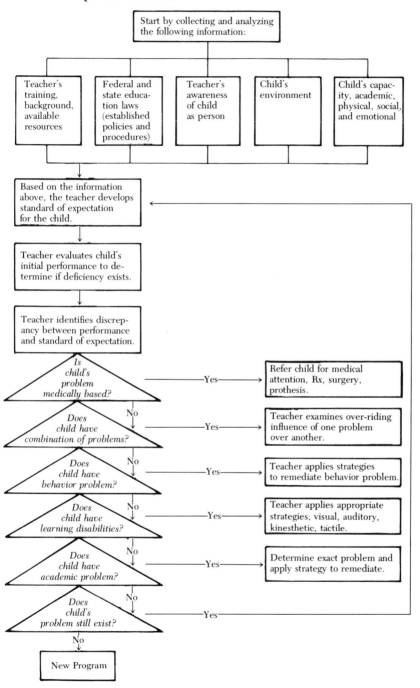

Parental expectations must also be considered. Parents or guardians provide a valuable source of information as well and can be the vehicle by which an educational program can be successfully carried out. The parent can provide insight about the child that the teacher just does not have. This insight is critical in making decisions about the expected levels of the child's behavior and eventual use of that information in planning an instructional program.

Expectations can be derived from reviewing the *resources* available and *capabilities of the teacher* to deliver an *appropriate* educational program. That is, the expectations should be set somewhere within the boundaries of the available resources that can meet those expectations. Further, to meet the expectation effectively, in most cases, will not exceed the teacher's capabilities to deliver. For example, if the expectation is to correct a child's speech problem and the teacher is not trained to provide therapy or the school does not have the services of a speech clinician, this will obviously effect satisfactorily meeting that expectation.

Finally, the *state* and *local education* agencies, plus the *school* policies and procedures for governing what is to be taught at specific age and grade levels, will provide another means of deciding what the expectations of the child should be. The teacher must be familiar with what these agencies expect of children's academic, social/emotional, and physical/motoric behaviors in terms of age and grade levels.

Analyzing the information given, it can be seen that Mark is a child with a chronological age of 9-5 and from test information available, several pieces of information can be found to assist in extracting Mark's expected level of performance or behavior. That is, the WISC-R full scale IQ score (92) is within the normal range of intelligence. This is somewhat supported by the Slosson Intelligence Test IQ score (95), as well as the mental age derivative from the DAP (9-6). From the analysis of this information, it can be concluded that expected performance levels of Mark should be comparable to those of his age and grade peers; that is, Mark should be functioning on a peer level with his fourth-grade classmates. Further, from the observation of the classroom teacher, his social/emotional behavior appears to be on a par or equal to his peer group. His communication skills also appear adequate. In the area of physical/motoric performance based on the anecdotal

Figure 13-3   A Profile of Mark's Expected and Actual Performance
Levels

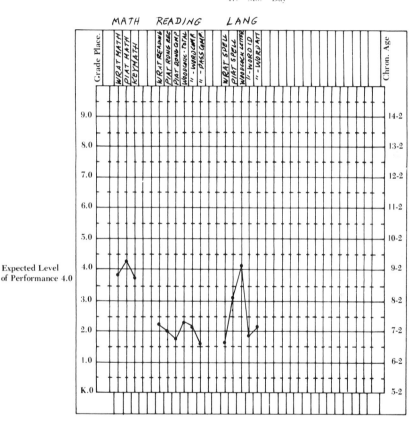

PROFILE CHART

Name __Mark__ Date _____ Profiler_____
            Yr.   Mo.   Day
School_____ B.D. _____ Report to _____
            Yr.   Mo.   Day
Grade _____ Age: _____ Address _____
            Yr.   Mo.   Day

information provided, Mark appears to be functioning adequately in this area.

When an analysis is made of his academic performance from the normative data provided in the sample, it appears that there are some weaknesses and overall he appears to be functioning below his fourth-grade placement. To assist in answering this question, Figure 13-3 is an illustration of Mark's academic performance profile. The profile reveals, when the assessment information is analyzed, that the reason given by the teacher for referring Mark may be valid—that is, a majority of Mark's academic behaviors, especially reading, are below those expected of a child in the fourth grade.

Mark's actual grade placement and his expected grade placement are very closely related. In planning educational programs, the teacher should keep in mind the goal of meeting a level of performance commensurate with that of grade placement. In Mark's case, the teacher has less of a problem than if the child had had a greater discrepancy between placement and academic performance. However, an analysis of available information to determine expectancies does make available to the teacher information from which decisions, as to instructional strategies, can be made. It gives the teacher at least a direction in which to plan. Profiling illustrates the expected level of performance both from an actual grade placement standpoint as well as the derived expectancy level taken from a number of sources (see Figure 13-2). The profile lends itself to illustration of academic areas more readily than perhaps the social-emotional or physical areas, especially in the sample provided since there are no criterion or norm-referenced data available to give direction as to Mark's performance in these areas. Upon review of the anecdotal and behavioral observation information provided, it appears that there is nothing to suggest that the child is having problems in either of these areas and the expected level of performance in the social and motor areas should parallel that of his age and grade peers.

What is Mark's actual performance?

After profiling derived expected level of performance, the test scores from the standardized measures can be plotted. From the information provided in this sample, Mark appears to be performing adequately in a number of academic areas as can be readily ascertained from the profile in Figure 13-3. It becomes now a question of how best to profile the information that has been given. In the illustration found in Figure 13-3, the test information is profiled by academic area, math scores are grouped together as are reading scores, as closely as possible. However, each test and its subtest could have been profiled together.

What are Mark's strengths and weaknesses?

From this illustration, the profile reveals a number of strengths and weaknesses in relationship to Mark's derived expectancy level or grade placement. His academic strengths and weaknesses can be more readily discerned from this graphic display. For example, Mark's overall academic strength appears to be in the area of math. His Key Math, WRAT Math, and PIAT Math scores were all at approximately grade level. Judging from the anecdotal information, his social/emotional and motoric levels of performance appear to be adequate and comparable to other fourth-grade children. These strengths should be noted and considered in planning the educational program. Distinct weaknesses appear to be in the area of general reading ability and more specifically in the area of comprehension of words and content. Given this area of weakness, the teacher can make some decisions related to the instructional objectives to be written for Mark as well as the strategies to be used.

Are there any underlying factors that may be affecting Mark's performance?

As was mentioned earlier, a thorough scrutiny of the assessment information is required to determine if there are any behaviors or performance variables symptomatic of failure in the identified academic areas. From the information provided in the sample, the answer to this question cannot be readily made and is, perhaps, an area in which further assessment, either of a formal or informal nature, should be conducted. Further assessment is especially important if the teacher feels that Mark is experiencing problems in another area that may be indirectly affecting his performance in reading.

Even though the observation of Mark's social-emotional and motor performance in the physical education program have revealed adequate behavior or performance, the two assessment devices used to assess auditory and visual performance in this case provide information that reveals potential problem areas. The Wepman Auditory Discrimination test score, as well as the Slosson Drawing Coordination test score, reveal potential problems. The question that now confronts the teacher is determining if these areas are interfering with Mark's overall performance and if they warrant spending instructional time in correcting them. In other words, is the Drawing Coordination or Auditory Discrimination performance actually affecting other areas; is the concern great enough to warrant spending time in correcting these two areas; and, if the correction of these deficits is made, will it affect overall performance? In the sample provided above, it may be best to collect additional assessment information related to these two areas. The teacher may wish to refer Mark to a specialist or someone trained in assessing these types of problems.

Through a review of the completed profile (refer to Figure 13-3), an abundance of information for programming purposes can be readily identified. Further, if this had been the initial assessment completed on the child prior to program development and implementation, the profile becomes a good evaluative measure for use later on in determining the effectiveness of selected instructional strategies.

Conclusions

The assessment information which has been profiled is merely an illustration of one way in which a child's *relative* strengths and weaknesses can be identified. It now becomes the task of the classroom teacher to more specifically determine what is to be done with the child, what the instructional objectives are to be, and what the instructional strategies will be in meeting those objectives. For example, in the case of Mark, it was identified that he had a reading problem. The reading task must then be broken down to a level commensurate with the child's actual performance level and specific to the subtasks involved in the reading task. From the assessment information given, it appears that Mark's word identification and understanding of words is his weakest reading area. A further breakdown, following procedures outlined in Chapters 6 and 7, would assist in further specifying what the reading problem might be as well as giving direction to the teacher for developing specific program objectives.

In considering the profile, it must be pointed out that nothing within the profile or assessment information should be used for any other reason than program planning. An inefficient use of the assessment information would be to label or categorize the child as being mentally retarded or learning disabled. The label or category will have little if any positive effect in making the child a more efficient or proficient learner. The information should be primarily for instructional program planning. As Reynolds (1975) suggests, a teacher's decisions must be based on sound information. The profile and assessment information in this illustration provides that information from which specific program objectives can be developed. Utilizing that information, the teacher can better manipulate factors in the learning environment or the instructional system to best fit the child's learning abilities and to make the child a more efficient learner.

Can You Answer These Questions?

Following is a similar exercise to the one just completed. Answer the questions below by profiling and analyzing the information and data provided.

1. What is the child's expected level of performance?
2. What is the child's actual level of performance?
3. What are the child's strengths and weaknesses?
4. What are the possible underlying factors related to the problem?

Assessment Information

Name: Carolyn
C.A.:   12.0
Present Grade Placement: 6th
Current Test Results Available:

WISC-R   VS 118
            PS   95
            FS 114
SIT   IQ 109
PIAT   Math: 4.0
            Reading Recog.: 3.5
            Reading Comp.:   3.7
            Spelling: 6.6
            Gen. Info.:   7.5
Woodcock Reading
            Letter Ident.:   12.9
            Word Ident.:   4.5
            Comprehension: 5.4
            Passage Comp.:   4.7
            Total Reading: 4.5

Behavior Observation:
Carolyn has been referred for planning an educational program, especially in the area of reading. Her teacher has indicated that Carolyn is very inattentive and off task when working on assigned tasks. Carolyn has been observed to interact well with her age peers and is a leader in most of the playground activities even though she avoids many games requiring eye-hand coordination. Her handwriting is very illegible and she has a number of reversals. She appears to try hard to complete her reading assignments, but is easily distracted from the task by almost any noise or movement in the class.

References

Reynolds, M. "Trends in Special Education: Implications for Measurement." In W. Hively and M. Reynolds (eds.), *Domain Referenced Testing in Special Education.* Minneapolis: Leadership Training Institute/Special Education, University of Minnesota, 1975.

Strang, R. *Diagnostic Teaching of Reading* (2nd ed.). New York: McGraw-Hill, 1969.

chapter

14

The Impact of Public Law 94-142

Objectives

The reader, at the conclusion of this chapter, should be able to:

1. identify the salient features of Public Law 94-142 that will have impact on those persons responsible for the education of handicapped children;

2. discuss the reasons behind enactment of Public Law 94-142;

3. specify the components of the Individual Education Program (IEP) as outlined in Public Law 94-142;

4. outline procedures for the development of goals and objectives to be used in the IEP;

5. present evaluation procedures that should be considered when evaluating the effectiveness of strategies outlined in the IEP in meeting the objectives specified in that program.

Introduction to Public Law 94-142

Public Law 94-142 (PL 94-142) or the Education for All Handicapped Act was enacted by the 94th Congress as its 142nd piece of legislation. The purpose of this law is to provide an appropriate and equal education for educationally handicapped individuals. The act was signed into law in November of 1975. PL 94-142 resulted from the efforts of many people but primarily the parents and advocates of handicapped or exceptional children. This act, in the opinion of the author, is having and will continue to have a great impact on not only the exceptional child in the public school system, but also the teachers and administrators who will be responsible for developing, implementing, and evaluating educational programs for that handicapped child.

In August 1977, the United States Office of Education (USOE) published the regulations that are used to govern how the law is to be implemented (Department of Health, Education, and Welfare, 1977) by State and local education agencies (SEA and LEA). Essentially, PL 94-142 is a funding law and its regulations are designed to provide guidelines to SEA and LEAs in requesting funds for serving handicapped populations found within their boundaries. The regulations specify several unique features that directly impact on teachers serving handicapped children. These features will be highlighted in the following discussion. The reader is invited, however, to request from the USOE a copy of the December 29, 1977, Federal Register and to refer specifically to pages 65082–65085 of the document for the most exact reference to the law.

Even though the law is of recent origin, it has created tremendous interest and concern on the part of educators in terms of what effect it will have in changing or altering the educational system as it now exists. The purpose of this chapter is not to overburden the reader with the full account of the law but to identify those features that might have the most immediate and direct impact on the classroom teacher.

History and Background of PL 94-142

It is estimated that there exists in the United States more than 8 million handicapped children. Many of these children are not receiving an educational program based on their unique learning needs and capabilities. It has been reported that over half of the handicapped children in this country do not receive appropriate educational services. Over 1 million handicapped children are excluded totally from the public school system and do not go through any type of educational process with their peers (Department of Health, Education, and Welfare, 1977).

It was in 1954 that Congress enacted legislation to provide for equal education opportunities for all children attending public schools. Since that date, much has happened to stimulate the development of the Education for all Handicapped Children Act. Much of this activity has been centered around the concern that parents and educators have had related to the existing educational system's inability to provide equal and appropriate educational opportunities for handicapped children. Some of this concern is directly related to the inadequate financial base provided at the LEA and SEA level and to a lack of well-trained professionals available to deal with the learning problems of exceptional children. The law was enacted as a means to assist state and local efforts in providing programs to meet the educational needs of handicapped children.

Salient Features of the Law

Within this section, the law will be summarized in terms of those features and parameters that would have the most immediate impact or effect upon the classroom teachers. A broad overview of the law can be found in a number of publications. The reader is referred especially to those by Jones (1976), Torres (1977), and Stolte (1978).

Prior to a discussion of the salient features of the law, a definition of special education and handicapped children is warranted to acquaint the reader with terms and concepts that will be used throughout this chapter. Special education, as defined in the regulations for PL 94-142, states:

Special education means specifically designed instruction at no cost to parents or guardians to meet the unique needs of a handicapped child including classroom instruction, instruction in physical education, home instruction and instruction in hospitals and institutions. Handicapped children are defined as those children who have been found to be mentally retarded, hard of hearing, deaf, speech impaired, visually handicapped, seriously emotionally disturbed, orthopedically impaired, other health impairments, deaf-blind, multiple handicapped, or having specific learning disabilities (Department of Health, Education, and Welfare, 1977).

The salient features that will have the most direct effect upon the classroom teacher are as follows.

1. The handicapped child must be placed in the least restrictive environment.
2. A free and appropriate education must be provided for each child.
3. A plan and documentation for the evaluation and placement of children into an appropriate education setting must be given.
4. There must be an Individual Education Program (IEP) written that illustrates the direction and outlines the goals and objectives to be met by the program in assisting the child.
5. There must be evidence of due process or procedural safeguards in which the child can contest being placed in or being kept from attending a specially designed educational program.

Least restricted environment. This statement is best characterized by saying that handicapped children, when at all possible, should be educated with non-handicapped children. How this is to be carried out is dependent upon the severity and type of handicap possessed by the child. For example, a severely motor-impaired child (cerebral palsy) that is confined to a wheelchair and lacks the verbal skills necessary for functional communication with peers and adults, may find placement in a regular school program rather difficult. The physical environment of the school may not be conducive to the condition of the wheelchair; and, the child's communication skills may not be conducive to interaction with peers and teachers which would result in acquisition of information needed for educational growth. It must be emphasized, however, that the placement in a regular school environment with non-handicapped children is clearly spelled out in the law and every effort to accommodate the handicapped child in the normal school environment should be made.

Removal or exclusion of a handicapped child from the regular education environment can only occur when the severity of the child's handicap is such that even with the use of supplementary services, an adequate educational environment cannot be satisfactorily achieved. The local education agency or school district must also provide a continuum of service patterns for the purpose of accommodating the handicapped child. These include instruction in regular classes supplemented with resource or professional help, special class placement within the regular school, special schools if required, home instruction, and instruction for children confined to hospitals and/or institutions.

Free-appropriate education. September 1, 1978, was identified as the deadline for providing services for handicapped children 3–18 years of age, while September 1, 1980, is the deadline for serving handicapped children 3–21 years of age. As the law specifies, serving these handicapped children is to be under free public education; free meaning at public expense, under public control, and without direct charge to parents. In terms of appropriateness, a child must be given and provided an educational program that meets or satisfies the child's unique learning characteristics. The appropriateness of the program is best described under the discussion of the IEP.

Evaluation and placement procedures. *Parental permission* must be obtained before any initial diagnosis or evaluation can be started relative to the development of an individual education program or for placement within a service pattern that is beyond that found within a regular education classroom. Evaluation that is to be performed must be done by a *multi-disciplinary team* of professionals that have been designated by the local education agency. The evaluations must meet the following conditions:

1. All tests and evaluations must be administered in the native language of the child unless it is not feasible to do so.
2. Individual diagnoses utilizing specific tests and diagnostic procedures must be validated for the specific purpose for which they are used.
3. The evaluation must be managed, controlled or administered under the direction of a trained professional and when utilizing

tests, these should be done following the instructions given by the producer of that test.

4. All tests and evaluation procedures must be nondiscriminatory. The cultural background of the person being tested must be taken into consideration and only those tests that are as culturally free of bias should be used.

The Individual Education Program (IEP). The Individual Education Program is a *written statement* developed for each exceptional child. This written statement is a statement that reflects the performance of the child's present educational skill level. It outlines *annual goals* that are to be met following the program guidelines. It is to include specific statements of *instructional objectives* that highlight what the child is to be learning through this program. *Educational services* are to be identified that should be most beneficial in assisting the child reach the specified goals and objectives (these to include the selected service pattern, i.e., self-contained special class resource placement, regular classroom placement with resource assistance, etc.) that the child will participate in, as well as the extent (all day, part day, two days a week for three hours per day) to which the child will participate in the regular education program. The written statement should also include the procedures and criteria to be used for *evaluating* the effectiveness of the program in meeting the objectives and goals specified.

The IEP must be developed, implemented, and evaluated by a *multi-disciplinary team.* This team should include representatives of the LEA such as the child's teacher, school principal, an advocate of the child, and even the child when appropriate. This team does not necessarily have to be the same team that completed the initial evaluation of the child. However, in the development of the IEP, a representative from that evaluation team or a representative familiar with the evaluation procedures used must be included in the development of the IEP.

Due Process.   This feature of the law was designed to accommodate the potential grievances that may arise between parents and school districts relative to the placement or exclusion of a child from participation in a special education program. An impartial due process hearing that involves the parent or an advocate of the child and representatives of the school district is conducted by a third party not employed or affiliated with the school district. Both parties who are involved, either child advocate or school representative, can be accompanied and advised by legal counsel. Each party can present evidence, cross-examine, and/or prohibit the introduction of evidence by either party. Either party can appeal the results of the hearing to the State Education Agency who conducts another due-process hearing at that level. Dissatisfaction of either party at this level can result in a civil action suit being presented in a State or U.S. District Court.

Individual Education Program

As directed by PL 94-142, each exceptional child found in the public school system is to be provided with an individual education program (IEP). This program is to be composed of specific types of information and is to be found on file with the child's school records. The IEP is to include:

1. the present educational level of performance of the child;
2. annual goals and statements specifying short-term instructional objectives;
3. statements concerning the service patterns, be they special education or related service patterns, that are to be provided for the child;
4. the extent to which the child will be participating in the regular educational program;
5. a projected date specifying the duration that special education services will be provided and when those services will begin;
6. an evaluation plan outlining the procedures to be used in determining if annual goals and instructional objectives have been met and a statement reflecting how effective the service patterns have been in meeting goals and objectives.

There is no specific way mentioned to format this information and data. The following are suggestions for how an IEP can be constructed and can be used as guides in organizing the information to facilitate ease of implementing and accounting for the effects of the IEP on the child.

Figure 14-1 An Example of Individual Education Program (Used by permission of the Provo School District, Provo, Utah).

① – ⑭

Individual Education Program—I.E.P.

Student _____ ①

School _____

	Percent of Time	Team: Parents	Support Services	Re-Evaluation Date:
Grade___ Date Programmed___	Reg. Prog./Sp. Ed.	Res. Teacher	⑤	⑨ *at least annually*
	⑦	Psychologist ⑩	*Relates to*	Additional Data Needed:
Mode of Learning ③	*Relates to*	Class. Teacher	*objectives set.*	⑫ *as needed during staffing and/or instruction*
Services Initiated_____	*objectives set.*	Comm. Spec.	Include P.E.	
Anticipated Duration ⑧ *estimate date*		Other		

(Level of Functioning)

Strengths   Limitations

←②→

Summary statements which consider all tests given, not scores

Goals, Objectives & Evaluation

Goals (Long Range)

④

Describe performance and level to which the student will achieve at the end of the school year and how it will be measured.

Goals should relate to level of functioning and handicapping category assigned.

Person Responsible _____

⑥

to carry out objective

③ *above*

Determine mode of
learning based on
strengths and limitations.

Objectives (Short Term)

⑬

For each annual goal there should be 2–4 short term goals.
These can be written following staffing of the student.

Placement Decision

⑪

Committee recommendations for procedure, techniques, materials, equipment, etc.

⑭

Listing of ideas as recommended by team during staffing.
Include suggestions that will be helpful in planning instructional program.

1. Whatever the format selected, it should be clearly written and easily interpreted.
2. The data from which goals and objectives are derived should be easily discerned.
3. The strengths and weaknesses from which goals and objectives are written should be concisely stated and should relate to the stated goals and objectives within the program.
4. The selected instructional strategies or service patterns should be clearly outlined and specify what is to be provided.
5. The specific kinds of media and materials to be used in assisting the child in meeting the specified goals and objectives should be identified.
6. In the evaluation section, the procedures should be precisely written in order to facilitate ease of implementation and to insure the information collected will adequately evaluate the effectiveness of the program in meeting goals and objectives.

In Figure 14-1 can be found a sample Individual Education Program that highlights the component parts of the IEP as outlined in PL 94-142. Each circled number in the figure corresponds to a major component in the IEP.

Writing Annual Goals and Short-Term Objectives

As Hayes (1977) points out, goals and objectives provide accountability. They can be used to facilitate parent and teacher communication, assist the teacher in preparation for more relevant teaching strategies and learning activities, and as a means to motivate students. Dever (1978) seems to support this when he indicates that a teacher, who can discover precisely what the child needs to learn, is in a much better position to make methodological changes. He further states that the critical part of the teacher's role is the ability to discover what it is the child must learn and, once this is understood, the methodology can be more functionally specified.

From the comments of Hayes (1977) and Dever (1978) as well as the work of many others (Mager, 1962; Bloom, Hastings, and Madaus, 1971) specifying what the child is to learn is the initial and perhaps most important step in the construction of educational objectives. In terms of the programmers for the IEP, they must have the information relative to the child's actual level of performance, what the expected level of performance is, and what resources are necessary and available to take the child from the actual to the expected. Having this information will help the IEP developers in specifying what the child is to learn.

In developing goals, Hayes (1978) feels that after a determination is made about what the child needs to learn, it becomes important to then set *priorities* for those areas of learning that are most critical and in need of the most immediate attention. Priorities are identified on the basis of the environmental conditions and constraints that influence or will affect the acquisition of knowledge for each child in learning the specific skills. Setting priorities is based upon:

1. the amount of time left in the school year;
2. the availability of instructional materials;
3. instructor availability;
4. what ancillary and support services are available to support meeting the objectives.

After the conditions and constraints have been identified, the next items to be identified and completed are the statement of annual goals and short-term instructional objectives. *Annual goals* are based upon the best estimate of what the child is able to do within the school year. This estimate is derived by the team developing the instructional goals. After annual goals have then been stated, specific *short-term objectives* are outlined. These are the intervening steps the child must take in reaching the long-term or annual goals. There is no specific number of short-term goals as each annual goal will have its own unique dimensions that may require a sequence of one to many steps to accomplish it.

In the actual writing of goals and objectives, it becomes a matter of how measurable the goal has been stated, which will facilitate deciding if the child's performance has met the measurement criteria. Lilly (1977) indicates no performance can be measured unless it "can be reliably observed and reliable observation depends on behavioral descriptions of problems" (p. 28). If this is the case, perhaps a reflection of Mager's (1962) schemata for writing instructional objectives should be considered. Under Mager's directive, objectives must communicate: (1) what the teacher's intent is, and (2) what the student is to do or be able to do as a result of engaging in and completing specified learning activities.

Mager (1960) defines behavioral objectives as containing at least three elements: conditions, behavior, and criterion. Under *conditions*, the definition of what the learning environment will be is specified; for example, "given paper and pencil," or "without the use of a calculator," or "when presented with a series of colored objects," the child will perform the task. Behavior statements are made concerning what the student will do that can be observed; "the student will write the alphabet," "the student will add one and two digit numbers," "the student will name all the members in his family." The last of Mager's elements is the *criterion* which is a reflexion of the acceptable level of performance expected from the student. Again, the criterion is stated in observable terms and should be indicative of either mastery or grasp of the task. The statement should clearly specify what is expected from the child in terms of performance: "the student will answer correctly four out of five comprehensive questions"; "the student will complete a minimum of seven minutes of uninterrupted on-task behavior"; "the student will complete the assigned math task with 90 % accuracy."

To summarize preparation of annual goals and short-term objectives, it is important to remember that all the persons responsible for the child's individual education program should be involved in the identification and specification of the goals and objectives. In doing so, priorities as to what the child is to learn, based upon some sound diagnostic information either from standardized information or observation of the child's performance related to the task to be performed, should be made. These priorities should focus on the identification of critical areas that need immediate attention on the part of the child, as well as the constraints and environmental conditions under which the objectives can be functionally met. Annual goals should then be identified that are realistic for the child. Once the annual goals have been identified, short-term objectives can be analyzed by identifying the incremental steps necessary to meet that long-range goal. After the teacher has identified the short-term objectives, he or she can put them in measurable terms, which can help to identify media and materials that may be helpful in meeting the goals, to identify strategies that may be effective in meeting a particular objective, and to provide a sound base from which to evaluate the effectiveness the strategies have had in meeting objectives. A measurable objective should contain at least three parts: the conditions under which the behavior will occur, the actual behavior that the student will engage in, and the criterion that specifies the acceptable level of performance the child is to meet. Following these suggestions, a more functional IEP can be constructed.

Evaluation Procedures

As stated within the regulations of PL 94-142, each IEP must have appropriate objective criteria and evaluation procedures outlined on an annual basis to determine whether instructional objectives are being achieved. Lilly (1977) outlines a model for collecting data designed to assist teachers in evaluating the effectiveness of their IEPs. He states that data collection is one area in which the requirements of the law can be used to improve classroom instruction; and, that the teacher will generate information to make program decisions that will be based on student performance. Five steps are outlined in Lilly's data-based instructional model that should be found in any evaluation system. These are:

1. *Specification of instructional problems in performance terms.* As stated earlier, if the effectiveness of the program or instructional strategy is to be determined, it is perhaps best to state the performance expected in the most measurable terms. As Lilly contends, no performance can be measured unless it is reliably observed, and a reliable observation is dependent upon behavioral descriptions of the problem. The emphasis again here appears to be writing statements or instructional objectives in objective, measurable terms.

2. *Collection of pre-intervention (baseline) data.* The value of maintaining a profile sheet, as discussed in Chapter 13, comes into play here. It is only on the basis of such baseline data, that a determination can be made as to what effects instructional strategies have had in meeting specified objectives. A caution should be given, however, as the individualized program can be violated if

it is not child-based. Using a profile based on test data and measuring objectives with one standardized test may reflect writing strategies for the test and not for the child. It is felt that both norm-referenced and criterion-referenced data can be valuable tools in establishing the baseline performance of the child. The important concept is that there must be some evidence of where the child was prior to beginning the program. The teacher has many information sources available to assist in establishing the child's beginning point.

3. *Initiation of instruction.* Both the development as well as the initiation of the instruction can be more realistically completed when instructional objectives have been specified in measurable objective terms. Even though the federal regulations do not specify that teaching methods have to be identified, it is suggested that the strategies to be used in taking the child from where he or she is now to where he or she is going to be, the instructional objective should be identified and specified. This will allow for a more thorough analysis of the program at the conclusion of the evaluation. If the instructional strategies are not written down, the evaluation can be for no purpose.

4. *Collection of progress data.* Data collected during this phase must be comparable to those data collected during the baseline. To make this part of the evaluation program more productive, it is suggested that data be collected at least on a weekly basis and preferably twice a week.

5. *Instructional decision-making.* At the end of the evaluation, a decision must be made relative to the effectiveness of the program. In other words, can it be shown that the child reached or did not reach the specified instructional objectives? If the teacher has collected data on both a baseline and progressive basis, decisions can be made as to the effectiveness of the program by comparing those sets of data. The teacher can then make adjustments or alterations in the overall instructional program based upon the discrepancies found from the data comparisons.

Other complex instructional decisions must be made by the teacher (Lilly, 1977) relative to PL 94-142. These include the following.

1. Is progress sufficient to justify a continuation in the present instructional setting?
2. Do progress data indicate that the instructional objective is appropriate or inappropriate for the student?
3. Is the criterion level appropriate for the instructional objective?

4. If the objective has been reached, what is the next appropriate step (p. 29)?

The evaluation component of the IEP is, perhaps, the most important as well as challenging component that faces the teacher. It is most important in that it allows the teacher to monitor and generate information about the overall effectiveness of the program. Following the steps outlined by Lilly above is merely one method that the teacher can use in generating evaluative information concerning the program. Constructing an evaluation program is challenging in that most teachers are ill prepared to develop and implement such a system. If the model proposed above is followed, teachers will be better equipped to develop an evaluation system.

It appears from the discussion that the IEP is to be more than a task completed in a few extra moments of a teacher's busy day. It is to be a thorough and complete document outlining in specific terms, what, when, and how a child is to be educated. In order to meet this responsibility, the teacher or person responsible for the development of the IEP must be able to interpret diagnostic information and translate that information into specific goals and objectives. Once the goals and objectives have been specified, a plan of action is then developed. All of this requires the teacher to be aware of instructional strategies, techniques and materials appropriate for meeting each identified objective. Successful completion of the IEP requires the teacher possessing a great number of professional behaviors.

Can You Answer These Questions?

1. What are the salient features of PL 94-142 that will most directly affect classroom teachers?
2. Define least restricted environment.
3. Define what is meant by due process.
4. Define what is meant by free appropriate education.
5. What is the IEP and who is responsible for its development?
6. What are the components of the IEP?
7. Can you define what is meant by a measurable objective?

8. What elements comprise a measurable objective?
9. Can you discuss Lilly's evaluation model presented in this chapter?
10. What are some of the complex instructional decisions that must be made by the teacher relative to PL 94-142?

References

Abeson, A., and F. Weintraub. "Understanding the Individualized Education Program." In S. Torres (ed.). *A Primer on Individualized Education Programs for Handicapped Children.* Reston, Virginia: The Foundation for Exceptional Children, 1977.

Bloom, B. S. (ed.). "Taxonomy of Educational Objectives." *Handbook I: Cognitive Domain.* New York: McKay Publishing, 1956.

Bloom, B. S., T. Hastings, and G. F. Madaus, (eds.). *Handbook on Formative and Summative Evaluation of Student Learning.* New York: McGraw-Hill, 1971.

Department of Health, Education, and Welfare, *Federal Register,* Washington, D.C., December 29, 1977, pp. 65082–65085.

Dever, R. B. "Language Assessment Through Specification of Goals and Objectives." *Exceptional Children,* 1978, 45, 124–129.

Hayes, J. "Annual Goals and Short-Term Objectives." In S. Torres (ed.). *A Primer on Individualized Education Programs for Handicapped Children.* Reston, Virginia: The Foundation for Exceptional Children, 1977.

Jones, John. "Federal Aid to States." *Exceptional Children,* November 1976, pp. 138–139.

Lilly, S. "Evaluating Individualized Education Programs." In S. Torres (ed.). *A Primer on Individualized Education Programs for Handicapped Children.* Reston, Virginia: The Foundation for Exceptional Children, 1977.

Mager, R. F. *Preparing Instructional Objectives.* Palo Alto, California: Fearon Press, 1962.

Stolte, J. B. (Project Director) *Clarification of PL 94-142 for the Classroom Teacher.* Philadelphia, Pennsylvania. Research for Better Schools, 1978.

Torres, S. (Ed.) *A Primer on Individualized Education Programs for Handicapped Children.* Reston, Virginia. The Foundation for Exceptional Children, 1977.

Answers

Chapter 1

1. The purposes of assessment include placement, classification, and research. However, in considering the teacher role, the primary purpose for conducting an assessment should be to plan the most appropriate educational program for the child.

2. Educational assessment can be simply defined as the systematic application of a process of diagnosis that results in identifying a child's school-related problems. In completing an assessment, all the factors that could possibly be affecting the child's performance are taken into consideration. These factors include the child's intellectual, social, and physical conditions that could affect performance in school-related activities.

3. An intra-individual comparison is a comparison of the child's performance against what would be expected of that particular child. Inter-individual comparison is a comparison of the child against expected behaviors of the child's peers.

4. The seven points to be considered in organizing an assessment team as outlined by Higgins (1977) include the following:
   a. The public agency responsible for assessing the child will use a team in the evaluation.
   b. The official of the education agency responsible for administration of special education programs is also the person responsible for identifying and appointing the evaluation team members.
   c. The team should be composed of the child's teacher, or a licensed teacher who has been appointed by the responsible official in charge of the evaluation.
   d. An individual that has been certified or is licensed by the State education agency to conduct individual diagnostic examinations (for example, a school psychologist, or speech clinician) must be included on the assessment team.

e. Team members must be chosen on the basis of their knowledge of evaluative procedures used in the assessment of children's learning abilities.

f. The individual team members must be qualified to perform these specific assessment tasks that have been assigned to them.

g. Upon completion of the evaluation, the team should meet at least once to discuss the evaluation and to reach a decision concerning the child's overall performance.

5. A standardized test is usually characterized by having specific administration procedures, definite scoring criteria, and distinct methods for interpeting scores has been outlined in detail.

6. Buros Seventh *Mental Measurements Yearbook* (1972).

7. In planning an assessment the reasons for that assessment must be clearly outlined by those involved. Is the assessment being conducted for placement into a particular type of educational setting (special education, self-contained classroom, resource room, etc.) or for the purpose of identifying the child's reasons for failing one or more of the academic school tasks. The teacher must also take into consideration the child's environmental background and physical capabilities. Both formal and informal instruments and/or assessment procedures can be more appropriately selected if information is provided relative to these points.

8. Teacher considerations in conducting the assessment must include an understanding of the child's background, the expectations of the school related to the child, the child's expected level of performance, as well as the reasons the assessment is being conducted.

9. It appears that a pre-selected battery of tests may be detrimental in that not all the tests for the battery would be necessary nor will they generate, in specific areas, needed information about the child. Further, time can be wasted in the administration of inappropriate instruments and in not administering instruments that would be helpful in identifying needed information about the child. Pre-selected batteries usually include standardized instrument which, if not used appropriately, can be detrimental to the child in terms of labeling, or in terms of limiting the teacher's perception of the child to just a standardized test score.

10. In conducting an assessment, permission must be obtained either from the parent or guardian. Next, the conditions under which the assessment is to be conducted must be approved by the local education agency. The assessment site should be one that is most con-

ducive to collecting the best information about the child. In interaction with the child, rapport must be established by the examiner and in all cases the standardized instruments if used must be administered following the procedures outlined within the administration manual. Confidentiality of the information collected, either prior to or after the assessment, is essential and should be a continual point of emphasis on the part of the individual teacher responsible for the results of the assessment.

Chapter 2

1. Norm-reference-testing refers to the use of standardized or norm-referenced tests, the results of which are used to compare an individual's score against that of a peer group.

2. In criterion-reference-testing, an individual's performance is being measured against the task and that individual's ability to complete the task. In other words, if the task is completing the skills within a fourth-grade math program, the individual is measured on the basis of how well and to what degree he or she understands and applies fourth-grade math skills.

3. The use of a criterion-reference test would be recommended if the teacher is to plan an individualized program for a child, particularly in the academic areas. In using norm-reference tests, the teacher should be aware of reliability and validity data that are available and the test should be used cautiously—especially if the results are to be used in decisions concerning placement in a special education classroom. Norm-referenced devices can be used, however, for screening to determine potential deficit areas in a child's performance.

4. Simply stated, reliability is dependability or stability. If a test is reliable, it is said to produce the same results over and over again.

5. Validity is defined as the ability of the test to measure what it purports to measure. If the test is to measure an individual's math skills, the results from the math test should reveal something about that person's mathematical ability.

6. Split-half reliability is a method in which half of the test is administered to a population and is readministered to the same or similar population after a specified period of time. The results from both administrations are correlated. In equivalent form reliability, two equally weighted forms of the same tests are administered to a population, and the results are co-related to determine the reliability of the two forms.

7.   Concurrent validity is a comparison of a new test against the results of an accepted measure. For example, in developing a test of reading ability, the results of the new test could be compared with those of an already accepted standardized test, such as the Woodcock Reading Mastery Test. Content validity is determined through a thorough analysis of the content or individual items comprising the test. A simple example is: If a math test is to be validated, the items should be reviewed to determine if they measure math skills. Therefore, the items from the math test should contain mathematical problems. Predictive validity allows for making accurate predictions or estimations about a person's performance in the future based upon that person's score from the test. Predictive validity is determined by measuring the test score against future performance.

8.   Mean, median, and mode. The mean is simply the arithmetic average of a series or set of scores. The median is a point or score in which half the scores occur above or below that point. The mode is the most frequently occurring score; it is the least sensitive of the three measures of central tendency.

9.   Standard deviation and standard scores are most valuable in determining the relative position of a person in relationship to that person's peers. For example, an individual's raw score in comparison with all of the other raw scores of persons completing the same test may be of little value; however, when those raw scores are translated into standard deviations and standard scores, they allow for a more sensitive look at where the person would fit in relationship to the total group and, especially, the group mean.

10.   The standard error of measurement is a means to account for possible error within a test. A test score is a relative measure of a person's ability to perform that particular test item. The test score itself may not be an indication of the individual's true score. The standard error of measurement is an attempt to provide a range of scores in which that true score would fall. The example given in the chapter was taken from the Key Math Diagnostic Arithmetic Test in which the standard error of measure is 3.3. A person's raw score, say of 150, could be used to generate a range of scores from 146.7 to 153.3 in which the person's true score would in all probability be found. A percentile illustrates a person's ranking. For example, a percentile of 75 would indicate that of 100 persons, 74 would have a ranking below and 25 a ranking above 75. Age and grade norms reflect a person's position relative to age or to grade criteria. A person scoring at the 2.5 grade level would indicate skill

and ability competence expected of or found at that specific grade. A person scoring at the seven year, six month, age level would be indicative of a person's being able to complete all tasks and skills expected of that age group.

Chapter 3

1. *Systematic Procedures for Conducting an Assessment*
    I. Discrepancy Analysis
        A. Expected performance level compared to actual level of performance
            1. inter—child's performance to that of peers
            2. intra—child's performance to own capacity
    II. Task and Behavioral Analysis
        A. Determine requirements of task
        B. Establish child's behavior in relation to task
    III. Analyze Factors Affecting the Problem
        A. Process analysis—method in which task is to be learned
        B. Child's understanding of task
        C. Social/emotional—environmental factors
    IV. Synthesize Results into Program Plan
    V. Monitor and Evaluate the Program
2. These factors are classified into areas of:
    a. Process—modality influences vision, hearing, etc.
    b. Understanding of the nature of the task
    c. Social/emotional—how the child feels about himself and others feel about him
    d. Environmental factors—physical factors—temperature, noise, light, etc.
3. Procedures for conducting task analysis
    a. Specify the main task
    b. Identify sub-tasks at the preceding level of complexity
    c. Treat each sub-task as a main task and repeat the analytical procedure
    d. Continue the analysis until the sub-task reaches the entry level of the study.
4. Definition of terms:
    a. Intra-individual comparison. A comparison of a child's actual performance against the child's capacity to perform.
    b. Inter-individual comparison. A comparison of a child's actual performance against the performance of the child's peer group.
    c. Formal assessment. The use of standardized normative testing instruments.

    d. Task analysis. A sequence of activities that pinpoints a child's learning problem and guides the teacher in planning effective remedial sequence of instructional tasks.

    e. Behavioral analysis. An analysis of a child's actual behavior in relationship to the task to be performed.

Chapter 4

1. The mental age is a means of reflecting an individual's performance level. For example, a mental age of five years indicates a performance level comparable to what would be expected of children at five years of age. Therefore, the mental age is a reflection of expected performance behaviors at any particular age level.

2. The MA given an IQ of 75 and a CA of 12.5 would be approximately 10.5. Remember $\dfrac{IQ \times CA}{100} = MA$.

3. The block design, coding, mazes, digit span, and picture arrangement subtest would give an indication of a child's sequencing ability.

4. A wide intersubtest scatter of the WISC-R of five or more points would indicate possible emotional disturbance or a specific learning disability.

5. An item analysis of the Slosson may reveal information about a child's auditory sequential memory, general information, visual motor skills, and general math computational skills.

6. The WPPSI, Vision-Up, and the McCarthy Scales of Children's Abilities are designed for use with very young children.

7. A cognitive assessment must include an individual's actual performance in a number of different areas—including the social-emotional, academic, or physical—in conjunction with that information obtained from a test of intelligence. A child's cognitive capacity cannot be determined by an IQ test alone, only information from the child's composite world will aid in the identification of the child's cognitive abilities.

8. Many concerns are expressed about the use of IQ scores. Primarily, the IQ score is said to be a very inaccurate predictor or insensitive guide to determining the overall capacity of the child performing academic or school-related tasks. Several authors believe that the Intelligence test and resultant IQ are an invasion of privacy and, therefore, should not be used. Other authors indicate that the tests used to generate IQs are constructed around inappro-

priate or culturally biased items and, when used with minority groups, do not reveal a true picture of cognitive abilities.

9. IQ tests and the IQ scores appear to be a prevalent feature of the educational community. As such, they should be understood more thoroughly in terms of what information they can generate for use in program planning.

10. The Slosson Intelligence Test, the Primary Mental Abilities Test, and the Kuhlmann-Anderson Intelligence Test are all devices easily administered and utilized by classroom teachers.

Chapter 5

1. a. Language development of children includes at least some of the following:
   1. Within the first year of age, meaning begins to be associated with sounds, the child begins to use some discernible words, usually nouns such as "mama" and "dada";
   2. Prior to the second year of development, the child's language is characterized by one- or two-syllable words and the child's verbal vocabulary is, at best, at simple object-word association;
   3. At the end of the second year and the beginning of the third, the child is using simple sentences that communicate distinct meaning;
   4. Within the third year language acquisition is greatly enhanced. The child's vocabulary increases dramatically, including the utilization of an increased number of words;
   5. By the fourth year the child has approximately a 2500 vocabulary that is actively used.
   b. In motor development:
   1. The child at one month is able to raise chest and head;
   2. Somewhere close to the third month, the child is reaching for objects;
   3. The fourth month a object can be grasped and manipulated;
   4. The ninth through the eleventh months the child is able to stand while holding onto furniture and can creep and walk when led;
   5. The twelfth through the fourteenth months is characterized by the child pulling on an object to stand. The child can ascend and descend stairs and stand alone;
   6. Somewhere prior to the fifteenth month the child should be able to walk unassisted.

2. The preschool child's tested intelligence is very unstable, especially if the child is under the age of four. There can be a great deal of change in the child's tested intelligence prior to the age of four. As indicated in this chapter, intelligence test scores of children two and three years of age when compared with their scores at five and seven years of age were significantly different. Yet, when scores of children five and seven years were compared with their scores at ages over ten they were less similar than the first comparison.

3. Piaget's developmental stages include: (a) the sensory motor stage, which occurs first in the child's life and lasts until approximately two years of age. This stage is characterized by six substages; (b) the pre-operational stage of cognitive development, which occurs between the ages of two and seven years of age and involves the child's making judgments primarily based on perceptual clues that are dealing with one variable at a time; (c) the concrete operational stage, which occurs between the ages of seven and 12 years and is characterized by the child's manifesting logical thinking; (d) the formal operations stage, which occurs around 12 years of age and carries the child into adulthood. This stage is characterized by the child's ability to form and respond appropriately to abstract reasoning and to apply problem solving similar to that used within the scientific method.

4. The Preschool Attainment Record (Doll, 1967) is a device to assess a child's ambulation, manipulation, rapport, communication, responsibility, information, ideation, and creativity. This device should be used with children six months to seven years of age. The Test of Basic Experiences (Moss, 1972) is designed to assess the child's experiences and preparedness in completing school tasks. This test can be used as a group test. It can be used to assess a child's language, math, science, and social studies understanding at a pre-school level. The Boehm Test of Basic Concepts (Boehm, 1971) will measure the child's understanding of concepts considered necessary for achieving in the primary grades. It is a group test designed to assess the child's concept of space, quantity and time. The Evanston Early Identificaiton Scale (Landsman and Dillard, 1967) can be administered either individually or to a group and should be used for children between the ages of five and six years of age. The purpose of the test is to identify high-risk children to those children who have a high probability of failing in school. The child draws a picture of a person. That picture is then analyzed by identifying the component parts of the person drawn. Raw scores are then translated into high risk, middle risk, and low risk (children who will be expected of having few or any problems in completing school related tasks).

5. *Project Vision-Up* by Robison and Croft (1976) is strictly a criterion reference device.

6. The value of Project Vision-Up is it diagnostic and prescriptive composition. The developmental behavior specified that can be used in determining a child's developmental level have associated with them the remediation procedures that can be followed in correcting a child's problem.

7. In order to conduct an assessment of preschool abilities, the teacher must be armed with information concerning the expected growth and developmental patterns of children in the areas of cognitive, language, motor, and social/emotional developmental. In other words, the teacher must be aware of what behaviors the child is expected to manifest at the preschool level (from birth to at least five years of age). Equipped with this information, the teacher can then make an assessment either through observation interviews with the parent or by having the child complete a formal test to determine if the child is performing at the expected level and what discrepancies might exist. The teacher must have an awareness of the school curriculum that the child is to participate in to ascertain the academic behaviors that will be required of the child.

8. According to Haring and Ridgeway (1967), teachers are very good at identifying and predicting which children will eventually have difficulty with school tasks. This is similar to the finding of Keogh and Smith (1970): that there is a very positive relationship between the teacher's rating of the child's actual achievement on academically related tasks.

Chapter 6

1. The essential elements of the reading process include readiness, perception, discrimination, vocabulary, and experience background development, letter identification, word identification, word attack, comprehension, and higher level skills.

2. Definition of terms
   a. Reading. Meaningful interpretation of printed symbols including recognition and comprehension.
   b. Perception. Ability to organize and interpret sensory information.
   c. Discrimination. Ability to differentiate between stimuli received by the senses.
   d. Letter and word identification. Accurate knowledge of letters of the alphabet and instant recognition of words.

e. Word attack. Method of decoding words by association of the printed letters with sounds they represent.
f. Comprehension. The process of understanding or obtaining meaning.
g. Sight word. A word instantly recognized by the child not requiring the process of decoding.

3. I. Categories of reading instruction
   Three levels of reading ability:
   A. Independent
      1. Comfort and mastery of material with no assistance
   B. Instructional
      1. Adequate functioning with supervision
   C. Frustration level
      1. 50 percent comprehension, frequent errors—emotional symptoms

4. Formal instruments. Any from Figure 6-3.

5. Informal procedures
   a. School records
   b. Parent interviews
   c. Checklists
   d. Word lists
   e. Performance-based activity charts
   f. Interest inventories
   g. Teacher observation

Chapter 7

1. Discrepancy Analysis
   a. Establish expected level of performance by utilizing IQ data to generate an MA

$$MA = \frac{IQ \times 100}{CA} \qquad MA = \frac{102 \times 100}{9.8}$$
$$MA = 10.4$$

   b. Establish grade expectancy by subtracting 5 from the MA

$$GE = MA - 5 \qquad \begin{array}{r} 10.4 \\ -5 \\ \hline \end{array}$$
$$\text{grade expectancy} \quad 5.4$$

   c. Compare performance to expected level of performance (intra-individual).

PROFILE CHART

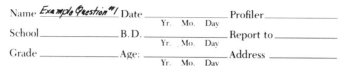

Name _Example Question #1_ Date _____ Profiler _____
School _____ B.D. _____ Report to _____
Grade _____ Age: _____ Address _____

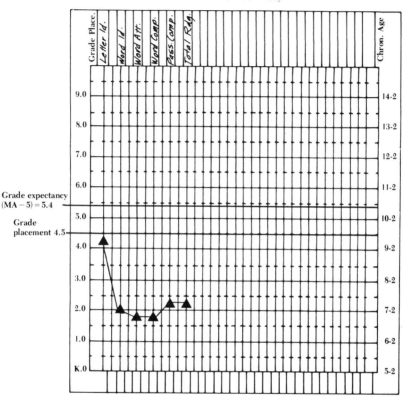

expected	5.4
actual performance	2.4
discrepancy	3.0

d. Compare performance to peers (inter-individual).

grade level placement	4.5
actual performance	2.4
discrepancy	2.1

By either method of comparison, a serious problem exists. The following example profile illustrates the discrepancy analysis.

2. Subtasks involved in the reading process include reading readiness, letter recognition, word recognition, word attack, and comprehension.

3. Subtask areas for basis of remediation:
    a. from Example 1—recognition of letters S, V, r, I, Q
    b. from Example 2—insertions, reversals, omissions, substitutions, rule of silent K

4. Factors that can influence reading performance include: methods the child uses to process information, understanding of the task, the child's social status, motivation, physical environmental conditions.

5. Item analysis is defined as an attempt to determine the specific functions the test is composed of. This provides a more functional basis for remediation.

Chapter 8

1. The important skills required of a child to complete a spelling task successfully include the following.
    a. The child must possess the visual and auditory capabilities necessary to process visual and verbal information required in spelling, including adequate visual and auditory acuity.
    b. Further, the child must be able to differentiate between different sets of auditory and visual stimuli—for example, to differentiate visually between a "b" and "d" and to discriminate auditorily between sounds that have minimal contrast such as fat and cat.
    c. The child must possess a capacity for the receipt, storage, and retrieval of written and auditory stimuli.
    d. The child must have the necessary motor skills, such as eye-hand coordination and fine-motor manipulation of fingers, to complete the spelling task.
    e. The child must be able to enunciate words adequately enough so that distortions will not result in spelling error.
    f. The child must also possess some understanding of rules of spelling. The child does not need to know the name of the rule itself but must be able to apply the content of the rule in spelling words.
    g. The child also needs to understand that the spelling rules include consistent letter pattern sounds for consonants, vowels, diagraphs, blends, and the rules that govern syllables as well as an awareness of what common inconsistencies are found within these rules.

2. The teacher must possess the following skills in order to make a proper assessment of the child's spelling.

    a. The teacher must know the components of language that apply to spelling, such as phonemes, morphemes, graphemes, and syllables.

    b. The teacher must be aware of common rules that are applied within the English language to the structure of words as well as the ability to specify the inconsistencies that are common to those rules.

    c. Further, it is important that the teacher understand the sequence in which spelling develops in children or, in other words, what the expected spelling behaviors of children are at particular stages of development.

    d. Finally, the teacher must be familiar with phonic and structural analysis of words.

3. The components of a spelling assessment include an understanding of letter-sound relationships (grapheme-phoneme combinations) as well as those that apply to syllables are some important components of a spelling assessment.

4. Spelling demons are those words that do not lend themselves to analysis, either in a phonic or structural sense. These are words to which none of the rules discussed in the chapter, seem to fit, or are words just commonly and consistently misspelled by children.

Chapter 9

1. The components of the oral language system include phonology, morphology, syntax, semantics, and vocabulary. Phonology is the study of sounds and the composite use of those sounds in producing words and sentences. Morphology is the study of units of language. Characteristically we think of the structure of words in terms of syllables or those units of words that represent some meaningful part of language. Syntax refers to the arrangement of words that transmit meanings. They are usually found in the form of sentences or phrases. Semantics refers to the meanings of words, phrases, and sentences. Vocabulary is defined as those words that are understood in either written or oral form.

2. Written language includes grammar, punctuation, and handwriting. Grammar is the manner in which order and structure is given to language to facilitate meaningful communication. Punctuation provides a means in which the organization and structure of language can be made. Punctuation gives written communication meaning as

well as organization. Handwriting refers to the structuring, spacing and legibility of written expression.

3. There are a number of formal tests mentioned within this chapter for assessing oral language capabilities. They include the Goldman-Fristoe Test of Articulation which assesses a child's understanding of sounds and words, the Templin-Darley Test of Articulation which is a phoneme inventory, and the Carrow Elicited Language Inventory which assesses the child's understanding and the use of grammar. These are three relatively good instruments which can be used to assess a child's oral language ability.

4. The California Achievement Test, the Metropolitan Achievement Test, Stanford Achievement Test and the Iowa Test of Basic Skills all have components to assess one or more areas of written language abilities.

5. Commas are use to separate parts of the date and day of the year, to separate city from state, to separate words in a series, after clauses in an introduction, to set apart short direct quotations, used before and after paranthetical expressions.

6. The two usual functions of the question mark are placed at the conclusion of an interrogative statement and for use at the end of a direct question within a sentence.

7. The readiness skills for handwriting include the skills of the child being able to sit in the proper position, to draw shapes including triangles, circles, and squares, being able to print from left to right, grasping the writing instrument in a three finger hold near the top of the pen or pencil, and being able to copy words from the chalkboard correctly.

8. A phoneme is the smallest unit of sound. A grapheme is the graphic representation of that phoneme.

Chapter 10

1. How well the child learns academic information is related to how well the child feels emotionally or how well the child perceives being accepted by peers. A child who is upset about a distressing event at home or who is overly concerned about being rejected from the peer group is not a good candidate for learning academic material.

2. The expected social behaviors of children three to six years of age include:
   a.   having one or two best friends, usually of the same sex;

b.   being involved in small, not highly organized, play group;

c.   frequent quarrels of short duration with friends;

d.   enjoying dramatic play;

e.   beginning to be aware of sex roles.

3.   The expected emotional behaviors of adolescents 12–15 years of age include:

a.   likely to be moody, temperamental, and unpredictable;

b.   boisterous behaviors, sometimes used to hide lack of self-confidence;

c.   intolerance, opinionatedness, and self-centeredness;

d.   anger outbursts.

4.   Formal social/emotional devices include:

a.   The California Test of Personality;

b.   Vineland Social Maturity Scale;

c.   Preschool Attainment Record;

d.   Walker Problem Behavior Checklist.

5.   Informal assessment techniques include:

a.   Behavior checklist and rating scales;

b.   Teacher observation;

c.   Sociogram;

d.   Sentence completion.

6.   Behaviors descriptive of adequate assessment of a child's social/emotional behavior:

a.   withdrawal from class participation;

b.   fighting during reading.

The important concept here is to develop a statement of behavior that describes the problems (that is, hitting the person in front while standing in the lunch line) and not to merely label the act (that is, the child is socially maladjusted).

7.   Strategies for overcoming inhibition and shyness:

a.   Magic Circle;

b.   role playing, creative play;

c.   DUSO—Developing Understanding of Self and Others and TAD—Toward Affective Development.

Chapter 11

1.   Simply defined, modalities refers to the pathways of learning. Discussed in this chapter, were three primary modalities: (1) the visual; (2) the auditory; and (3) the motor modality.

2.   This is the ability to select a figure from a background of confusing or irrevelant visual stimuli.

3. Visual stimuli are presented and integrated with one of the other modalities. For example, a visual motor integration task would include copying from the black board, or moving efficiently through a complex obstacle course utilizing only the visual sense to control the motor functions.

4. Acuity involves the mechanisms required to hear, see, touch, and feel. Acuity would involve determining if the child has a hearing deficit, a visual deficit, or a motor handicap. Perception on the other hand, refers to how information is processed by the child, how well the child can discriminate auditory and visual stimuli to store and recall that stimuli, and then to integrate that information into all the areas of learning.

5. One of the most widely discussed formal tests of visual perception, is the Marianne Frostig Test of Visual Perception. This test is composed of five areas: Eye-motor coordination, figure-ground, form constancy, position in space, and spatial relationships. The test has received a great deal of controversial discussion in terms of its utility and the development of educational programs for children. The developmental test of visual motor integration by Barry is designed to assess visual motor functions of the child. This test should be utilized primarily as a screening device. The memory for designs test, assesses the child's visual perception ability through having the child reproduce 15 different designs from memory. The resultant score gives an indication as to the person being brain-injured.

6. The Wepman Auditory Discrimination Test which is an easily administered test, requiring the child to differentiate similarities and differences in word pairs. The test will give an indication of the child's ability to discriminate sounds of letters and words, a gross indication. The Goldman-Woodcock Test of Auditory Discrimination assesses the child's discrimination of speech sounds within both the quiet and noisy backgrounds. The Rosewell-Chall Auditory Blending Test, assesses auditory skills in children.

7. The answer to this question rests primarily in the area of assessment of perception and with acuity. The greatest controversy rests in the area of semantics; those semantics used to describe what perception is. Further, the controversy is enhanced when professionals in the field attempt to find consensus as to what part perception plays in learning. There are many researchers and educators who contend that without an adequate perceptual base children will fail in school, yet on the other hand, several researchers have found little evidence to support discontention.

8. What would be included in an informal assessment of motor functions? To accomplish an information assessment of motor functions, can be facilitated through a number of procedures. First of all, the teacher must know the motor skills involved in the task to be assessed, as well as have some idea of the developmental level that those skills occur. Having an idea of the skills and developmental sequence of those skills, a checklist of behaviors can be constructed, and the child's actual behavior observed in attempting to complete the task with those motor functions being identified that he is unable to complete successfully.

Chapter 12

1. Four formal measures that can be used to identify the child's actual performance level in math, include the Key Math, Disagnostic Arithmetic Test, Stanford Achievement Test, Metropolitan Achievement Test, and the Wide-Range Achievement Test. Others that could be used include the California Achievement Test and the Peabody Individual Achievement Test.

2. Determining a child's expected level of math performance could be accomplished through an analysis of the child's abilities and interests within the total school environment. Expectancy behaviors can also be extracted from a scope and sequence chart or from a skill level chart outlining the sequence of behavior necessary in performing progressively more complex math skills. These are usually obtained from a standardized commercial math program or from the efforts of the local education agency (that is, school district) math program. These lists specify the expected behaviors of children at either age or grade levels. Figure 12-1 in this chapter is a breakdown of specific math skills according to grade level and could be used as a means of identifying expected math behaviors.

3. The three procedures in developing an IAI are: (1) construction, (2) administration, and (3) interpretation.

4. Behaviors expected of children between the second and third grades in the area of numerals and numbers would include skill in the ability to read and write numerals through 999, identifying and locating numbers through 999 on a number line and rename numbers through 999 with expanded notation.

5. BESI is an excellent tool for pinpointing specific math deficits, the math subtest of the BESI will allow collecting information from a number of different areas to include naming, recognizing, and uti-

lizing numbers basic addition subtraction, multiplication, and division facts and computations, as well as determining the level of understanding for fractions and time and money concepts.

6. Two of the diagnostic strengths of the Key Math Test is found in the profile and in the behavioral objectives that correspond to the individual test items, that comprise the test. The test will yield both a norm-referenced score as well as the test items can be identified in terms of behavioral objectives which allows for the teacher to better understand the task being tested, as well as to identify the direction for programming to correct the child's dificient math behavior.

7. To informal procedures for assessing math skill include the anecdotal record and the information arithmetic inventory.

8. Tests for use in screening math skills conclude all formal or standardized measures. To determine a general level of math ability and to identify potential math problem, the math subtest from the PIAT and WRAT could be used, as they lend themselves to generating information in a short period of time.

9. The IAI can generate information in the areas of: the approximate level of the child's math achievement, relative strengths and weaknesses as they pertain to math skills, and the identification of those math areas that need to be further assessed.

10. The value of the Kay Math Profile allows the user to graphically display relative strengths and weaknesses on each of the subtests of the Kay Math.

Chapter 13

1. From the assessment information provided, it appears that Carolyn's expected level of performance should be equal to that of her age and grade peers. The WISC-R and SIT IQ scores reveal an intellectual capacity in the above average range of functioning. These scores alone may lead to an expected achievement level a little above her actual grade placement. However, in consideration of all information available relative to Carolyn's interaction with peers and age mates, plus her performance on the playground and in the classroom, the expected level of performance can be comfortably set at her present grade placement.

2. From the test data, Carolyn's actual performance in the academic areas is her expected level of performance with the exception of her Spelling and General Information test scores from the PIAT. It

would appear from the behavior observation information that her social-emotional performance is comparable to that of her age mates. Yet, her fine motor abilities may be somewhat suspect in consideration of her avoiding eye-hand coordination activities as well as her poor handwriting performance.

3.   Through comparison of the actual achievement level to the expected level, discrepancies can be readily identified. It appears that Carolyn's General Information and Spelling from the PIAT should be considered strengths in the academic program, while her overall reading and math performance might be considered a weakness. From the information provided, a more thorough analysis would have to be made for each of these academic areas. Utilizing information from Chapters 6 and 7, the reading task could be more specifically analyzed through an in-depth item analysis of the Woodcock Reading Test. In the area of math, it may be wise to conduct a further assessment utilizing either the Key Math or a criterion-referenced test designed to measure the specific math skills of interest to the teacher.

4.   The discrepancy between the verbal and performance scales of the WISC-R may be indicative of a potential learning problem. Each of these subscales should be more thoroughly analyzed. The procedures outlined in Chapter 4 for analyzing this particular test should be valuable in generating information for deciding what might be the underlying factors to the child's problem. Further, the information as to the child's eye-hand and overall motor abilities should be further investigated to see if these areas may be interfering with the efficient completion of assigned academic tasks. Another area of vital importance is to assess the effect external stimuli, noise and movement, is having on Carolyn's ability to attend to a task. It could be within this one area alone that significant changes in academic performance could be enhanced by providing an environment that would stimulate and increase her attending to the assigned task.

Chapter 14

1.   What are the salient features of PL 94–142 that will most directly affect classroom teachers?
     a.   Handicapped children will be placed in the least restrictive environment which will have a dramatic effect upon both regular and special classroom teachers in providing educational programs.
     b.   Due process. The child, child advocate, and parent have the

right to contest the child being placed in or being kept from attending a special education program.

   c. An Individual Education Program is a written document that specifically outlines the goals and objectives to be met by the instructional program in assisting the child in meeting those goals and objectives.

2. Define least restrictive environment. The handicapped child must be placed within an educational setting that closely approximates the regular classroom. That is, the handicapped child should be provided an educational opportunity that approximates that which is found within the regular or normal public school system.

3. What is meant by due process? This feature of the law is designed to accommodate potential differences between parents or the child's advocate and the school district. These differences may be in terms of placing a child in a program or excluding a child from a special education program. The due process is a legal proceeding conducted by a third party that neither represents the parents or the school district. During the hearing the child advocate or school representatives can be accompanied and advised by legal counsel with each party having the opportunity to present evidence, crossexamine, or prevent the introduction of evidence by the other party.

4. Define what is meant by free-appropriate education. Simply stated, free-appropriate education means at public expense, under public control and without direct charge to parents or child advocate.

5. What is the IEP and who is responsible for its development? The Individual Education Program, is a written statement developed for each exceptional child. This statement reflects the performance of the child's present educational level, it outlines annual goals and specific instructional objectives to be met by instructional strategies. It must be developed, implemented, and evaluated by a multi-disciplinary team which represents the professional expertise of the school system. It should at least include the child's teacher, an advocate of the child, and a representative from the school district.

6. What are the components of the IEP? Components include: a statement relative to the child's present educational level of performance; a statement of annual goals and instructional objectives; the identification of service patterns in which the child will participate, such as a self-contained special education classroom, a placement in a regular classroom with support or assistance coming from a

special education teacher, etc. Within the IEP a statement must be made concerning the amount of time in which the child will be participating in the designated program. A projected date specifying the duration the child will be participating and receiving services should be stated, as well as an extensive evaluation system provided to illustrate how the instructional program is to be determined effective.

7. Can you define what is meant by a measurable objective? Simply stated, a measurable objective clearly indicates what the child is to learn and what behaviors the child will manifest having reached or met that objective. These are behaviors that can be observed and therefore measured.

8. What elements comprise a measurable objective? Mager outlines three elements in a behavioral objective: conditions, behavior, and criteria. Conditions define what the learning environment will be, behavior specifies what the child will be doing that can be observed and therefore counted or measured, and the criterion is a specification of the acceptable level of performance expected from the child.

9. Can you discuss Lilly's evaluation model presented in this chapter? Lilly outlines several steps in the development of an evaluation system. These include specification of instructional problems in performance terms or measurable instructional objectives written to reflect what the child should be capable of doing at the conclusion of the instructional program. Next in Lilly's scheme of evaluation, is the collection of pre-intervention (baseline) information. This is merely an indication of what the child actually participates in the instructional program. Data is then collected throughout the child's participation in the instructional program. This data is compared with the initial baseline data for comparison purposes from which instructional decisions can be made. Discrepancies found between the two data comparisons allows for realistic decisions to be made concerning the effectiveness of the instructional program.

10. What are some of the complex and instructional decisions that must be made by a teacher relative to Public Law 94–142? The teacher will be expected to make decisions concerning: the continuation of a child within the instructional program; deciding if the instructional objectives are appropriate for each student; assessing the criterion levels to ensure they are appropriate for each instructional objective; deciding if the objective has been reached by the child and then determining what to do if it has or has not been met.

Glossary

Acuity. The child's physical abilities to hear, to see, and to move physically throughout the environment.

Age Norms. Those expected behaviors that are anticipated at a particular age level or from a certain age group.

Age Scale. A scale that differentiates between older and younger children. Certain items on the scale should reflect the performance expected of a five-year-old child; other items may reflect the performance expected of a twelve year old.

Anecdotal Record. A record of the child's behavior. It is collected in a number of different forms to include: completion of work assignments, actual observed measurable behavior, or description of the child's interactions with other children, adults or school tasks.

Case-Study Method. An assessment technique in which the teacher reconstructs the child's history to determine underlying causes for the child's current problem. This includes looking at the child's developmental history, medical background, and physiological and psychological make-up.

Cognitive Capacity. Differentially defined as the ability to deal with abstractions or the global capacity to act purposely, think rationally, and work effectively within the environment. To assess a child's cognitive capacity requires more than a single measuring instrument and should involve looking at the child's overall physical, psychological, and environmental make-up.

Criterion Reference Tests. Measure the individual's mastery of a specific skill. The criterion test measures an individual's ability or mastery of the necessary skill needed to complete a specified task successfully.

Criterion Task-Base Method. A method of assessment in which the child's ability to complete a task is measured against the requirements of the task. In other words, can the child perform the necessary behaviors to complete these specified tasks?

Discrepancy Analysis.   A method of assessment in which a child's expected level of performance is determined through formal or informal means. The child's actual performance is then determined and the two sets of information are then compared and discrepancies identified to determine a child's relative strengths and weaknesses in the area of academic, social/emotional and motor areas.

Distractibility.   A reflection of a child's inability to focus on a task for any length of time when conflicting stimuli are present. The child is characterized by attending to all competing stimuli within the learning environment and not specifically to the task to be learned. Therefore, the child's distractibility interferes with learning the materials presented.

Due Process.   A legal proceeding available to contest a child being placed into or being kept from participating in a specially designed educational program. The due process is a procedure that can be exercised by both parents of exceptional children as well as the public school that is to provide an appropriate educational program for that handicapped child.

Educational Assessment.   The application of the systematic process of diagnosis that results in identification of the child's school-related problems. It provides information relevant not only to the problem but to the remediation procedures that should be used in correcting the problem.

Formal Assessment.   The use of standardized norm-reference tests.

Free Appropriate Education.   Public education at public expense under public control, meaning that parents or guardians of handicapped children are not obligated to pay for educating their handicapped children.

Frustration Reading Level.   That level of the child's reading behavior in which only 50% or less of the material is comprehended.

Grade Expectancy.   What would be expected of a child in a particular grade level.

Grade Norms.   Those behaviors or performances that would be expected of children at a particular grade level.

Grammar.   The manner in which structure is given to oral and written language to facilitate meaningful communication. Grammar consists of having an understanding of the usage of nouns, verbs, adjectives, adverbs, conjunctions, prepositions, singular and plural forms, relationships between subject and verb.

Grapheme.   The graphic or letter representation of phonemes. *I.A.I.*

or the Informal Arithmetic Inventory is an easily developed informal assessment of a child's math abilities.

Independent Reading Level.   The level at which a child can read materials with comfort and with complete mastery of concept, vocabulary, sentence structure and comprehension.

Individual Education Program.   A written statement developed for each handicapped child that reflects the performance of the child at his present educational skill level with specific goals and objectives and procedures to be followed in meeting those goals and objectives.

Informal Assessment.   The use of procedures that will reveal information about a child's educational strengths and weaknesses and includes the use of criterion-referenced measures, observation, checklists of behavior, case studies, anecdotal records, plus analyzing the child's performance in relationship to the individual behaviors required to complete the task.

Instructional Reading Level.   The level at which a child can functionally read with supervision. Comprehension of this material is at a 75% or higher level.

Inter-individual.   The comparison of the individual with his or her peer group. This is usually characterized by having the child complete a standardized test and using that test score as a means or basis for comparing how the child did in relationship to his or her peers.

Intra-individual.   A comparison of the individual's performance with performance in other areas. The child's performance in math is compared with his or her performance in other academic areas as a means of determining if math is a strength or weakness in the child's overall academic performance.

Item Analysis.   A task analysis of an individual test to identify the individual component parts that comprise the overall test. The examples used in this text for an item analysis were the Woodcock Reading Mastery Test and the Slosson Intelligence Test. The items comprising both of these tests were analyzed into more specific category. The reader is referred to Chapter 4 for the Slosson Intelligence Test and Chapter 7 for the Woodcock Reading Master Test to identify item analysis done on both tests.

Language Development.   The analysis of a child's language abilities to include the application and use of phonemes, morphemes, syntax, semantics, and vocabulary.

Least Restricted Environment.   The type of learning environment in which the child should be placed. This environment should closely approximate the normal public school environment yet still be conducive to meeting the educational needs of the handicapped child.

Magic Circle. A method of exploring children's positive and negative feelings, thoughts and actions. It employs a procedure of grouping approximately ten children together and having them respond to questions such as, What did you do that someone liked you? What did you do that someone disliked?

Maturation Level. The stage of development in the child's life at which the child can perform specified tasks. That is, the child has the necessary level of hearing development or speaking development to understand properly and utilize oral communication or the ability to properly hold a pencil for use in writing. An understanding of maturational levels is essential to the person making the assessment in order to understand the expected and actual performance of children better.

Measurable Behaviors. Those behaviors that can be seen and observed occurring throughout the course of an activity. They may be indicators of a child's actual performance on completing an academic task or may be behaviors that reveal a child's social/emotional make-up or behaviors that reveal a child's motor capability. They are behaviors that can be seen and counted.

Measures of Central Tendency. The mean, mode, and median. The mean is simply the arithmetic average of a set of scores. The median is the mid-point at which half of the scores occur above and half of the scores occur below. The mode is a score that occurs most often.

Mental Age. Defined as what would be expected of children at a specific age in performing a particular task. A child with a mental age of six theoretically should manifest behaviors expected of six-year-old children.

Modalities. The pathways of learning. Modalities are usually thought of in terms of visual, auditory, and motor pathways of learning. That is, the child learns through the visual, auditory and motor pathways.

Morpheme. The smallest meaningful unit of language which represents something in the real world or is used to communicate meaning between a speaker and listener.

Morphology. A study of the units of language. Morphemes are an integral part of morphology.

Neurological Processes. The child's ability to receive as well as express information that is directly associated with the neurological system.

Norm-Referenced Tests. Those measurement tools that have been designed to reflect the standing of an individual against other like individuals completing the same norm-referenced measure. Norm-reference tests provide a distribution of scores and allow the examiner to discriminate among the performances of individuals completing the norm-reference measure through identifying where that individual's score fits within the overall distribution of the scores.

Percentile.   A means in which a child's performance can be compared to other children's performances. It reflects the percentage of those children who performed above or below a particular child's performance. Given 100 possible scores, a child performing at the 45 percentile reflects that 55% of the population had a higher score, while 44% of the population had a lower score.

Perception.   Determining if a child has the ability to discriminate between visual and auditory stimuli, to store and recall that stimuli and then to integrate the stimuli into other areas of learning.

Perserverance.   Where the child is unable to change from one activity to another. The child continues working on one task or one item within that task over and over again.

Phoneme.   The smallest unit of sound.

Phonic Analysis.   An understanding of the rules for vowels and consonants in order to analyze the component parts of the words to assist in pronouncing that word.

Phonology.   A study of sounds and the composite use of those sounds in producing words and sentences. Phonemes are an integral part of phonology.

Point Scales.   Reflect how individual test items are arranged to illustrate levels of difficulty. These are sometimes associated with grade equivalents. That is, test items should reflect what would be expected of an individual in the first grade, or the fifth grade, etc.

Profiling.   A means in which diagnostic or assessment information can be presented in graphic form. It allows for easy visual analysis of the assessment information in determining relative strengths and weaknesses of the child, as well as the effects the instructional program has had in correcting or remediating specified problems.

Rapport.   A necessary component of a successful educational assessment, in that the person making the assessment must develop a good relationship with the child or children being assessed to insure that the environment will be conducive to optimum performance on the part of the child throughout the assessment session.

Reading.   Everything from the child's ability to word-call to making meaningful interpretations of printed symbols.

Reading Readiness. A child's ability to successfully complete or participate in the reading task. The child must be developmentally ready to read in that the child must have the necessary perception and discrimination abilities to participate in the reading task.

Reliability. Synonymous with dependability. If test is reliable, it continues to test and give the same scores over and over again.

Semantics. The meaning of words, phrases, and sentences.

Sociogram. A method of assessing a child's social acceptance by a peer group or individuals within the classroom. The device is used to reveal the child's social position within the class.

Spelling Demons. Words that consistently and constantly are misspelled. It appears that in some cases, spelling rules do not fit; however, in many cases words that are spelling demons are words to which spelling rules can be applied. Simply stated, spelling demons are those words that seem to pose a spelling problem to children.

Standard Deviation. An identification of how scores can be distributed and interpreted. It is a measuring device to illustrate how individual scores differ one from another.

Standard Error Measurement. An attempt to account for possible variability or error involved in a test.

Standard Scores. Means in which the teacher can determine the child's relative position in a distribution of unrelated scores. Standard scores equate seemingly diverse raw scores into comparable entities for comparison purposes.

Structural Analysis. A means in which a word is broken down into its component parts. For instance, prefixes, suffixes, and root words may be the component structural parts of a word.

Syntax. How words are arranged to produce meaning in the form of phrases and sentences.

Task Analysis. An evaluative and assessment procedure to determine the component parts of the task to be performed as well as the behaviors expected of the child in performing that task.

Validity. Simply defined as the ability of a test to measure what it purports to measure. If a test is designed to measure reading skills, then the results of that person taking a reading test should provide an indication of reading ability if the test is considered valid.

Vocabulary. The words understood and produced either in written or oral form by the individual.

Appendix

Following is a list of commercially available tests that could be used in the assessment process. They are organized under headings that best describes their function.

COGNITIVE ASSESSMENT INSTRUMENTS

Author Adaptation of the Leiter International Performance Scale. Grace Author, C. H. Stoelting, 1950, Chicago Illinois.

This measure is a nonverbal measure designed to assess the intelligence of children two to 12 years of age. The test if not appropriate for children who have difficulty with verbal construct, are deaf, hard of hearing, bilingual, lack an English language base, or have different speech patterns. During the test the child is required to categorize objects, match colors and shapes, and duplicate patterns.

California Mental Maturity Scale (CMMS). B. Burgemeister, L. Blum, and I. Lorge, Harcourt Brace Jovanovich, 1972, New York.

The CMMS assesses the general reasoning ability of children 3 years 6 months to 9 years 11 months of age. It is administered individually and requires that the child discriminate between pictures on a card. The child looks at all the pictures on a card, then identifies the picture that is different from the others.

McCarthy Scales of Childrens Abilities. D. McCarthy, Psychological Corporation, 1972, New York.

The McCarthy Scales are easily administered and interpreted tests for the classroom teacher. The Scales were designed to assess the general intelligence of children from two years six months to eight years six months. There are 18 subtests within the Subscales: verbal, perceptual, motor, cognitive memory and quantitative. The test results are a mental age score, as well as an index of cognitive ability.

SRA Primary Mental Abilities. L. L. Thurstone and Thelm Gwinn Thurstone, Science Research Associates, Inc., 1962.

The PMA is designed to measure aptitude in five areas: verbal meaning, number facility, reasoning, spatial relations, and perceptual speed. The test batteries are constructed for six grade levels (k–1, 2–4, 4–6, 6–9, 9–12, and adult); however only one of the batteries (grades 4–6) includes all of the five mentioned areas of aptitude.

Slosson Intelligence Test for Children and Adults (SIT). Richard L. Slosson, Slosson Educational Publications, Inc., 1971, East Aurora, New York.

The SIT can be a useful individual screening instrument for both children and adults. The ease and brevity of the test lends itself to use by teachers, counselors, and many others who might not otherwise be qualified.

Stanford–Binet Intelligence Scale—1972 norms edition. Lewis M. Terman, Maud A. Merrill, Houghton Mifflin Company, 1973, Boston.

This edition of the Stanford–Binet is a revision of the 1937 edition. It is a single scale intelligence test. The Stanford-Binet is an age scale test that uses age standards for performance.

Wechsler Adult Intelligence Scale (WAIS). David Wechsler, The Psychological Corporation, 1955, New York.

The WAIS is another IQ test developed by David Wechsler. The first edition was called the Wechsler Bellevue Intelligence Scale. The WAIS was especially developed to test adult intelligence. The WAIS consists of eleven tests, six of which are grouped into the verbal scale, while five comprise the performance scale.

Wechsler Intelligence Scale for Children–Revised (WISC–R). David Wechsler, The Psychological Corporation, 1974, New York.

The WISC–R was designed and organized to test general intelligence. Recently, however, the WISC–R has established itself as a useful clinical and diagnostic tool in the areas of educational assessment and appraising learning and other disabilities. The WISC–R consists of twelve subtests, six of which constitute the verbal scale and six the performance scale.

Wechsler Preschool and Primary Scale of Intelligence (WPPSI). David Wechsler, The Psychological Corporation, 1967, New York.

The WPPSI is an individual intelligence test designed for subjects between the ages of four and six and one-half years. The WPPSI has eleven subtests divided into verbal and performance scales.

PRESCHOOL ASSESSMENT

Boehm Test of Basic Concepts. A. E. Boehm, Psychological Corporation, 1971, New York.

The Boehm Test is used with children of primary grades to measure their mastery of 50 concepts necessary for achieving within the primary curricula. The test has two forms of 50 pictorial items arranged in order of difficulty and aids the teacher in planning an instructional program, inasmuch as it measures one important aspect of school readiness. This test is a group administered device.

Denver Developmental Screening Test. W. K. Frankenburg and J. B. Dodds, LADOCA Project and Publishing Foundation, 1970, Denver.

This test attempts to detect delayed development in children aged two weeks through six years and four months. The test consists of four sections: personal-social, fine motor–adaptive, language and gross motor. The Denver Test is a screening device for children with learning and behavior problems. The test is relatively easy to administer and interpret.

Evanston Early Identification Scale. M. Landsman and H. Dillard, Follett Educational Corporation, 1967, Chicago.
The Evanston Early Identification Scale is intended to identify those children five years to six years three months who may be expected to have difficulty with school related tasks. It can be administered individually or in a group. The child draws a person and is classified as low-risk (no problems expected in school), middle-risk (some difficulty expected in school), and high-risk (problems requiring special help in school) based on a scale of point values for missing body parts. This scale is a good screening device for assessing preschool aged children.

Metropolitan Readiness Test (MRT). G. H. Hildreth, M. Griffiths, and M. E. McGauvran, Harcourt, Brace Jovanovich, 1969, New York.
The MRT measures readiness for first grade instruction and provides information helpful in classifying students and predicting success in early school learning. The subtests are similar to other reading readiness tests but contain, in addition, a numbers subtest, a general measure of number knowledge, and a measure of auditory discrimination.

Preschool Attainment Record (PAR). Edgar A. Doll, American Guidance Service, Circle Pines, Minnesota.
The PAR assesses physical, social, and intellectual functions of preschool aged children with or without various types of handicaps, including socio/cultural. It provides a record of performance which is a baseline for educational planning, treatment, or management. It is meant for children from birth to seven years.

Project Vision–up. Noel B. Croft and Lee W. Robinson, Educational Products and Training Foundation, 1976, Boise, Idaho.
Project Vision–up is a developmental scale used in conjunction with a prescribed curriculum. It has been designed for children from birth through six years of age. It consists of items measuring development in the following areas: fine motor, intellectual, language, physical, self help, and personality development. The curriculum package includes materials and instructional strategies for use in remediating, correcting, or teaching skills for each of the above-mentioned areas.

Test of Basic Experiences (TOBE). M. H. Moss, California Test Bureau/McGraw Hill, 1972, Monterey, California.
This test is designed to assess the preschool, kindergarten and first grade child's conceptual understanding of language, social studies, science, and math. The test is group–administered. There are two levels to the test, one for preschool to kindergarten and the other for kindergarten to first grade.

READING

Durrell Analysis of Reading Difficulty (DARD). D. D. Durrell, Harcourt, Brace, Jovanovich, 1955, New York.
The DARD is used for children of nonreading through sixth grade reading levels

to assess reading difficulties. It contains a series of tests in oral and silent reading, listening comprehension, word recognition, word analysis, and supplementary tests in visual memory and auditory analysis of word elements, spelling, and handwriting. The Durrell manual can be useful in organizing remedial teaching and planning teaching programs. The DARD, even though somewhat outdated, is an excellent diagnostic reading test.

Gates–MacGinitie Reading Tests. Arthur I. Gates and Walter H. MacGinitie, Teacher College Press, 1972, Columbia University, New York.

The Gates–MacGinitie Reading Tests are a series of group reading tests which measure vocabulary, comprehension, speed, and accuracy. The vocabulary tests measures the student's reading vocabulary, while the comprehension test tests the ability of students to read complete prose passages with understanding. The speed and accuracy test is an objective measure of how rapidly students can read with understanding.

Gates–McKillop Reading Diagnostic Tests. A. I. Gates and A. S. McKillop, Teacher College Press, 1962, Columbia University, New York.

The Gates–McKillop is a complete diagnostic test of word analysis skills. There is a battery of subtests contained in two forms. The advantages of the battery are its variety and range of word analysis skills. Its disadvantage is its length; however these are very good diagnostic tests of reading.

Sucher–Allred Reading Placement Inventory. Floyd Sucher and Ruel A. Allred, The Economy Company, Oklahoma City, Oklahoma.

This reading inventory is used to group children according to ability in the reading area. It gives the level at which a child is functioning in reading from kindergarten through ninth grade compared to his grade level. It helps to pinpoint the different levels of achievement in reading: for example, where a student is reading at an independent level, where he is doing so at the instructional level, and where he is doing so at frustrational level. Thus it enables the teacher to know what help to give the students.

Woodcock Reading Mastery Test. Richard W. Woodcock, American Guidance Service Inc., Circle Pines, Minnesota.

The Woodcock is a screening test that assesses reading abilities in letter identification, word identification, word attack, word comprehension, and passage comprehension in children from kindergarten through grade 12. It is an individual test designed to assist the teacher in assessing the children's knowledge of letters of the alphabet and helps to point out areas of strengths and weaknesses in reading.

SPELLING

Webster Diagnostic Spelling Test. Webster Division of McGraw Hill, 1978, St. Louis.

The Webster Diagnostic Spelling Test assesses the child's spelling abilities from grades two through eight. The test is designed to assess phonic and structural analysis skills, to determine the child's understanding of long and short vowels;

to assess the final *y*, *c*, *g*, and *s* sounds; and to determine understanding of suffixes, prefixes, root words, and compound words. The test score obtained by the child can then be applied to a graph to determine percentile ranking for the individual child in relation to grade level.

Test of Written Spelling. S. Larson and D. Hammill, Empiric Press, 1976, Austin, Texas.

The Test of Written Spelling analyzes the child's written spelling performance from a dictated word list. The words are then analyzed to determine types of errors made by the child. The test is primarily designed to estimate the child's spelling ability or level in order to assist the teacher in identifying specific spelling deficiencies.

LANGUAGE

Carrow Elicited Language Inventory. E. Carrow, Learning Concepts, 1974, Houston.

The Carrow Elicited Language Inventory (CELI) evaluates a child's use of grammar. The CELI consists of five sentences and one phrase which are read by the teacher and imitated by the child into a tape recorder. Some of the sentences are in the active voice, others are passive, affirmative, negative, declaration, interrogative, and imperative. The average time for administration, transcription, and scoring is 45 minutes.

Slingerland Screening Test for Identifying Children with Specific Language Disabilities. Beth H. Slingerland, Educators Publishing Service, 1970, Cambridge, Massachusetts.

The Slingerland Screening Tests screen young children for potential language impairments related to reading, writing, spelling, and speaking. There are nine subtests which measure visual copying, visual memory, visual discrimination, auditory perception, auditory memory, and auditory–visual association. It can be administered individually and in a group setting.

Templin–Darley Test of Articulation. M. C. Templin and F. L. Darley, Bureau of Educational Research and Service, 1960, University of Iowa, Iowa City.

The Templin–Darley Test of Articulation assess ability in articulation. Although diagnostic in nature, some of the items may also be used for screening purposes. The specific items test the child's ability to produce vowels, dipthongs, single consonants (in initial, medial, and final positions), and consonant blends in varying combinations.

Test of Language Development. P. L. Newcomer and D. D. Hammill, Empiric Press, 1977, Austin, Texas.

The Test of Language Development (TOLD) is a comprehensive measure of language ability. It is used with children ranging from four years to eight years 11 months. The five principle subtests measure aspects of syntax and semantics, and include: (1) picture vocabulary, (2) oral vocabulary, (3) grammatic understanding, (4) sentence imitation, and (5) grammatical completion. Two supplemental subtests focus on the phonological skills of word discrimination and word articulation. Approximately 40 minutes are required for administration.

Utah Test of Language Development. M. Mecham, J. L. Jex, J. D. Jones, Communication Research Associates, 1967, University of Utah, Salt Lake City.
It is designed to assess expressive and receptive verbal language skills in children from one to 15 years of age. It is a test originally meant for brain damaged children, but it can be used with children who give evidence of language disorder.

SOCIAL/EMOTIONAL

Vineland Social Maturity Scale (VSMS). Edgar Doll, American Guidance Services, Circle Pines, Minnesota.
An individual assessment test of social maturity for persons from birth through 30 years of age. This device is *not* directly administered to the individual, but a confident who knows the individual quite well is questioned. The VSMS assess eight aspects of social ability, including self help skills, locomotion, occupation, communication, self direction, and socialization. This device, while providing some good information, is somewhat out of date and in need of revision.

Walker Problem Behavior Identification Checklist (WPBIC). Hill M. Walker, M.D., Western Psychological Services, 1970, Los Angeles.
The WPBIC Checklist is a tool for identifying children with behavior problems who should be referred for further psychological evaluation and treatment.

MODALITIES

Auditory Discrimination Test. Joseph M. Wepman, Ph.D., Language Research Assoc., Inc. 1973, Balm Springs, California.
The Wepman Auditory Discrimination Tests measures the child's ability to recognize differences between phonemes in English speech. The child is asked to listen as the examiner reads pairs of words and then to indicate whether the words read were the same (a single word repeated) or different (two different words).

Bender Visual–Motor Gestalt Test for Children. Lauretta Bender, American Orthopsychiatric Association, 1938.
The Bender Visual–Motor Gestalt Test for Children (BVMGT) is composed of nine geometric figures that the subject is required to draw from memory or reproduce while the stimulus is present. This test primarily measures visual–perception abilities but has been used to evaluate social and emotional adjustment, intelligence, and brain damage. A trained clinical psychologist should administer and interpret the BVMGT.

Bruininks–Oseretzky Test of Motor Proficiency. R. H. Bruininks, American Guidance Service, 1977, Circle Pines, Minnesota.
The Bruininks–Osteretzky Test for Motor Proficiency gives a general estimate of gross and fine motor abilities. The specific subtests include: (1) running speed

and agility; (2) balance; (3) bilateral coordination; (4) strength; (5) upper-limb coordination; (6) response speed; (7) visual–motor control; and (8) upper-limb speed and dexterity. Test results are reported as age equivalents and percentile ranks. It is a very thorough test of a child's motor skills.

Developmental Test of Visual–Motor Integration. Keith E. Beery and Norman A. Buktenia, Follett Educational Corporation, 1967, Chicago.
This is a popular technique with teachers for assessing visual–motor functioning in children and adolescents. It is appropriate for children from two to 15 years of age. The test is also useful for preschool and early primary grade children. When used for screening purposes, it may be administered in group settings.

Goldman–Fristoe–Woodcock Auditory Skills Test of Auditory Discrimination. Goldman, Fristoe, Woodcock, American Guidance Service, 1970, Circle Pines, Minnesota.
This test assesses speech sound discrimination under quiet and noisy conditions.

Goldman–Fristoe–Woodcock Auditory Skills Test Battery. Goldman, Fristoe, Woodcock, American Guidance Service, 1976, Circle Pines, Minnesota.
This test battery provides a comprehensive diagnosis of auditory–perception for individuals from three years of age to adulthood. It measures auditory selective attention—ability to listen in the presence of noise that varies in type and intensity. This test also measures auditory discrimination, auditory memory, and sound symbol.

Illinois Test of Psycholinguistic Abilities (ITPA). Samuel A. Kirk, James J. McCarthy, and Winifred D. Kirk, University of Illinois, 1969, Urbana.
The object of the ITPA is to delineate childrens' abilities and disabilities in processing information through auditory and visual channels. The ITPA has a total of 12 subtests, and each subtest is either included under the receptive process (decoding), the organizing process (association), or the expressive process (encoding) covering auditory and visual functions.

Purdue Perceptual–Motor Survey. Eugene G. Roach and Newell C. Kephart, Charles E. Merrill Publishing Co., 1966, Columbia, Ohio.
The Purdue Perceptual–Motor Survey (PPMS) is an informal survey evaluating motor performance and its relation to perceptual awareness. Skills in the areas of (1) balance and posture, (2) body image and differentiation of body parts, (3) perceptual–motor matching, (4) ocular control, and (5) form perception are surveyed. Eleven subtests consisting of 22 items total are presented.

MATH

Keymath. Austin Connolly, American Guidance Service, Circle Pines, Minnesota.
The Keymath is an individual test intended for children from kindergarten through eighth grade. Keymath assesses skills possessed by children in 14 areas of mathematics (enumeration, fractions, geometry and symbols, addition, subtraction, multiplication, division, mental computation, numerical reasoning,

word problems, missing elements, money, measurement, and time). It is primarily a diagnostic test giving dependable information that aids in interpreting the subject's performance on subtests and individual items. It provides raw score grade placement and grade equivalent performance. Scores can be profiled to graphically illustrate a child's strengths and weaknesses in math. The manual that accompanies the test is especially good for interpreting test results, since each test item is referenced to a behavioral description that provides a distinct guide for program planning.

Stanford Diagnostic Arithmetic Test. L. S. Beatty, R. Madden, and E. F. Gardner, Harcourt Brace Jovanovich, 1966, New York.
This diagnostic test is best used with children from Grades 2 through 8. Throughout the test, the child is expected to work with numbers to demonstrate how well they are understood and used in computations. The manual that accompanies the test provides very good information for interpreting and using test results.

GENERAL ACHIEVEMENT

California Achievement Tests (CAT). Ernest W. Tiegs and Willis W. Clark, CTA/McGraw-Hill, 1970, Monterey, California.
The CAT generally measure the ability to understand and use the content of the Standard school curriculum. The child's performance in applying rules, facts, concepts, conventions, and principles of problem solving in the basic curricular materials is measured. The students' level of performance in using the tools of reading, mathematics, and language in progressively more difficult situations are also provided through this device.

Metropolitan Achievement Test (MAT). Walter N. Durost; Harold H. Bixler; J. W. Wrightstone; G. A. Prescott; G. A.; and I. A. Barlow; Harcourt Brace Jovanovich, 1971, New York.
The MAT comprises a coordinated series of measures of achievement in the important skill and content areas of the elementary and junior high school curriculum. The MAT is organized in five levels or batteries, primary I through advanced, covering kindergarten through ninth grade. It is a group administered test yielding information about a child's understanding and skill in reading, math computations, math concepts, math problem solving, science, social studies, and word analysis.

Peabody Individual Achievement Test (PIAT). Lloyd M. Dunn and Frederick C. Marwardt, Jr., American Guidance Service, 1969, Circle Pines. Minnesota.
The PIAT is used to measure general academic achievement. It is a wide-range screening instrument for achievement in the areas of mathematics, reading, spelling, and general information. The test may be given individually to persons from ages five–adult and can be used with the handicapped, as well. It gives grade and age equivalents, a percentile rank, and a standardized score which, when profiled, aids in comparing each subtest and the total test scores with other data.

Stanford Achievement Test (SAT). R. Madden; E. R. Gardner; H. C. Rudman; B. Karlsen; and J. C. Merwin, Harcourt Brace Jovanovich, 1973, New York. The SAT was designed to assess skill development in different areas, such as vocabulary, reading comprehension, word study skills, mathematics concepts, spelling, language, social science, science, etc. There are three forms of the test, A, B, and C, and these three forms are available from grades 1.5 to 9.5. The 11 subtests of the SAT occur at some levels but not at others, and the skills assessed by these subtests are different at the different levels. Two manuals are also available: one which groups the items by their major instructional objectives; the other manual provides an item analysis and instructional objectives and ways to teach these objectives.

Wide Range Achievement Test (WRAT). J. F. Justak and S. R. Justak, Guidance Associates, 1965, Wilmington, Delaware. The WRAT is used as a screening device for academic performance in reading, spelling, and arithmetic. It detects general skill in spelling, ability to read words in isolation, and to compute a variety of math problems. The test has two levels to assess children kindergarten through sixth grade (Level I) and sixth grade through adult (Level II). This test is quickly administered and scored.

Iowa Test of Basic Skills. E. F. Lindquist and A. N. Hieronymus, Houghton Mifflin, 1956, Boston. The Iowa test includes subtests measuring vocabulary, reading comprehension, language skills (spelling, capitalization, punctuation, usage), work–study skills, and math skills from a third to ninth grade level.

Index